to Napier Putney

AN ENERGETIC LIFE

— "to know"

AN ENERGETIC LIFE

The Memoirs of Peter R. Odell from 1930 to 2010

by

PETER R. ODELL

A Professor Emeritus of International Energy Studies at
Erasmus University Rotterdam

Formerly a Lecturer and later a
Visiting Professor at the London School of Economics

The Memoir Club

© Peter R. Odell 2010

First published in 2010 by
The Memoir Club
Arya House
Langley Park
Durham
DH7 9XE
Tel: 0191 373 5660
Email: memoirclub@msn.com

Peter Odell has asserted his rights under the
Copyright, Designs and Patents Act 1998
to be identified as the author of this work.

All rights reserved. Except for brief quotations in review,
this book or any part thereof, may not be reproduced,
stored in or introduced into a retrieval system or transmitted,
in any form or by any means, mechanical, photocopying,
recording or otherwise, without the prior written permission
of the author or publisher.

Unauthorised duplication
contravenes existing laws.

British Library Cataloguing in
Publication Data.
A catalogue record for this book
is available from the
British Library

ISBN: 978-1-84104-515-3

Typeset by TW Typesetting, Plymouth, Devon
Printed by Charlesworth Press, Wakefield

Dedicated to my family
and to Carol Klug for her outstanding
secretarial help over more than two decades

Contents

List of Illustrations		ix
Preface		xiii
Acknowledgement		xv
Chapter 1	From a Working Class Birth in 1930 to University Admission in 1948	1
Chapter 2	The University Years, 1948–54	27
Chapter 3	1954–58: As an Officer of the Queen; a Belated Marriage; a Year in the United States and the Search for a Career!	51
Chapter 4	1958–68: A Ten-Year UK Career; and our Evolution into a Family of Six	70
Chapter 5	As Migrants to The Netherlands for Better or for Worse?	84
Chapter 6	Mid 1977 to Early 1978 – A Sabbatical Intermission; with Hard Work and Multiple Failures	98
Chapter 7	Fifteen More Very Energetic Years in Rotterdam, 1978–92	106
Chapter 8	From 1992 to 2000: On Rejoining my Family in Ipswich and a Formidable Range of Activities	122
Chapter 9	Back to Life in London after 32 Years	148
Chapter 10	Five Twilight Years from 2005	164
An Epilogue		179
Appendix 1: Books, Papers and Articles Written between 1961 and 2010		181
Appendix 2: Professor Odell's Appointments, Affiliations and Awards from 1954 to date		201
Index		208

List of Illustrations

1. The author's Mother b. 1903 d. 1954, Grace Edna Randon ... 8
2. The author's Father b. 1901 d. 1978, Frank James Odell 8
3. My Father and Mother's Wedding, May 1928: with Odell and Randon relatives 8
4. The author's very early childhood – say 6 months! 9
5. Cycling already! In the garden 9
6. Growing up a little – say 3 years with Park Road houses behind me 9
7. As a pageboy with my cousin Margaret Randon at Aunty Doris' wedding in the mid-30s 10
8. Growing up – to 9 (?) years with my younger sister of 6 years . 10
9. A donkey and me on the beach in the early 1930s 14
10. Mum, my sister, an unknown boy and me on a late 1930s beach 14
11. Mum, Aunty May, my cousin Ken and me at Prestatyn about 1933 14
12. Me and my cricket bat plus Mum, Dad, Granny Randon et al. in Llandudno 15
13. Myself and other family members this time on Llandudno beach 15
14. An early post-war gathering of the Odell and Randon families: in our small Park Road garden 23
15. The winter of 1945/6; 'snowbound' in a neighbour's garden .. 23
16. Coalville Grammar School's 2nd XI Soccer Team in 1947/8 – but one player didn't make it! 23
17. My geographical coverage from Coalville at the centre: but sparsely so beyond the 30km 'ring' – thereafter un-bikeable distances! 26
18. Birmingham University staff and students of the Geography Department, 1949/50 31
19. July 1951: Graduation Day on the campus outside the Great Hall 31

20. 1st Class Honour's Degree now awarded at Birmingham University	31
21. After Degree Day, a visit to Skien in Southern Norway	32
22. Our Norwegian families' daughters guide us in their local countryside	32
23. Discussions in Budapest in 1951 between us and our hosts	37
24. On returning to Birmingham we hand over a gift from the Hungarian Student Union to our Union's president	37
25. In East Berlin at the IUS meeting in 1953, I speak on behalf of the British National Union of Students' decision to leave the International Union	37
26. Bharat Airways DC4 for the Paris/Bombay flight	42
27. A stop-over at the small 'airport' in Bahrain	42
28. The Maharajah of Mysore welcomes us to his palace	42
29. We are greeted by a march-past in the city	43
30. Our invitation to the Town Hall of the City of Mysore	43
31. My ex-army uniform meets the requirement of hot weather	44
32. Five of us gather together as participants from five countries	44
33. How my post-1951 activities engendered several journeys across Europe: and into the Levant (beyond Cyprus)	49
34. RAF Jurby, Isle of Man: 'on guard'	53
35. 'Comrades in Arms' ready for a march – with rifles and other kit – over many miles!	53
36. The 1954 Passing Out Parade – after 3 months training: PRO in the foreground awaiting instructions	53
37. RAF Halton House for the officers – from the front	56
38. Rear view of the House	56
39. Myself and four colleagues awaiting instructions!	57
40. Sister F/O Jean M. McKintosh based at the RAF Halton hospital later to become my wife!	57
41. The Wedding Approaches: with the best-man	60
42. The bride and I – now married – leave the Methodist Church	60
43. The two families gather: Odells to the left, McKintoshs to the right	61

LIST OF ILLUSTRATIONS

44. The family plus other guests assemble prior to departure to the wedding feast 61
45. Shell's new clan of potential managers, September 1958 71
46. Our family completed with Nigel, Deborah, Mark and Susannah 79
47. Our arrival in Rotterdam at Oudorpweg 9 in early September 1968 85
48. The family in Rotterdam in the mid-1970s 86
49. Meeting with Shell's North Sea Exploitation Team in Aberdeen 93
50. Lecturing on the UK's Developing Offshore Oil and Gas Production and Potential 102
51. The staff of my Geographical Institute in 1980: on my resignation 108
52. Reflections on my Energy Institute's future 110
53. The author's international visits to different countries and regions around the world 120
54. Our Edwardian house – now 108 years old 123
55. The garden of the house 123
56. Our 'pied à terre' in Islington, London 124
57. My 1991 IAEE award, presented in May 1992 126
58. Presentation of my award at the 1993 Annual Meeting of the Royal Scottish Geographical Society 127
59. My attempt to become a Euro MP 129
60. Volume 1 of the collection of my important global articles and lectures 131
61. Volume 2: Europe's Energy Entanglement 131
62. My book on the future of carbon fuels, published in 2004 150
63. The London Underground showing the location of Highbury and Islington stations 163
64. My presentation from the rostrum at a large conference in Abu Dhabi in September 2005 165
65. A photo of me receiving the 2006 OPEC International Award 171

Preface

This book is essentially based on my memories – except, of course, for the first few years of my life. Even so, from within that very short period I can still visualise a largish number of memorable events. For example, I can still remember my rides down the garden path of a neighbour on the back of a large but friendly dog. And more extensively, I recollect almost every corner and attribute in my home.

Subsequent societal developments in the late 1930s, followed by the six years between 1939 and 1945, widened my horizons. These developments lead to consequential memories which have established never-to-be forgotten elements in my subsequent long life, some of which are described throughout this book. And so they were: initially through my studies in Birmingham (UK) and Boston (USA), subsequently leading to academic appointments in the London School of Economics (from 1961–1968 and 1988–2001) and the Netherland School of Economics from 1968, later to become Erasmus University Rotterdam in 1973. My initial economic geography interests – over 10 years from 1968 to 1980 were then moved to International Energy Studies, subsequently maintained to this date.

Previously, schools, Chapels, the Boy Scouts' movement and other entities – additional to those exclusively in my family – in the earlier period of my life led me through to the unexpected opportunities. In doing so they created an ultimate set of plateaux of sunlit proportions on which it seemed my 'futures' could be established. And so it proved.

These are presented in each of the ten chapters and one epilogue: within which family and friends, supplemented by colleagues – favourable and unfavourable – helped open up and challenge the opportunities which were presented to me – though not perhaps as broadly or as deeply as I should have secured.

Thus, in these, my memoirs, there are relatively few people named and admired (beyond the members of our closely knit family) who have helped me tread the 'energetic life' of the book's title. Sometimes, indeed, quite the contrary, as my prospects were sometimes diminished rather than enhanced by my compatriots, both British and Dutch!

So, with many examples of positions and ventures undertaken, there have seldom been more than modest successes for my actions and presentations: for reasons which are presented in this book's chapters. There is, nevertheless, one entity in particular which has repeatedly welcomed my views and activities; most notably over the past couple of decades in which I have emphasised the emergence of global changes in the relative importance of the producers of oil and natural gas. The entity so concerned is the Organisation of the Petroleum Exporting Countries – better known as OPEC, the member countries of which now have over 77% of the world's known reserves of oil.

Finally, my efforts over the past 12 months to write this book have been rewarded. This satisfies not only me, but also my wife, Jean, who has had to withstand the impact of the time involved on my part over the year. It has also involved my secretarial assistant, Mrs Carol Klug, who in her repeated need to read my handwritten text and to produce the word processed material has always kept to the timing of the work as required.

Peter R. Odell
peterodell2@btinternet.com

Acknowledgement

To OPEC's Secretariat for its generosity in contributing to the costs of producing these memoirs and thus ensuring the publication of my book in 2010.

CHAPTER 1

From a Working Class Birth in 1930 to University Admission in 1948

I WAS BORN IN THE MATERNITY home in the small town of Coalville, Leicestershire in the early hours of 1 July 1930 during which, I was later told, the town was in the throes of a violent thunderstorm.

The family into which I came lived in Park Road – at number 23 – only about 150 metres from the maternity facility on the town's main thoroughfare of London Road and opposite to the Anglican parish church, Christ Church, which had been build in the mid-nineteenth century. In this context it reflected the growth and expansion of the town, newly-named in 1914. Prior to this formal designation its name had been Long Lane, a road which passed through the medieval parishes of Whitwick, Hugglescote, Snibston and Swannington en route from Leicester to Ashby.

Even more than almost half a century later my July 1930 birth certificate recorded me as having been born in the ecclesiastical parish of Whitwick, the market place of which was some two miles away to the north-west from the location of the maternity home, close to the then recently built new offices of Coalville Urban District Council. More about my somewhat convoluted birthplace follows later in the chapter.

Meanwhile, I need to set out the antecedents to my coming into this world, in the Odell and the Randon families, both of which had initially established themselves in Coalville in the 1890s, subsequent to which my father – an Odell – and my mother – a Randon – were born in 1901 and 1903 respectively.

The Odells were from Bedfordshire, where there was and still is a village with the name of Odell, about ten miles north of the county town. This part of middle England is thought to have received many eleventh century immigrants from Normandy following William the Conqueror's success over the Anglo-Saxons at the Battle of Hastings in 1066. His soldiers who survived the battle and remained loyal to their leader were accorded land rights, with the acreage dependent on rank and the perceived quality of each individual soldier. One such beneficiary was one of Norse background from the period of the Vikings' successes in populating Normandy. His name was Wadl (or Wadul) from which the name of Odell has been long since derived. The Odell village/family appears to have successfully established itself, with some survivors through the medieval plagues and, thereafter, over many generations through to the nineteenth century.

Thereafter, growing population numbers in the village of Odell led to inter-village marriages within the northern part of Bedfordshire, and later in the county town itself which expanded on the basis of a steadily rising range of traders and manufacturers. My great-grandfather, George Odell, resettled in Kempstone (some twelve kilometres south of the village of Odell) where, at the time of his marriage in 1865, he was designated as an agricultural labourer. His choice of Kempstone (closer to Bedford) in which to set up home and raise a family seems likely to have reflected the county town's expanding range of urban activities and its role as a centre of the emerging railway routes – southwards to London; to Leicester, Derby and Nottingham to the north; to Cambridge, Norwich and Ipswich in Eastern England; and to Northampton, Stratford-upon-Avon and Oxford, to the west Midlands and the west country.

Indeed, the Midland Railway Company's Bedford 'hub' appears to have provided a job in the early 1890s for the eldest son – Frederick Charles – of my great-grandfather. My paternal grandfather was, however, soon moved north to Long Eaton in south Derbyshire to take a job as a railway freight train guard based on the newly expanded Totton marshalling yards through which coal produced from the many Derbyshire and Nottinghamshire mines was forwarded in trainloads to London and other parts of south and east England.

He lodged in Long Eaton where he met and subsequently married a girl six years younger than him, Lucy Clark, on 25 December 1895. Subsequently, later in the mid-1890s my grandparents were moved to Coalville where the Midland Railway Company deployed my grandfather to work the coal and ballast trains to Peterborough, Wellingborough and Birmingham. He and his wife Lucy were now able to buy and settle into a newly-built 1898 house in Park Road. This lay within walking distance of the rapidly developing Coalville town centre and of the Midland railway marshalling yard.

The house in Park Road was spacious enough for a family and had a garden capable of fruit and vegetable production for the whole year, together with space enough left over for a pig sty and a sizeable hen-house with an accompanying fenced run. Thus, the steadily growing family was guaranteed much of its annual food requirements.

My father, Frank James, was born in 1901 in the family's Park Road house as the third of the five children – and as the first boy of Coalville's only Odell family. Each of the children received at least some education, generally to the age of twelve, prior to taking jobs, mostly during the later years of the First World War. Happily no-one in the family became involved in the armed services of the time.

I was the second Odell family grandchild, just six weeks younger than an older cousin, Ken Turner, also born in 1930 to one of my father's three sisters. As already indicated above, I also became a Park Road inhabitant on leaving the nearby maternity home. Number 23 in Park Road was a mere seven doors away from my grandparents' former house so that in the earliest years of my life I was able to help out (or sometimes to hinder) his successors with the productive garden and hens: and also to witness the annual slaughter of the pig late in each year whereby meat and offal could be prepared for eating over the winter months. Prior to 1930, however, my grandparents, together with their still unmarried children, had somehow become wealthy enough to move to a detached house which they had had built on the much more salubrious Forest Road, immediately adjacent to the railway line on the east side of the town. There was land enough on the property for more hens and fruit trees, together with a tennis court. It also had direct access from the bottom of the garden to the extensive Forest Road Allotments Society, the establishment of which in the 1920s my grandfather had, together with a number of his railway colleagues, brought into being as a working men's venture. In the context of low wages and high unemployment in Coalville in the post 1914–18 war and the great depression of the late twenties and early thirties, the more than one hundred and fifty allotment plots (300–600 square yards in size) were constantly in use. As the annual reports of the Society (now in Leicestershire's County archives) show, there was, indeed, a more or less continuous waiting list of applicants for securing a plot, usually secured only in the event of the death of a member of the Society without a son to take up the vacancy.

Prior to my going into greater depth on my boyhood, I need first to present the details – in as far as I know them – of the maternal side of the family, namely the Randon's antecedents. I have been unable to establish anything more than their births in Hathern, a Leicestershire village some ten miles north-east of Coalville, lying in the valley of the River Soar (a tributary of the River Trent) close to the Nottinghamshire boundary and only a little further from Nottingham itself. This location was to be critical for the future of the Randon family.

My great-grandfather, George Randon, was born in 1834 and his wife-to-be, Elizabeth, three years later in 1837. In the population census of 1881 the Randons in Hathern numbered no fewer than 66 in eleven families, compared with only four other Randon families shown to be living in two other Leicestershire villages. The census indicated that almost all of the Randons of twelve years or more were designated as 'framework knitters of worsted'. This indicates an 'out-sourcing' activity for each household whereby their dependence on Nottingham's entrepreneurs' production system generally led to little more than subsistence wages.

One of the many children of George Randon (born in 1834) was my mother's father – also named George – born in Hathern in 1867, as one of the eight siblings produced in the thirteen years from 1863 to 1976. He was thus also registered as an 'out-worker' of Nottingham's industry. However, by the 1881 census year, such outworking had gone into permanent decline as a consequence of the growth and increasing sophistication of Nottingham's factories systems of production.

As a result of this growth in factory production, migration from the villages of north Leicestershire, including Hathern, became well-nigh obligatory. Much of this was to Nottingham, Loughborough and Leicester, in all of which factory labour expansion was required. However, in the case of my grandfather-to-be, George Randon born in 1867, he decided late in the late nineteenth century to move to Coalville where there were employment opportunities in the town's expanding coal mining and associated industries. He was then in his late twenties or early thirties and, it seems, already married to a Miss Fisher (birthplace unknown) who was, of course, to be my future maternal grandmother.

As far as I know, the newly built late-nineteenth century house in James Street, Coalville, which Grandad Randon bought or rented, remained the home of my grandmother until after the end of the 1939–45 war. By that time she had survived my grandfather for well over twenty-five years. He had died in his early fifties as a result of the dangerous coal mining conditions in which he had worked for upward of thirty years by 1927. Three of his four sons (my uncles Bill, Reg and Albert) had, nevertheless, all followed in his footsteps into the coal-mining industry. Soon after his death, however, and in the context of bad pay and conditions for coal miners in the 1930s, they all switched to alternative work. Two of them went into factories in Coalville and the other one into a Leicester industry.

Meanwhile, my mother-to-be had been born in 1903 and after a short period of schooling to the age of twelve she became a Burgess' factory worker in the expanding textile industry in Coalville. Her working years were, however, quite short-lived – only to the age of twenty-five when she married my father-to-be on 12 May 1928.

Her husband – my father – had by then, after about eight years as a shop-worker (from groceries to men's clothing), finally secured employment with the Midland Railway in 1921 – hopefully following in his father's footsteps with a job that offered continuity of employment in a period of great uncertainties and unemployment in the country's economy. His initial work as a railway man was, however, as a station porter at Bardon Hill, a country station on the Leicester to Coalville and Burton-on-Trent line. This was to be an initial familiarisation job at which 'lessons' on railways' rules and procedures could be absorbed and tested on an annual basis. He was successful in meeting these requirements for potential promotion to his father's job as a freight-train guard or to becoming a signalman; but disaster struck when his annual medical examination in the late twenties showed him to have a progressive deafness (the result of a childhood disease). Such a condition eliminated the possibility of his attaining any railway operational job, so that the company (now the London Midland and Scottish Railway Company) – one of the big four companies which were created in 1923/4 in a consolidation procedure from the score of separate railway companies which existed until then – could do no more than tell him that his only option was to remain a porter. In the economic difficulties of the 1920s he had little alternative but to stay in the job he had, eventually almost until his retirement in the mid-1960s. Year by year he had to hope that his medical examination would not reveal too much deterioration of his hearing difficulties.

His acceptance of a modest – and an even more relatively modestly-paid – job with the LMS railway company through the 1920s is somewhat difficult to understand given existing evidence of the serious efforts he had made to enhance his educational background, having left school at the age of twelve with a good school report. The following books (still in existence on my bookshelves), used by my father for home and spare-time study closely reflect his post-school interests and his apparent search for admission to another occupation:

The Principles and Practice of Farm Valuations, 1905; *Pitman's English and Shorthand Dictionary*; *Pitman's Shorthand Teacher*; *Pitman's Shorthand Reporter*; *Pitman's Commercial Geography*; *Pitman's Book-Keeping*; *Pitman's Salesmanship*; *The Student's Business Methods*, all of 1913; *The Student's Complete Commercial Book-keeping* was of 1915. Whichever of this range of text books were studied, little effective use appears to have been secured from them as a basis for seeking up-market jobs. Except, perhaps, for the skills and knowledge he secured for some of his tasks at Bardon Hill station where the station-master and his clerk worked from 9 a.m. to 6 p.m. from Monday to Friday, though only from 9 a.m. to 1 p.m. on Saturdays and never on Sundays. Outside these hours Porter Odell had not only to sell tickets and to take care of milk churns, baskets of racing pigeons, parcels and luggage brought to the station for dispatch to other places, but also to accept responsibility for goods unloaded from the passenger trains for local delivery; together with frequent acceptances and dispatches of railway wagons and road carts which had to be loaded and unloaded with horses, cattle and machinery etc. A porter's job in the 1920s and '30s at a country railway station was not an easy one!

The 'swinging' 20s came before my time, but from the bedtime stories that I recall being told by my father (and since seen from the family photos which have now survived the near-to one hundred years since then), social life between the two families' youngsters (the Odells and Randons) in that period was intense and long-lived (inasfar as long working hours permitted). Most of such activities were built around the non-conformist chapels of the Methodist and Baptist faiths. The chapels were thus not only places of worship, but also institutions for furthering knowledge and for the provision of sports and other recreational facilities. It was, indeed, within this context that liaisons were formed and from which marriages such as that between my mother and father in 1928 emerged.

Thus, my birth in 1930 was into a respectable working class family, largely living within the confines of the town of Coalville but including some members who, during the 1930s, decided to move to live in Leicester with its more prosperous industry and commerce. My bi-lateral family consisted of one grandad (the other had died in the late twenties), two grandmas, eight uncles, nine aunties and, by 1942, no fewer than twelve cousins; plus more distant relatives of great-uncles, great-aunts and second cousins. These extended family members were, however, geographically more dispersed: scattered, in the main, in the Bedfordshire, Derbyshire and Nottinghamshire birthplaces of my grandparents. Regular visits were made *en famille*, usually on 'grand occasions' such as birthdays, weddings and funerals in both the 1930s and the 1940s, both during and after World War II. Now, no such contacts remain: not even with one of my second cousins, now Sir Paul Smith of Beeston!

As a child of the 1930s my life, in part, reflected the way of life in earlier decades of the 'respectable working class'. The latter social standing of my father and mother was, however, difficult given the former's close-to-poverty wage from a basic working week of 48 hours, yielding only between 32 and 38 shillings, depending on whether or not Sunday work at Bardon station had to be done. Consequently great care over expenditure was required and implemented, partly by having a lodger in the two-bedroom plus a third bedroom-cum-bathroom house. For much of the 1930s, and into the early '40s, there was thus an 'Aunty Evelyn' in the house. She was 'almost family', as the widow from the early death of her husband who was the brother of the husband of my mother's sister! I suspect that Aunty Evelyn's contribution to our household costs was critical for our family's survival. It also helped secure better access to medical treatment in Leicester hospitals through an ability to make a weekly payment of a sixpence or two into the National Deposit Friendly Society, through which medical costs incurred could be secured.

Fortunately, such facilities for me in my healthy boyhood did not have to be much used. I did survive a hot-water scolding as an eighteen-month-old baby when I pulled a kettle of boiling water off the hob on to my chest (making scars which still remain visible seventy-nine years later!); and then, as an eight-year-old in the playground of Bridge Road Primary School where I slipped (or was pushed!), so falling onto the concrete capstone of a low wall and opening up a gash on my forehead. This was made good by our family doctor (Dr Hamilton, whose daughter I much admired – though only from a distance, given our societal difference!). The marks of the clips the doctor used to close my head-wound can still be clearly seen more than seventy years on.

Our family access to medical services – preceding the NHS by almost two decades –was, however, much more important for my three years younger sister, Patricia Mary. She was born as a somewhat fragile child and only just able to survive childhood consequent upon frequent illnesses. She

1. The author's Mother b.1903 d.1954 Grace Edna Randon

2. The author's Father b.1901 d.1978 Frank James Odell

3. My Father and Mother's Wedding, May 1928: with Odell and Randon relatives to left and right respectively

4. The author's very early childhood — say 6 months!

5. Cycling already! In the garden

6. Growing up a little — say 3 years with Park Road houses behind me

7. As a pageboy with my cousin Margaret Randon at Aunty Doris' wedding in the mid-30s

8. Growing up – to 9 (?) years with my younger sister of 6 years

thus had to go to the Christ Church Primary School – just a hundred metres or so at the top-end of Park Road – rather than to the new, more distant County Council Bridge Road Primary School which I attended from 1935 to 1941. Over the six year period of primary schooling, I lost no more than a few days of absence through ill-health. I also went home twice a day on foot – every day for a midday meal – without any parent having to take or collect me! The name of the school was derived from two railway bridges used by pedestrians. One was of wood with twelve steps up and down and the other of steel with sixteen or seventeen steps. Apart from their utility for watching the passing trains, the bridges also offered a boyhood challenge, namely to jump from top to bottom of both bridges' steps on the way home. All such acceptances with the other lads fortunately left me unscathed – as both Dad and Mum had forbidden me to take part in these 'exercises'!

Returning, however, to money and health problems: both my parents suffered from incidents in their childhoods. Some youthful illness of my father had led to his deafness which, as shown above, got steadily worse and inhibited his hopes of advancement to higher status and better pay. Fortunately, during his forty-plus years as a station porter he had only one accident when attending to his duties on the railway sidings as a train 'dropped off' wagons en route to the Bardon stone quarry served by rail (as still happens today some sixty years on). Apart from this incident which kept him away from work for several weeks, he rarely missed out on his scheduled duties. Some evenings and weekends (when the station master was off-duty), I joined my father at Bardon Hill station and helped out as required in the station office, out on the lines, on the station platforms and, best of all, in the signal box, with its roaring fire and its plethora of signalling equipment and the manual procedures required for the safe operation of both passenger and freight trains; plus the 3–4 feet diameter iron wheel which had to be physically turned to open and close the gates across the adjacent highway. Had I not been a successful pupil at Coalville Grammar School, I think I would have taken employment as a railway signalman! And subsequently, as a member of the National Union of Railwaymen, I would probably have entered politics via the Labour Party and possibly have become a Member of Parliament!

Meanwhile, as my father continued to work his way through his 'daily round and common task' in spite of his worsening deafness, my mother's health continued to deteriorate. This eventually led to her admission to the famous medical spa facilities in Buxton, Derbyshire, in the hope that a cure could be achieved. The access to such a facility at near zero cost was secured by my father's weekly contribution over many years to a 'railway-servants" health fund: otherwise, access to the spa would have been financially impossible.

Her stay in Buxton lasted for several weeks, so necessitating regular visits by my father to the institution. On some of the visits I accompanied him on the out and return-train journeys of about 150 miles between Coalville and Buxton, with changes at Burton-on-Trent, Derby and Matlock, so that journey times totaled up to six hours. Fortunately for our family's low weekly income, travel costs were much reduced by the low-cost privilege tickets issued to railway employees and their families.

Regretfully, the facilities and expertise in Buxton Spa were unable to eliminate the cause of my mother's ill-health: but at least the treatment which was given set her up sufficiently to be able to meet the enhanced problems of the late 1930s and those of the Second World War years from 1939 to 1945: a period, indeed, when my father's continuing low wages necessitated my mother earning some shillings per week by taking in other peoples' laundry for washing and ironing, and in so doing, enabling us as a family to have an annual week's holiday in various seaside resorts.

Such an annual holiday event was also facilitated by the LMS railway's issue of the five free passes per year to each of its employees for use on its passenger train services across the system. This railway system then stretched out from its heartland in Derby in the midlands of England to distant locations as far away as North Wales; Blackpool, Morecambe, the Lake District and southern Scotland; Cromer and Yarmouth in East Anglia; Bournemouth and Torquay on the south coast; and, of course, London and even Southend!

As far as I can recall, the details of the 1930s and the early '40's gave us as a family enjoyable breaks some half-a-dozen times. In the two years after my sister's birth in 1933, however, such a family holiday became impossible, so that I was handed over to my father's sister, Aunty May, and her husband, Uncle Ernest Turner, a freight steam-locomotive driver at the Coalville depot and hence much better paid than my father. Their son, Kenneth Turner, had also been born in 1930, just six weeks prior to my birth, so that as four-, five- and six-year-olds we could enjoy each other's company.

In the 1930s, until the outbreak of the Second World War on 3 September 1939, members of our extended family of Odells and Randons all plodded their way through the tough economic situation of the period. There was much coming and going between the ten families created by the children of Grandad and Grandma Odell and of Grandma Randon. With most of the folk of the previous generation living within walking distance of each other in Coalville, such visits were often made to deliver or receive messages and information in the absence of telephones; or as visits when difficulties arose for one particular part of the family; or – and most important – to celebrate birthdays and – yet more important – to get together over the Christmas period. The latter occasions were marked by traditional dinners and abundant teas with sandwiches, pies, fruit, jellies, blancmanges and, finally, a homemade Christmas cake suitably decorated. Before and between meals there was an equally wide variety of party games and sing-songs around the piano (one of which was to be found in each of the separate homes). Such celebrations often went on until well past midnight – when the family guests had to walk their various ways home through generally poorly gas-lit streets – or, during the six war years from 1939, in utter darkness without lights. Unless, of course, the moon was shining brightly enough making for easier walking!

The three families that had migrated to Leicester for better jobs in the late twenties and early to mid-thirties had become relatively isolated (in the absence of cars), but there were, nevertheless, occasions of reciprocal visits, related frequently to a special occasion such as a birthday. Only infrequently in that decade were there visits for funerals. The most memorable of these were of my paternal grandparents; they died in 1936 and 1938, while still in their early sixties. I do not recall, however, being allowed to attend their funeral services and their burials in the cemetery provided by the Coalville Urban District Council.

In the second half of the 1930s my hitherto gradual process of consolidation within the extended family for the first five years of my life was slowly expanded to take other elements of living into account. First, was my inevitable involvement in neighbourly concerns with the other four families who shared the single entry from Park Road to the rear of all the five houses so as to provide access to their back doors. It was also used by numerous visitors, plus the coming and going of tradesmen's deliveries of coal, milk, bread, fruit and vegetables; and also with insurance agents and credit/debit collectors concerned with the five families' fortunes. Strangely, all four neighbours had family names beginning with 'H': the Harrisons, Hornbuckles, Harts and Harpers, with, between them, seven children

9. *A donkey and me on the beach in the early 1930s*

10. *Mum, my sister, an unknown boy and me on a late 1930s beach*

11. *Mum, Aunty May, my cousin Ken and me at Prestatyn about 1933*

WORKING CLASS BIRTH TO UNIVERSITY ADMISSION

12. Me and my cricket bat plus Mum, Dad, Granny Randon et al. in Llandudno

13. Myself and other family members this time on Llandudno beach

(three girls and four boys) – of which five were from six to twelve years older than me. This age difference was to make a world of difference in the near-future evolution of our lives following the beginning of the Second World War. In such a crowded, short row of houses we all knew – or got to know – each others' businesses, expectations and problems.

There were, of course, differences that emerged from the various husbands' jobs – from that of a coalface worker to an operator of the lowering and lifting of the cages in the Whitwick colliery mine shaft, to an employee at one of the Coalville Co-operative Society's many branches and to a metal-factory worker; plus, of course, my father as a railway porter. The contiguity of our houses made for much reciprocal helpfulness, in both our homes and our gardens. Spring, summer and autumn evenings were taken up with back doorsteps' and garden seats' chatter and discussions over events ranging from local town and institutional issues to matters of national concern. There were also discussions – and even arguments – over the role of the chapels in our lives: with two of the other families who were not chapel-goers, except perhaps for special occasions; with two families strongly attached to the very close-by London Road Baptist Chapel and its tennis courts at the bottom of our gardens; and with the remaining family who were members of the Primitive Methodist faith. By and large, however, the cohesive behaviour of the twenty-plus inhabitants in the five houses far out-weighed the occasional tiff or dispute!

My other post-1935 involvement was, of course, with the primary school to which I went in August 1935 at the age of five years and one month: and from which I moved on to secondary school at the end of August 1941, aged eleven – and almost two years into the Second World War. The Bridge Road primary school was newly built on my entry but was adjacent to a Victorian/Edwardian secondary modern school for 11–15 year-olds and also to a new educational facility for Coalville, the Technical College for training artisans. The location was, however, relatively tranquil, with very little traffic along Bridge Road from which the primary school buildings stood back, well over a hundred metres from the road. It had large playgrounds – one for boys and one for girls – and an extensive playing field for team games and for 'physical' training. This was a 1930s phenomenon, not, unhappily, one which lasted many years after the end of the war in 1945.

The primary school had twelve classrooms – with two for each of our six years of passage through the school. Each class had its own teacher responsible for the range of lessons which had to be taught. Discipline was strict but not unkind, and I have no recollection whatsoever of any disorder – except, perhaps, occasionally in the playground. One or other of the headmaster or headmistress opened each school day with an assembly with hymns and prayers held in a hall large enough to take all the staff and pupils. The hall was also used for music lessons – particularly choral – and for indoor exercises in inclement weather. My fellow pupils were a cosmopolitan lot, albeit all of English, Irish and Scottish stock, reflecting in large part the inflow to Coalville of miners from other coalfields in the country. There were, as far as I can recall, no pupils (nor any member of staff) from other ethnic groups, but there was a social mix with pupils ranging from sons and daughters of doctors, dentists, solicitors, teachers and tradespeople to the children of working class families – most notably from the coal mines and from the railways, as well as the children of factory workers, bus drivers and shop employees.

I enjoyed those school days and generally got good annual school reports – except for repeated references to my talkative nature! There were also activities external to the school which served me well, in addition to the positive influences of my father and mother and of their relatives. These were the London Road Baptist Chapel, our family doctor and the Cub Scout movement. The Chapel, as already indicated, was not only a place for the weekly Sunday school and attendance at the services; it was also a social centre led by a Minister who encouraged us to take advantage of our schooling and to express ourselves as appropriate. Our family doctor – of Scottish ancestry and with a robust Scottish accent – not only took care of us as patients (in as far as possible given the fact that doctors' bills had to be paid), but also in another respect which probably determined my future, namely the letter which he sent to the headmistress – a Miss Lager – of the lower three classes of my primary school, stating that I was not to be forced to write with my right hand as he had noted I was left-handed! The school accepted this requirement of Dr Hamilton, so that I did not have to spend all the time which would otherwise have been needed in order to overcome my left-handedness for the 'normal' right-handed phenomenon in the society of the time!

Both the external factors – plus the efforts of the school itself and of my parents' attitudes – collectively enabled me as a working class lad to achieve success in the 11+ Scholarship examinations and thus secure a Leicestershire County Council Grade A scholarship for my secondary education, at the then 32-year-old King Edward VII Coalville Grammar School. At that time the Grammar School was largely for the sons and daughters of the town's professional and trading families (the lower-middle classes). Such children were normally selected for places, with their parents usually having to pay fees – albeit of very modest dimension – until the 1944 Education Act terminated the procedure. The 'scholarship' I was awarded was for a place in the school for which no fee was payable, thus opening up the possibility of my securing a 'middle class' education. But the school required standardised uniforms and the possession of the 'tools' that would be required for progress through it for matters academic, sporting and social. On my father's railway porter's wage, at that time still less than £2 per week, together with my mother's needs for regular medical attention and the loss of the rental income hitherto paid by Aunty Evelyn when she found a second husband who, with a house and his work ten miles away in Loughborough, took her away from our house, my entry to the grammar school was by no means a certainty. However, in the few weeks or so between the announcement of the results of the 11+ examination (taken in the last term at primary school) and the beginning of the grammar school's new academic year in mid-September 1941, my father somehow managed to put sufficient funds together – though I know not how – to pay for some of the costs involved for uniforms and sport needs; and then with the balance outstanding paid, through, I think, the Minister at the Baptist Chapel and its middle-class members with whom he had close contacts. Moreover, I was offered the balance of the money required from the Grammar School's own Harley Trust Fund designed to help pupils financially, in cases such as mine.

It is perhaps necessary at this point to recall the desperate situation which existed at that time in the UK, the second year of the Second World War, with all its negative impacts. Family-wise, the consequences were not traumatic, with only one of my uncles being called up to military service in the Royal Air Force. Even he then served mainly in the UK on airfields around the country, where dangers from German air attacks were no greater than those for the population at large. His overseas posting came late in the war – and then only to the RAF's large and important base in Gibraltar.

All my other uncles – and a few of my male cousins who were past their school years – were in 'reserved' occupations, thereby contributing to the required war efforts in industry and transportation, with additional out-of-working-hours' responsibilities as air-raid wardens and in the 'Home

Guard'. Coalville was initially designated as a town to which evacuees were sent from London and Birmingham, albeit not in very large numbers – and then, indeed, not for long, as the town's coal mines and railways also became potential targets for air attacks. Happily, these turned out to be infrequent and relatively light in terms of actual attacks made. But there was one notable exception on a Sunday night in 1942, when just one large bomb was dropped by a German bomber directly onto the town. My father, on his way to work, was either blown or fell off his bicycle as the bomb whistled down to the ground! This air attack was unknown to us at the time as my sister and I plus six or seven cousins were, following the air raid warning, huddled together in the air-raid shelter which Uncle Bill (Randon) had had built in his rear garden (this was paid for by his profitable activities as a market-trader, selling 'seconds' in ladies and children's clothing, thus outside the requirement for clothing coupons, with which purchases from shops were severely limited). From inside the shelter we heard the bomb coming down from overhead and then a 'thump' as it hit the ground in very close proximity. There was, however, little by way of an explosion so the strength and effectiveness of the shelter remained untested! Over the next few days the hole made by the bomb in the middle of the nearby farmyard became a site visited by large numbers of adults and children – including myself. On arrival on site, however, there was very little to see as the bomb was deep in the ground under the farm's manure heap! The pilgrimage, though, was soon cut short as the large bomb was defined as being unexploded – and thus still capable of endangering lives and of causing damage to nearby buildings. These included the homes of Grandma Randon and Aunty Doris (whose husband was in the RAF) and of Uncle Bill – to say nothing of the back-garden air-raid shelter in which we had been ensconced. A short-term evacuation covering a mile or so in diameter from the bomb site was ordered. The bomb was then successfully defused and taken away by one of the army's bomb-disposal units.

This proved to be the height and more or less the end of the dangerous war-time conditions, needing the blanket black-out of lights each night, the requirement for the tape on the windows to inhibit flying splintering glass from explosions and, in my home, the requirement for my sister and me to sleep on a narrow mattress under the stairs in a 3 x 2 metre space which was considered to be the safest part of the house in the event of bombing. From mid-1943 such dangers were considered low risk and we were allowed to renew the use of our bedrooms – except when there were air-raid warning sirens, which necessitated 'going under the stairs' until the all-clear was sounded.

Such nefarious activities did not, of course, help with progress in grammar school where the now mainly female teachers did their best to keep us up with the required syllabus for the Northern Universities School Matriculation Certificate Board whose exams were taken after four to five years of grammar school teaching. The Certificate's requirements involved five compulsory subject passes including English language and literature; mathematics embracing arithmetic, algebra and trigonometry; a modern foreign language (usually French); at least one science (chosen from physics, chemistry and biology); and then two to four other subjects including additional sciences, history, geography, a second language and so on. For success, at least seven 'passes' had to be achieved. These had to include all of the five compulsory subjects, plus any two others in order to secure the award of the Certificate.

There were also higher grades to be earned, whereby job prospects at the age of sixteen were strengthened, or conditions for entry to the sixth form were secured. Most of the forty to fifty original intake to Coalville Grammar School in 1941 had a preference for the former; that is entry to job openings, which were plentiful in 1946, just over one year from the end of the Second World War. No more than fifteen or so of us of the 1941 entries to the school secured high enough grades in the School Certificate examination to stay on in the sixth form. School Certificate results generally determined the only choice that could be made for sixth form studies but, given my set of School Certificate grades, both options were open to me as I secured high enough grades across the board (except, I think, for French) to do either arts or sciences. Indeed, with Grade As in mathematics, physics, English, history and geography, both Mr Broomhall (the head of physics) and Miss Silk (head of geography) sought me to take their subjects at the sixth form level. I eventually chose the latter by virtue of my rapidly evolving interest in national and world affairs – a consequence, I think, of having had most of my secondary schooling to date under World War II conditions and in the context of the Labour Party's 1945 election to power through a campaign to which I had made a contribution to the successful efforts of the local party to win the seat in the Bosworth Constituency of which the residents of Coalville formed a major part.

In the five years prior to taking the School Certificate (1941–6) and then two years later in the sixth form for the Higher School Certificate (1946–8), my life was filled to over-flowing from a combination of many tasks. These started at home as my mother's health deteriorated under the impact of a failing heart (the result of childhood rheumatic fever) and in my contribution to the work required on my father's allotment (and in his role as secretary of the Association which owned the allotments). In the context of a family income only just sufficient to meet basic household needs, I also had to take part-time jobs including selling sweets and chocolates around the touchlines of Coalville Town's football ground, and as a butcher's-boy delivering meat to customers on a heavy bicycle on Friday evenings and Saturday mornings within a distance of about two miles of butcher Harris' town centre shop. Meanwhile, I attempted to keep up with my interest in the 4th Coalville Scout Group, involving not only weekly meetings, but also the time required to secure badges indicating competence in various sorts of activities! And, of course, the biennial visits to the Scout camps – riding to and fro in the back of furniture vans, as far afield as Stratford-on-Avon, almost 100 kms from Coalville.

The 'rest' of my time outside school remained orientated to participation in the religious and social activities of the London Road Baptist Chapel, culminating in the Baptist Church's procedure of adult believers' baptism; and in socialising with fellow school pupils, both boys and girls, in visits to Coalville's three cinemas and to the Adult School's Old-Time Saturday night dances – or even, on occasion, at the Saturday modern dance evenings, held in the town's multi-purpose indoor swimming pool building!

All the above, however, left just enough time from 1946 for the activities required at the Grammar School. First and foremost, of course, there were the intensive study programmes in English, geography and history. My chosen subjects in the two academic sixth-form years of study for the Higher School Certificate each involved up to eight class hours per week, plus all the 'private study' hours necessary for reading the set books and for writing the essays, as practice, of course, for the ultimate examinations of six unseen three-hour papers, spread over two to three weeks in June 1948. In the final academic school year, moreover, the requisite visits to the universities selected had to be made. For me Oxbridge was not in sight – given neither Latin nor Greek studies – together with the lack of the knowledge required for the entry examinations of the various colleges. Such possibilities only lay by staying on for a third year in the sixth form, given good enough results in the Higher School Certificate exams. This was not an option to which I aspired. Instead, I attended interviews at the three chosen provincial universities where, I thought, degree courses in geography would suit my temperament and abilities: namely the red-brick universities of Leeds, Sheffield and Birmingham. All three offered me a place, given my achievement of good enough Higher School Certificate exam results. I eventually chose Birmingham for its style and form and, moreover, because it was less than two hours' journey by train or bus from Coalville.

Meanwhile, other traditional grammar school responsibilities and activities occupied many hours each day of the week except Sunday. County grammar schools, such as that in Coalville, had taken on board many elements from the country's traditional public schools, as, for example, in school uniforms from socks to hats, taking in shoes, trousers, blazers and ties en route. No exemptions were allowed, as was also the case with designated sports equipment and dress-code, so making for heavy weekly washes at home in those days before washing machines and driers! The costs involved were quite formidable in low-wage working class households, so necessitating the continuation of paid work – in my case as the 'butcher's boy', together with other paid odd jobs for neighbours and friends – and, of course, I continued to help on my father's allotments and with his hens, whereby essential items of family foods could be secured – and even with some left-overs for sale to other families. All, of course, in the context of the continuing rationing of food, clothing, sweets/chocolate and furniture in the left-wing governments of post-World War II Britain between 1945 and 1951.

Other phenomena of grammar school life lived on. On entry to the school one was allocated to a 'House' – in my case the House of Broughton, with its yellow-coloured sports clothes. The four school Houses were competitive in terms of the formalities relating to success and behaviour. And each House had its captains – one boy and one girl – together with prefects drawn largely from the sixth form, plus 'trainees' from the upper fifth form. I recall that I started off as one of the latter and then became a full prefect in the lower sixth form; and was then made a House captain for the last school year in upper sixth. Responsibilities within each House were exercised by House masters and/or mistresses so that the hierarchy was fully complete. In general, the House system worked in terms of enhancing solidarity and accepting responsibilities as a matter of course.

14. *An early post-war gathering of the Odell and Randon families: in our small Park Road garden*

15. *The winter of 1945/6; 'snowbound' in a neighbour's garden*

16. *Coalville Grammar School's 2nd XI Soccer Team in 1947/8 – but one player didn't make it!*

In addition to House activities and responsibilities, there were also the school's football (soccer), cricket, rounders and hockey sports teams (with Saturday matches morning and/or afternoon) for appropriate seasonal games, against a sequence of teams from a dozen or so other grammar and similar schools in Leicestershire. These all added more to the solidity and formalities of the School: and undoubtedly enhanced the standing of the institution and of its staff and pupils.

At the end of my seventh year of secondary education at Coalville Grammar School, came the denouement in terms of the degree of success which finally emerged: one's results in the Higher School Certificate examinations. In parenthesis it should be remembered that out of the fifty or so entries to the school in 1941, no more than fifteen to twenty – well under half – made it to this final stage. The others – in greater number – had left the school at sixteen with their School Certificates and thus secured their entries mainly to a world of the lower middle class status. I did do well enough in the final examination to secure a Higher School Certificate – based on studies in three subjects – albeit at merely 'good' to 'very good', rather than 'excellent' results. The level achieved was, nevertheless, sufficient to secure my place in the University of Birmingham Department of Geography – though not good enough for me to win a County Major Scholarship from Leicestershire County Council. Each of these was worth the university's entry fees, plus about £200 to cover basic costs for each year of the course as required for securing a bachelor's degree. I, thus, did no better than secure a County bursary, with an annual worth of about £100, awarded to those students who had reached a certain standard of success in their HSC examination and who were prepared to accept the designated career that would emerge from a successful degree course, namely that of a secondary school teacher.

At this stage in my life I wavered over the prospect offered – but not for long as the only alternative at that time was to accept the requirement to do my two year period of National Service in the Army, Navy or Air Force. Thus, I accepted Birmingham University's offer of a place, with some six weeks or so remaining to earn some money to top up the bursary offered, plus a £20+ per annum bonus from the Harley Foundation which seven years earlier had helped financially to secure me a grammar school place.

By this time I had given up my butcher-boy's work, but with my eighteenth birthday behind me I was now able to become a temporary milkman – a six day per week job from 6:00 a.m. to 2:00 p.m. involving an ability to exercise control over the pony and trap whereby the milk could be delivered to customers around various parts of Coalville. Indeed, the delivery round stretched out over eight miles from dairy-back-to-dairy and required me to serve up to a hundred customers. Somehow I survived the dangers and difficulties of a pony with a mind of its own: a pony which always appeared to get restless as I was trying to pour milk from one of the three or four 50-gallon churns loaded onto the trap into the 3- or 4-gallon hand churns from which deliveries were made to the customers (except for the few wealthier customers who bought bottled and pasteurised milk at a premium price). The range of customers spread from the latter few to the much greater number who bought milk from the churn: making for a difficult procedure when trying to serve a customer by means of the pint and half-pint measures to hand from which the milk had to be poured into the receptacle offered by the customer. Such receptacles ranged from pristine fancy jugs to jugs at the other end of the cleanliness scale! Back in 1948 Coalville's milk drinking population ranged from a few relatively wealthy customers to the much greater number of families who managed to survive in a period of relatively low wages (often called the respectable working class); and then on to the smaller numbers of the so-called 'non-respectable' working class families. Doing a milk-round proved to be an eye-opener into the social structure of society in the coal-mining town, even after only seven weeks of exposure to the wide range of Coalville's inhabitants!

Eventually, one early October day in 1948, I boarded the 1.15 p.m. local train to Burton-on-Trent, where I changed to an 'express' to Birmingham. There I had previously sussed out a place to lodge which was relatively close to the University campus. This accommodation charged two guineas (=£2 and 2 shillings) a week for the thirty or so academic weeks each year for bed, breakfast and dinner. All this was in the context of an expected annual income of £130, leaving little more than £60 for all other costs of living, including 1s. 3d. daily lunch, the purchase of compulsory books, other study costs and occasional travel costs between Coalville and Birmingham. Overall, in the context of English academia, then accounting for less than 5 per cent of the country's eighteen-year-old age group – with its different social and systematic attributes – the prospective challenges of the 'New Order', in which I had to become a member, seemed formidable!

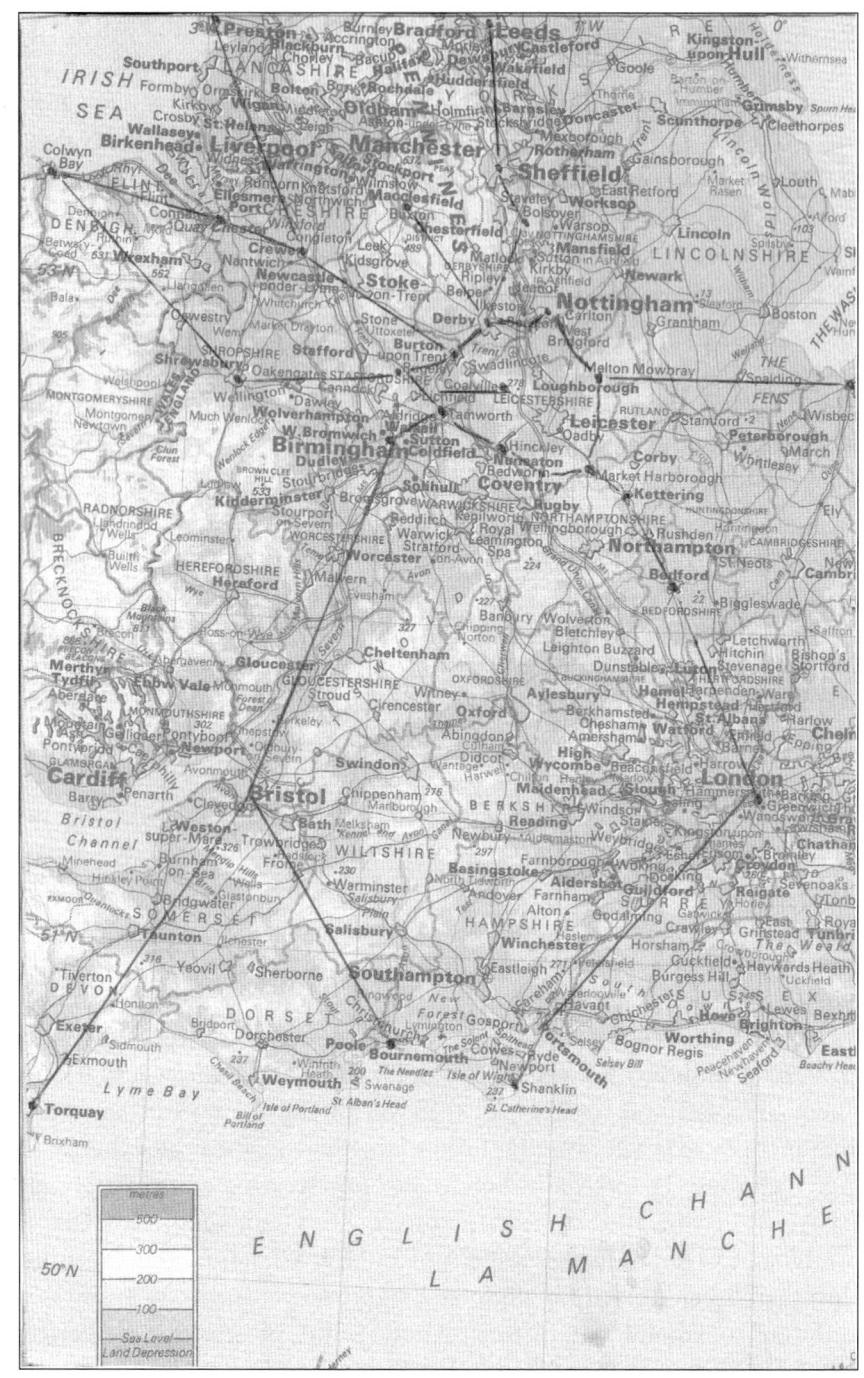

17. *My geographical coverage from Coalville at the centre: but sparsely so beyond the 30 km 'ring' – thereafter un-bikeable distances!*

CHAPTER 2

The University Years, 1948–54

Initial adjustments

FROM COALVILLE TO BIRMINGHAM is no more than 60 kilometres as the crow flies but it was close to a two-hour journey by public transport from my home in the former (only five minutes walk to the railway station) to Birmingham New Street station. From the latter there was an additional 20–25 minute tram ride costing costing 3*d*. from the city centre to the stop at the top of the road in the suburb of Northfield where I was destined to lodge for the next six years. Birmingham, over four times the size of Leicester, was, nevertheless, not unduly overwhelming; but the first part of the tram ride was both morbid and sordid, on a route through inner city slums, in which there were still areas of desolation from the heavy bombing that the city had suffered between 1940 and 1944.

The university's campus, adjacent to Edgbaston, the city's elitist area, was in marked contrast, with its tree-lined roads, most notably the central reservation on Bristol Road, along which the trams plied free of obstacles. This feature continued over the four kilometres or so out to Northfield from the Edgbaston cricket ground, except for the kilometre or so through the industrial and commercial areas of Selly Oak. Thereafter, there was a positive change from that Victorian-orientated suburb to the extensive development created by Cadbury's specially built, inter-war (1918–39) 'village' of Bournville. Here the employees of the company were housed to high standards of the time. Furthermore, potential 'decadence' was eliminated by the bans on pubs and fish and chip shops! Northfield, a further two kilometres or so down the Bristol Road, was a complete contrast, a medieval village which had succumbed to Birmingham's massive housing expansion in the 1920s and 1930s (with some post-World War II additions already there by 1948), in response to the location and continuing growth of the Austin car manufacturing and assembly plant at nearby Longbridge.

Three years of undergraduate geographical studies

My six years as an undergraduate and post-graduate at the University of Birmingham therefore extended over an area of the city which was more than ten times greater than that of my earlier years in Coalville. Nevertheless, in order to save time – and money – I took my Rudge free-wheel and three-speed bicycle, which had already served me well over several of the later years in my home town, to my lodgings in Northfields. It enabled me to cycle most of my four-kilometre journeys each way between there and the University Geography Department, then located in its 'temporary' premises in a part of a teacher training college, just off the formal campus of the University. From there it was little more than a five minute walk to the newly-opened Guild of Undergraduates' Union building with its student-run restaurant and bar, billiards room, debating hall, council room and a large hall used for student societies' meetings, lectures by visiting professors, election hustings (for the student council), performances of the Guild's drama society and, most of all, for the weekly Saturday-night 'hop' with a formal dance band (name now forgotten – but whose signature tune was the long-remembered 'The Rich Maharajah of Magador!). This weekly event – along with the bar and the billiard room (for male members only) – effectively provided the main social life for the great majority of the students, both undergraduate and post-graduate, who from their own towns and countries had chosen Birmingham for their university studies. Students who continued to live at home in the Birmingham area were not, however, insignificant in terms of numbers. Indeed, many students were then 1939/45 war soldiers, sailors and airmen who had waited for years after the end of the war to enter higher education and, having finally achieved this, had then settled down with wife and children within reachable daily travel distance of the University. Their relative numbers within the student population were clearly shown in the fact that twenty-five (or more) of them constituted about 75 per cent of the thirty-three or so undergraduates who were accepted by the University's Geography Department in 1948. Their formidable presence – and their higher ages, plus far greater experiences of life (and the death of comrades) – quickly and effectively diminished the gap between the professors/lecturers (still, in 1948, wearing gowns to lectures) and the members of the student classes.

Unlike Oxbridge and a few other English universities, Birmingham, with its three thousand students in 1948/9, was not a collegiate entity. For better or for worse, the Departmental framework established most of basic social cohesion. Indeed, for every student in a 'designated' hall of residence – within which there were some elements of collegiate formalities – there were nine other students with no such connections.

As a consequence, for most of the students, the Guild of Undergraduates with its plethora of societies ranging from religion and politics through to more playful and sporting associations within and around the Union building, provided many opportunities for non-academic challenges. More examples of these come later in the context of my own Union predilections, following on from my reasonable academic endeavours and, as things turned out, for my unexpected succession to higher responsibilities, within the student world.

Study for a BA in geography was not a continuation of Higher School Certificate grammar school methodology. Indeed, whilst geographical studies in themselves covered a much broader range of topics, each aspect was provided by a specialist member of staff in his or her field. There were also requirements to study two or more subsidiary subjects, as well as exposure to a foreign language. My choice of geology, economics and economic history in their respective faculties, in contrast to my original choice of an undergraduate geographical degree in the Faculty of Arts, was somewhat unwise, given that both the Faculty of Science and the Faculty of Commerce also offered degrees which involved a high level of geographical input. My grammar school had not acquainted me with the alternatives and it was too late to change once I had decided to go for an Arts degree. Thereafter, over many years ahead, the choice of a BA, rather than a BSc or a BCom, led me into uncertainties over my capabilities for alternatives to the pre-determined career as a geography teacher, which I had agreed to take up in order to secure a place at the university with an accompanying modest financial grant. In this context, my choice of which subsidiary subjects to study had to be taken seriously. Happily that was the case, so assisting my eventual entry to, and the choice of, a career which I eventually made after six years of university study and three years of military service in the decade 1948 to 1958.

My academic progress through the three undergraduate years at the University of Birmingham was eminently smooth, given a generally positive relationship with most of the lecturers responsible for the BA course work from 1948 to 1951. I seldom missed lectures and tutorials in which I established myself as a competent note-taker and a reasonably systematic student of the literature as listed by the members of staff, partly by the necessarily financially-limited purchases of the set books, but even more so by the use of the facilities provided by the Departmental library, the University library and the library of the City of Birmingham – all with easy accessibility and comfortable seating!

Through the three years, I steadily drifted from the physical side of the subject to the economic and social components, though not neglecting the geological, geomorphological and climatological elements of the course (with subsequent values in global events culminating in the concern about climate change in recent years). This paradoxically emphasised the then central meteorological thesis for a prospective onset of another global ice-age! Geographical excursions, both locally in Birmingham and in the Black Country, took up many Saturday mornings (and, sometimes, afternoons as well); and thereafter to other parts of the country during vacation periods, so opening up vistas of great geographical contrasts between the Derbyshire Peak District, the mountains of Wales and the coal mines and industries of County Durham.

The culmination of these observational events was ultimately reached in a third year visit in 1950/1 to the centre of France for an eye-opening, first-ever visit to another country, from which the austerity of post-war Britain was finally exposed. Meanwhile, the required BA dissertation, on a topic agreed with one's tutor, had to be formulated and prepared for submission before final exams. For this, my pre-university background in Coalville and its surrounding area provided a subject which could be done from home: the evolution of the railway system based on the north-west Leicestershire coalfield and associated extractive industries over more than one hundred years. Fortunately, data enough from my father's access to relevant railway documentation – to add to his personal observations over many years – proved to be sufficient to give me an A+ mark for the dissertation and, I suspect, just enough 'oomph' to take me through to my surprising award of the only first-class BA honours degree in the total of thirty-three class members.

This, together with the prestigious W.A. Cadbury prize awarded to me from the 1948–51 group of Birmingham geography students; and the award of a university post-graduate scholarship – covering both the entire fees and a bursary of around £300 per year – fundamentally changed my prospective career outlook. This success required the cancellation of the requirement initially put upon me by the Leicestershire Education

THE UNIVERSITY YEARS, 1948-54　　　　31

18. Birmingham University staff and students of the Geography Department, 1949/50

19. July 1951: Graduation Day on the campus outside the Great Hall

20. 1st Class Honour's Degree now awarded at Birmingham University

21. After Degree Day, a visit to Skien in Southern Norway

22. Our Norwegian families' daughters guide us in their local countryside

Authority to proceed from a bachelor's degree to a one-year teaching diploma and, thereafter, to a post as a secondary school geography teacher. Instead, I undertook a three-year research project, so leading to the potential award of a Ph.D.

This project began following the Arts Faculty undergraduate 1951 degree ceremony just three days after my twenty-first birthday. Unhappily, this ceremony could be attended only by my father and sister, as my mother was already too ill to make the railway journey from Coalville to Birmingham and back in the day. A twenty-first birthday celebration was thus also out of the question. Instead, after a month or so of familiar paid work as a milkman, a friend from earlier years' summer work in holiday fellowship centres, viz. Stan Glenny, and I went abroad for a month to southern Norway on the invitation of a couple of families in the town of Skien whose daughters had been at a Holiday Friendship centre the previous year, where Stan and I had been responsible for the guests' welfare and enjoyment. Norway turned out to be a humdinger of a holiday with the outward sea crossing from Newcastle to Bergen and a return trip from Oslo back to Newcastle. In Norway we travelled from Bergen on one of the world's most scenic railways to the capital city of Oslo, where we were greeted and entertained by our hosts, prior to the onward journey by train to Skien. In that year southern Norway revelled in perfect summer weather so that both local and regional visits – by car or public transport – were of the essence. Being smitten by the landscape and the family hosts (especially Liv, their elder daughter!), I considered the possibility of expanding my prospective graduate research project on the evolution of the social geography of Leicestershire towns over the 150 years since 1800 to incorporate a comparative element; namely that of the Norwegian 'county' of Telemark (of which Skien was the county town).

Unfortunately, the designated supervisor for my Ph.D. research, Professor Kinvig, Chairman of the Birmingham University Geography Department, would not accept my proposal and hence my potential Norwegian affiliations were frustrated. Though, as will be shown later in my memoirs, my Norwegian connection was resuscitated twenty years later, following the discovery and development of the country's formidable offshore oil and gas resources at a time when upstream oil and gas developments in North-West Europe had become my main research interest.

Post-Graduate Ph.D. Geography Research, 1951 to 1954

Over this three year period, my research efforts and their eventual production of the required thesis necessarily split my life between Birmingham and Coalville, but with other locations also involved, partly in the search for relevant data in the British Library, the National Newspaper Library and the Public Record Offices – all in London – and partly from my role as a member of the executive committees of the National Union of Students and the World University Service.

The time post-1951 spent in Coalville, in particular, and Leicestershire, in general, had two elements. First, there was the increasing severity of my mother's illness, leading to her confinement to bed in 1952, so that my help was required at home, given a situation in which my father continued to have to work shifts as a railwayman, combined with my sister's efforts to qualify as a nursery nurse for pre-school children at a centre in Leicester involving a daily approximately 45-minute bus ride in each direction. Such a situation necessitated my being available for my share of household duties, as and when I was able to postpone my researches in the county or able to forgo not only my analysis of the evidence in the Birmingham University geographical research centre, but also my responsibilities by this time for the British Committee of the World University Service.

Notwithstanding these other responsibilities, my work on the thesis went steadily ahead, culminating in the production and presentation by February 1954 of a two-volume study running to a total of 643 pages under the title, 'A Study of the Development of Urban Spheres of Influence in Leicestershire'. The two bound volumes of this thesis incorporated an Introduction of 108 pages plus three Sections of 502 pages in total, a Conclusion of 6 pages, three Appendices taking up 6 more pages and a three-part Bibliography (General Works of Reference (4 pages); Local Works of Reference (4 pages); and published Directories (2 pages). I assume that they all collectively remain in an appropriate section of the reference library of the University of Birmingham. Over the now more than fifty-six years since my thesis was accepted, I have never had a real motivation to seek it out. Moreover, I do not recall even one approach from an interested party seeking to find out more about my early-1950s study! Its total readership to date has thus probably been no more than four: namely, myself, Professor Kinvig, my supervisor; and the two external examiners (Professor Smailes, then head of the Geography Department of Queen Mary College in the

University of London and Prof. A.N. Other, whose name and university I cannot recall!).

With my Ph.D. an academic career opened up, but the opportunity to pursue other activities over the subsequent seven years to 1961 put what might otherwise have been an immediate prospect on the back-burner. Between times, the only utility engendered by the thesis was in the form of the publication of two short papers in British geographical journals of the period: first, 'The Hinterlands of Melton Mowbray and Coalville' in the *Transactions of the Institute of British Geographers*; and second, 'Urban Spheres of Influence in Leicestershire in the Mid-Nineteenth Century' in *Geographical Studies*, both in 1957, no less than three years after the award of my Ph.D.!

Extra-curricular student politics

I now need to go back to my pre-university years before 1948, in order to emphasise the continuation of my 1945/8 political activities. Coalville was, of course, a stronghold of the Labour Party right from the general election of 1945, from which a Labour government, led by Clement Atlee, secured overwhelming power for only the second time in its then fifty or so years as the country's socialist party. Given the party's promises of a national health service available free at time of need, for social security and educational developments, together with the promise of the nationalisation of the coal mines, the railways and the gas, electricity and water services, I was proud and enthusiastic to be able to 'do my bit' to help secure a Labour MP for the Bosworth constituency in which Coalville's domination by miners and railwaymen was formidable. At home we took the left-wing *Daily Herald* on weekdays, together with the equally socialist *Reynolds's News* on Sundays and the *John Bull* magazine on, I recall, Fridays. In addition, I became a youthful subscriber to the famous Left Book Club published by Gollancz – even though I could only purchase the regular productions from a specific book shop in Leicester. I still have on my bookshelf all fourteen of the much-read publications of 1947/8: namely *The Coming Crisis*; *Adventure in the Sun*; *Behind the Silken Curtain*; *Austrian Requiem*; *When Smuts Goes*; *So Many Hungers*; *Socialism of the West*; *The Cooperative Movement in Labour Britain*; *Labour Life and Poverty*; *Prisoners of Fear*; *Kaffirs are Lively*; *How Long the Night*; *The Tragedy of Austria*; and *The Men in the Pits* – the last of the series! After the 1945 election, with the help of the Leicestershire Branch of the National Union of Mineworkers, I and a fellow Coalville Grammar School boy – Terry Burke, the son of a miner and the owner of a collection of jazz records – had launched the Coalville Branch of the Labour League of Youth. As its meetings could not be held – as with every other Labour gathering – in the Labour Working Men's Club (with a liquor licence and sawdust and spittoons on the floor), we gathered fortnightly in the Branch Offices of the National Union of Miners. From this 'bastion of the left', Terry and I went forth to attack the local and national Tories by letters to the local newspaper, the *Coalville Times*; and we even put in regular attendances at Tory party meetings in order to barrack the speakers!

With this 1945–48 teenage background in the Labour Party, my move to the University of Birmingham took me into immediate membership of the Student Union's Labour Society and, through that link to work for the Northfield Constituency Labour Party – and others elsewhere in the City – as local and by-elections required. Needless to say, with a Labour government over those years that extended wartime austerity to 1950, there was a declining level of support for the party, and for its local and national standing. This culminated in its heavy defeat in the 1951 general election. By then, however, I had successfully won a seat on the Guild of Undergraduates' Council and, through that, subsequently became an elected member of the Student Union's Executive Council on which I was made responsible for 'external affairs'. This involved my representation of Birmingham University students at social and other events in other English universities and colleges, so taking me for days or weekends to many different parts of the country. Even more important was my representational function at the annual and other meetings of the National Union of Students – at most of which the central issue was that of student grants or of relationships with other bodies, including Trades Unions, of which many or even most university graduates would eventually become members.

From national to international interests

Also to come, however, was another level of contacts with European and international contexts. First, in 1951, I led a 'team' of just two students from Birmingham to Hungary for a couple of weeks of exchanges with our opposite numbers in a country within the Soviet bloc. This event preceded the development of affordable air services in Europe. Instead, we travelled

THE UNIVERSITY YEARS, 1948–54   37

23. Discussions in Budapest in 1951 between us and our hosts

24. On returning to Birmingham we hand over a gift from the Hungarian Student Union to our Union's president

25. In East Berlin at the IUS meeting in 1953, I speak on behalf of the British National Union of Students' decision to leave the International Union

by train – from Birmingham to London; then from London to Ostend (via Dover and a cross-Channel ferry); from Ostend to Cologne and thence to Prague in Czechoslovakia where we were welcomed, fed and watered by the executive committee and staff of the International Union of Students (the IUS) of which the NUS was then a member. Twenty-four hours later we were put on the night train to Budapest. The following morning we were received at Budapest's main station by a welcoming party from the Hungarian NUS, together with the press. It seemed that we were the first western European students to have visited post-war, Russian-controlled Hungary.

The programme presented to us was formidable in terms of how many people we were to meet and exchange ideas with and of how many places we were to visit. This prospect was made less strenuous and tiring when we discovered that our stay in Budapest would be at the famous Gellert Hotel, standing on the north bank of the Danube (in Buda). It was, indeed, what one would have expected if billeted and fed in the London Ritz Hotel. But it went even further than this, as it ranked at the top of a luxurious phenomenon that stood higher and mightier above the rank and file of the rest of the population than even the Ritz could have managed in 1951. The Royal Hotel on Woburn Place used by the NUS in London to accommodate its 'executives' and visitors for overnight plus breakfast for twelve shillings and sixpence was from another world – that of UK austerity. This UK situation contrast with the generous Hungarian hotel hospitality was still further enhanced when we discovered that the transport for our visits was to be door-to-door service by a limousine of formidable Russian proportions! Each day of the two weeks the car was waiting for us outside the Gellert Hotel to carry us to the appointments and meetings on the agenda for the day, all of which had been determined in advance.

The full details have long since been lost in a succession of moves from place to place as my career emerged, but there are a number of events which still remain in my memory. We were always chaperoned around with virtually no possibility of any changes to the schedule with the exception of a few free hours on the last day in Budapest. This, we thought, provided an opportunity to buy some souvenirs: but to no avail, as the city shops were so poorly stocked with goods, available only to the citizens with their ration cards (not unlike the situation at that time in the UK). The central market offered non-regulated purchases, but still with little choice. Indeed, the sole purchasable souvenir was a pair of gloves!

The official visits were largely based in Budapest, ranging from a reception in our honour at the city's university to a half-day in the main hospital including our presence at an operation. Then to the centre for the children's state organisation, the Pioneers: a derivation, it seemed, from Baden-Powell's Scouting system. The facilities for physical education activities, plus the training for marching and displays through to the 'railway' system which the children ran and to the indoctrination in words and music of the communist system, were all mightily impressive.

In addition to these and other visits in Budapest, we were also introduced to the beauty of Lake Balaton and then to the city of Miskolc, some 150 kilometres to the east of the capital. This long trip on a not-too-good road took us through essentially rural areas of northern Hungary, in which all the villages we saw appeared to be very poor. The city of Miskolc itself, on the other hand, was, as the country's centre for heavy industry, much more buoyant, with Hungary's major iron and steel plant strangely similar to those in the UK's Black Country between Birmingham and Wolverhampton. The highlight of our visit was, however, yet to come, when we were driven from Miskolc to a large state-owned collective farm to see something of the centrally-planned rural side of the country's economy. Discussion on the nature of the farming system was interesting, but this was soon overwhelmed by the invitation to take lunch. And what a lunch it was, with a great plethora of courses and dishes accompanied by Hungarian wines of never-ending availability. And it lasted for over five hours! Our invocation of fraternal greetings and solidarity through toast after toast, based not only on wine, but also on vodka, led to our stumbling exit from the farm buildings, fortunately over a very limited distance to our waiting limousine. Communist Hungary, we had discovered, was truly intoxicating!

Such international events thereafter ruled my timetable, given my subsequent nomination as one of the National Union of Students' representatives at meetings of the Prague-based International Union of Students. Of these several occasions, the one that stands out in my memory dates from March 1953 when I was dispatched to Berlin to convey the decision of the NUS to withdraw from the IUS, given the latter's Russian-dominated position. At the time this appeared to be a brief and perfectly straightforward venture with a direct two-hour plane journey from London to West Berlin in operation. On arrival I found a lodging for the night in the western part of the city with the intention to use the S-bahn to cross into East Berlin early the following day, so as to register my presence for the IUS Executive meeting in Humboldt University. My plan went smoothly – even more so than expected when, on exiting the S-Bahn station in the vicinity of the University, I was struck by the absence of vehicles and people on the streets and pavements. It was eerily quiet as I walked the few hundred metres to the university, on arrival at which it seemed to be closed! An armed policeman showed me to an entrance door behind which a reception desk for the meeting had been set. I stood alone for some considerable time until a receptionist appeared. In response to my inquiry as to why the members of the IUS were not yet there, I was in return asked why I had reported there, given the overnight news: 'Didn't you know,' I was asked, 'that comrade Stalin's death has been announced and that everything is on hold? And that only the police and the military are allowed on the streets!' I would therefore, I was told, be escorted to the hotel at which reservations had been made for me; and at which I was to remain until contacted. Thereafter, I watched the movements (and the lack of movements) on the streets of East Berlin from the window of my hotel room for the rest of the day and into the following morning. That morning a beautiful and charming young lady arrived at my room to inform me of the revised schedule for the Executive Meeting and that she would take care of my needs! On my near-immediate assumption that the room was bugged by hidden cameras and/or microphones, I declined to do other than to meet with her in the hotel foyer, as and when necessary!

It was forty-eight hours later before the meeting began. There I delivered the message of the NUS's decision to terminate its membership on the IUS, in the context of the latter organisation's unwillingness to make itself independent of Russian control. This was declared by the IUS executive committee as incorrect and unnecessary and I was asked to secure different instructions. I agreed to report back, but emphasised that the NUS had been firm in its decision and was thus very unlikely to change its mind. I then decided to leave the meeting in my own interest lest I was seen and even apprehended as a possible 'spy' in East Berlin. I thus proceeded back to West Berlin and then to Tempelhof airport for the first available flight back to London. Within days, the NUS executive confirmed its decision for the NUS to leave the IUS, and to consider the possibility of creating a Western-orientated alternative international student organisation. How much of this was due to pressure and/or from promises from the government and other bodies on the President and Vice President of the NUS, I was unable to discover. Thereafter, my term as a member of the NUS executive came to an end so that, outside the need for greater attention to my doctorate research, I now gave more attention to my role as a member of the executive committee of the charitable student organisation, viz. the World University Service. There upon another significant role for me in international student affairs soon emerged: a visit to India and the Middle East to participate in an international WUS seminar at the University of Mysore: and, thereafter, at a meeting of the WUS in Istanbul.

An Indian experience

My selection as the British participant (alongside a single representative from most other western European countries, as well as about thirty students from North America) to join in a close to two months' seminar at Mysore University in southern India, necessitated preliminary preparations in terms of inoculations and the purchase of tropical kit in time for the required departure from the UK on 2 June 1953 – the day of the coronation of Elizabeth II! Starting from Coalville, the first stage of the journey was a two-hour train ride to Birmingham and then by bus to its airport, followed by a two-hour flight to Paris where all the North American and European participants were scheduled to meet. This was for an initial briefing session prior to a chartered flight to Bombay the following day. Long distance air flights in 1953 were virtually unknown – especially by the planes of India's Bharat Airways. It was only a DC4 with fewer than a hundred seats and a maximum flying time with a full load of about four hours. As there was a total contingent in excess of the seating capacity – and probably of weight limitations as well – the journey seemed likely to be 'interesting'!

And so it was. At each intermediate stop for refuelling and meals, in Cyprus and Bahrain, the overload of passengers were instructed to sit at the rear of the aisle in the approach to landing and then, on instructions from the pilot as the plane touched down, they were told to run forward down the aisle in order to enable the plane's front wheel to hit the runway! The same happened on arrival in Bombay, by which time the plane's condition had worsened as the cowling on the starboard side engine was detached completely from the plane – and fell to somewhere in the Indian Ocean! The seriousness of the eventful flight eventually emerged when, on a return trip to Bombay from Mysore, I was invited to meet the head of Tata Ltd, India's then largest company. In the small-talk that preceded our discussion on my experiences in India, I was asked by my host how I travelled to his country. 'By Bharat Airways,' I responded. And I was then informed by

26. Bharat Airways DC4 for the Paris/Bombay flight

27. A stop-over at the small 'airport' in Bahrain

28. The Maharajah of Mysore welcomes us to his palace

THE UNIVERSITY YEARS, 1948–54

29. We are greeted by a march-past in the city

30. Our invitation to the Town Hall of the City of Mysore

31. My ex-army uniform meets the requirement of hot weather

32. Five of us gather together as participants from five countries

my host that he was Chairman of the company that owned and ran the airline. But then, he added, 'I would never ever travel by one of its planes!'

Earlier, our overland trip from Bombay to the ultimate destination of Mysore was by Indian Railways: first, by a relatively short 150 km train journey to Poona up in the Western Ghats (where the altitude somewhat reduced the monsoon's heat); and then on a train to Mysore on the almost 1000 km narrow-gauge track, but with comfortable privileged Class 1 accommodation for both the days and the nights across the essentially rural Deccan. Breakfasts, lunches and dinners were supplied at successive station restaurants – together with the china, the pots and the pans which were then collected an hour or so later down the line at the next main station. The train's average speed over the journey was no more than 50 kph and given that there were many station stops, our journey to Mysore took two full days and nights; by then our eventual arrival was some eight days from leaving the UK.

Mysore is located at an altitude of over 500 metres and so we found that its climate was less enervating than that of Bombay, making our many weeks' sojourn very acceptable and positive for the proceedings. The seminar, with the intention of evolving north/south relationships in the aftermath of India's independence from the UK, was located on the campus of the city's university and was comprised of an equal number of local Indian students and the fifty-plus foreign students from Canada, the US and Europe, together with an equal number of Indian and foreign academics as the contributing speakers. Accommodation was in the double rooms of the halls of residence, with one local student and one visitor in each room, while the university supplied all meals *à la* Indian cuisine.

Fifty-seven years on from the event makes it difficult to recall the details of the academic programme, but the topics of mid-twentieth century international politics and cultural differences were discussed in depth and at length, through the many days set out by the programme. It was, however, the formal and informal extra-curricular occasions that have left me with the more significant memories. These ranged from the ubiquity of the traditional bicycle (with British names, but manufactured in India) as the means of local transport, to the splendour of the palace and the elephants (in ceremonial dress) of the Maharajah of Mysore. All members of the seminar were invited to the Palace for 'afternoon tea', a guided tour and, if wished, an elephant ride. Other excursions which were organised took us on bus tours to some of the splendours of the antiquities of the state, as well as to examples of the area's agricultural and other economic activities. Out of all this eye-opening presentation of another world, well away from that of home-base, one event remains vividly in my memory.

The timing of the seminar was, of course, only a few years after the declaration of the independence of India from British rule. Thus, my physical European stature, my khaki uniform (ex-British army tropical wear) and my topee were still familiar to the people in the villages and on the streets of the city. On one day's lengthy cycle ride out of Mysore City into the countryside, I went well ahead of my Indian colleagues to reach a sizeable village. There I was stopped by the inhabitants on their assumption that I was the new Assistant District Commissioner (ADC) arriving after four long years in the village which had had no such appointee following the British withdrawal. As a result there had been no one to hear and determine villagers' disputes over land ownership issues, nor to try other misdemeanours that had occurred and which required legal examinations and decisions. I was thus invited by the villagers 'to fulfil my ADC responsibilities' in the context of long-overdue judicial procedures! My quandary was, however, short-lived as, by then, Indian colleagues from the seminar had also reached the village. They were eventually able, though with difficulty, to persuade the villagers that I was not an ADC and had no authority – or, for that matter, competence – to undertake the hearings. Embarrassment all round was the order of the day!

At the end of the month's seminar proceedings I took my leave of staff and fellow students, with many contrasting ideas on where to go to from Mysore to other parts of India. The British World University Service (the sponsor of my journey to India and to the seminar) had, however, asked me to visit a number of Indian institutions with which it had had earlier contacts. Thus I headed first to Madras – about ten hours by train from Mysore – to see how things were going at one of its university colleges in the aftermath of financial assistance provided by the WUS in London. And then, likewise in Hyderabad; and, finally, in Bombay. In the latter, in addition to endless discussions, I was provided with a car and driver to do the rounds of the city, with its still viable functions as the British port of entry. Thereafter, after an ex-British evening gathering which I was invited to attend and at which I learned much about India's post-independence period, I finally left from the Indian sub-continent as a much better informed student.

An inspiring Middle-Eastern and European journey home

My departure from India in late July was in marked contrast with my arrival on the Bharat Airways charter flight. Instead, I was provided with a ticket from Bombay to the Lebanon on a BOAC Comet airliner, the first jet-powered plane to enter passenger service (albeit briefly, following the subsequent loss of two such planes in mid-air flights between India and the UK). My flight from Bombay to Beirut had now become only a relatively short hop, so giving me a few days in the first Middle Eastern city I had visited. Local contacts through the American University enabled me to see both the city and its hinterland, with time and facilities enough to organise my flight to Istanbul on an uncomfortable ex-French military plane converted for civilian use. The object in Istanbul was to fulfil my role as a British delegate to the annual meeting of the World University Service Organisation. It was, of course, also a city of prime historical significance, and then, by the 1950s, one of great strategic importance between Europe, the Middle East and the former Soviet Union. What was there to be seen, in terms of historic and religious (both Christian and Islamic) attributes, turned out to be much more interesting than the content and procedures of the WUS meeting! Nevertheless, my knowledge and understanding was extended in both of these contrasting elements and opportunities.

Duty – and sightseeing in Istanbul – having been done, I then joined up with the three other British WUS representatives for the journey back to London – and home – via a number of European countries en route. Calls were thus made on various WUS national committees and facilities. The first stage was by coastal steamboat from Istanbul to Piraeus/Athens in Greece. There our hosts made sure we saw the main archaeological sites, both those in the city and those in its neighbourhood. We went from the then quite dilapidated Parthenon, following war-time damage in the first half of the 1940s, to the most famous and largest of the outdoor Athena theatres in proximity to Athens. Another boat trip then provided the second stage of our journey across Europe, from Piraeus through the Corinth Canal and on to Brindisi in southern Italy, also still showing residual elements of the Italian war front from 1943 to 1945. Thence, we travelled by train across the peninsula to Naples and its seemingly gross over-population, with a side trip to Pompeii and Vesuvius, as well as to viewpoints on the Bay of Naples and its famous sunsets. We went yet further on by train, this time to Rome, where Italian WUS representatives welcomed us and again took us to the city's main historic sites – as well as to the beaches on the Tyrrhenian Sea. There was basically nothing back in the UK which I could then put on a par with Rome and its surrounding areas.

From Rome – again by train – we headed north through Florence and Turin (but without time to stop for sight-seeing) to Chamonix in the French Alps. There we were due to make a visit to the hospital/convalescent home for European students suffering from lung diseases (tuberculosis and so on) made possible through financial help from various national-WUS affiliates. Once more – both for me and some of the companions on the journey – our eyes were opened to a locality and a facility quite unknown in the UK.

On returning home to a Ph.D. and my mother's death

Again with an overnight stop in Paris (my first earlier visit there had been in 1951 on a field trip arranged for final year students in Birmingham University's School of Geography), I finally returned to the UK in mid-September 1953, leaving only five months at most in which to complete my Ph.D. thesis.

Meanwhile, in the period of my absence abroad, my mother's medical condition had seriously deteriorated and a terminal diagnosis had been given, becaue of the failure of the then non-operable mitral valve of the heart, a consequence of her childhood rheumatic fever. After a further four months of bedridden survival in the home in which she had lived since her marriage in 1928, she died at home in the presence of our family, in February 1954, at the early age of fifty-one. After the burial service at the nearby London Road Baptist Chapel with a full congregation of families and friends, she was buried on a bitterly cold day in Coalville's Broomleys cemetery, in a grave next to that of her Odell parents-in-law.

On the side of the Randon family she was the first to die of her generation of the six siblings. Her limited life – and particularly that after her marriage – had been hard, given the sequence of adverse financial and wartime difficulties, together with the problems of my father's deafness and my sister's illnesses. Nevertheless, until her last few years of painful deterioration, she had been just what wives and mothers were then expected to be, viz., a good cook, in spite of the limited options to make the weekly wage go round, and an even better housekeeper in our small

Park Road house, where wind-driven grime from the burning waste banks of the two nearby collieries (Whitwick and Snibston) necessitated frequent dusting and polishing in our house; and even more so, with respect to the weekly – or more frequent – washing as it was hung out to dry in the garden. The winds blowing from the direction of the pits often necessitated a re-wash of many items. Almost all working-class homes in Coalville in the 1930s and 1940s were without washing machines and driers, refrigerators and any central heating and hot water heating facilities. The hard and continuing work so generated for the housewives of the period served to increase the early loss of life. My mother's later years of ill-health

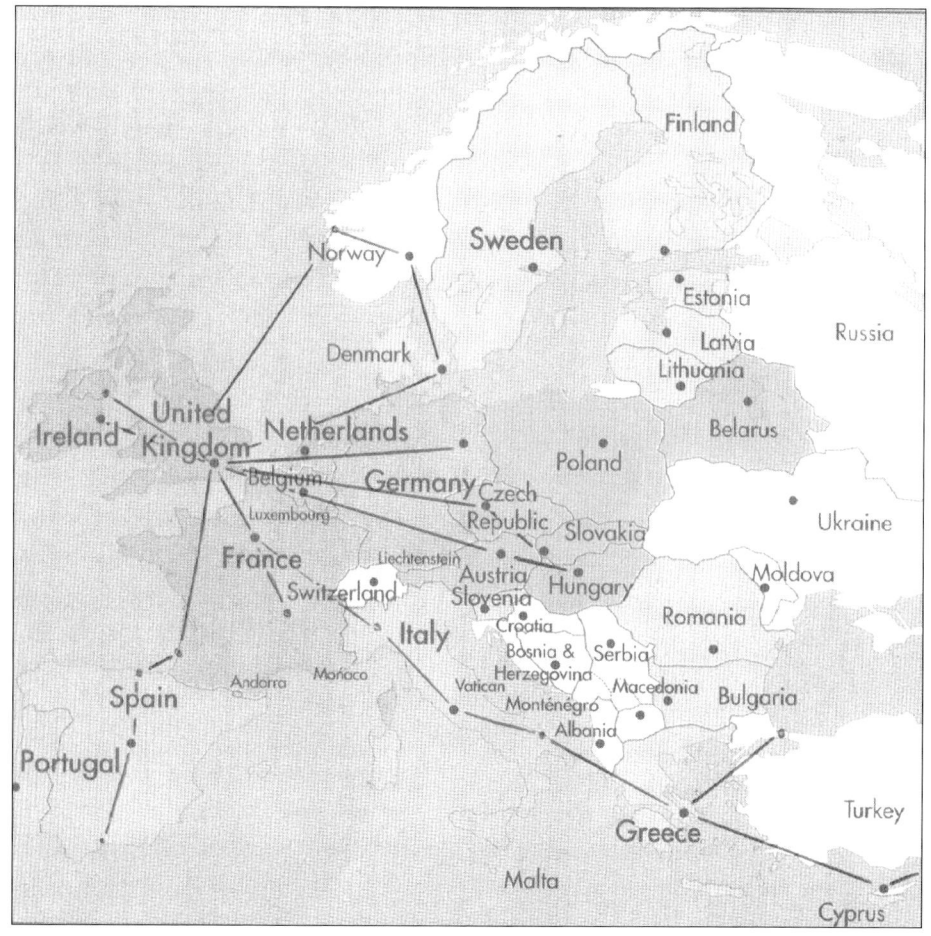

33. *How my post-1951 activities engendered several journeys across Europe: and into the Levant (beyond Cyprus)*

epitomised the phenomenon, and taught me to put my nose to the proverbial grindstone whereby to secure a longer and better life.

As with my mother's earlier inability to attend my graduation ceremony in the July 1951, so by her early death she also failed to see the formalities of the award of my doctorate in July 1954. What, however, I was able to tell her in her dying days was that Professor Kinvig, the supervisor of my graduate work, had told me that he was certain that my external examiners would accept my thesis as worthy of the award of a Ph.D.

By then, I think that my mother died still remembering and realising the potential validity of the advice she had been given by a doorstep gypsy in the early days of her marriage which she passed on to me many years later: namely that her 'son would become famous in London when he grew up'. That message did, I think, become a serious motivating element in my subsequent efforts to try to reach higher ground in the natural order of things over the second half of the century. With hindsight, would that I could – and should – have achieved that which the gypsy foretold! But 'twas not to be, except, for example, for my many appearances on TV and radio programmes concerning the initial exploitation of the UK's and other countries' oil and natural gas resources; and later as a special adviser on these matters to Tony Benn, the then Secretary of State for Energy in the late-1970s.

Chapter 3

1954–58: As an Officer of the Queen; a Belated Marriage; a Year in the United States and the Search for a Career!

Compulsory military service

Britain's compulsory military service for most eighteen-year-old men continued well after the end of World War II in 1945, but post-1947 conscription was delayed for those who were accepted for higher education. My call-up papers were thus not sent to me for the six years which I spent at Birmingham University, but were then immediately issued in mid-1954 following the completion and acceptance of my Ph.D. thesis. In the context of having zero savings at that time I decided to seek a three-year service commission which offered a higher rank and a significantly higher salary than that paid to those opting for the compulsory two-year stint of National Service. In addition there was £300 (a current value of about £4,500) tax free, and a lump sum payable at the end of the designated period. The references required were duly obtained and dispatched to the RAF's recruitment office in London and were then followed very quickly by a stiff interview and a thorough medical check-up. In spite of my radical political views and my participation in left-wing student union affairs, I was, much to my surprise, accepted for the RAF Education Branch. Early in June 1954 I thus received my instructions and my travel passes to proceed to Liverpool in order to catch the ferry to the Isle of Man at 11:00 hours on a specified day, and thence by the then still existing Manx railway passenger service from Douglas to Sulby Glen station some 40 km away. From there I travelled by RAF vehicles to the base for the Officer Training Centre on the Jurby airbase. I reported in at about 5:00 p.m. and was destined to be there until late mid-September.

Thus began the switch from my civilian to a military status, with the initial 13 weeks of training covering the whole range from learning the

Queen's Regulations to the use of weapons. In this context of the established physical and learning requirements of the RAF, without any permitted element of idiosyncratic behaviour or of challenges to the wisdom and logic of the rules and regulations, the solidarity and bonhomie within the officer-cadet ranks were of prime importance and were speedily learned! Physically it was a tough three months during which we seemed to have marched or crawled over every square metre on the Isle of Man, fortunately in extraordinarily good summer weather. Duties included march-training and how to clean, hold and use both rifles and Bren guns; and a requirement to read, mark, learn and inwardly digest the Queen's Regulations. Out of 'working' hours (some evenings plus Saturday afternoons and all day Sundays) relaxation on the base – including the requirement to set to shining one's own boots and to cleaning one's clothing and bed space – was modified by visits permitted on Saturdays to evening dances in the island's resorts – most notably with Joe Loss and his orchestra at the Villa Marina in Douglas – along with about 1500 holiday makers, and also on other occasions to the much nearer Ramsey swimming pool which was converted to a dance hall on most Saturdays!

Overall, the switch from academic research and student activities to service in the RAF was a positive addition to my life experience about which I had only one real grumble, viz. the refusal of my allocated Squadron Leader to release me from the four hours of training on the first Saturday in July, in order to permit me to be present at the 1954 Degree Congregation of the University of Birmingham for the collection of my Ph.D. degree (which was thus awarded *in absentia*). This was an unhappy event for me, but even more so for my recently-widowed father and other family members and friends from Coalville. As far as I can recall, no formal document was ever sent to me by the University for my Doctorate Degree which in 1954 was still an infrequent award outside of the Faculty of Science.

Thereafter, the remaining weeks were steadily written off over a period during which the formal passing-out parade was rehearsed and rehearsed to perfection. A very senior RAF officer took the salute! Then, following our last collective and somewhat alcoholic evening in the NAAFI canteen, we were taken the following day to join the Isle of Man train to Douglas at Sulby Glen station – and thence on the boat to Liverpool. This was followed by what I think was a week's leave, after which I was required to report to RAF Grantham in Lincolnshire for a month's training course on

1954-58 – AS AN OFFICER OF THE QUEEN   53

34. RAF Jurby, Isle of Man: 'on guard'

35. 'Comrades in Arms' Ready for a march – with rifles and other kit – over many miles!

36. The 1954 Passing Out Parade – after 3 months training; PRO in the foreground awaiting instructions

how to teach in the RAF's Education Branch. At this stage we were invited to nominate the RAF bases we preferred. Given my earlier international jaunts as a 'student politician', I selected an overseas posting – with a preference for Changi in Singapore, followed by Cyprus, Malta and Germany! Instead, those in charge of such matters decided I should be posted to RAF Halton in Buckinghamshire for which Aylesbury was the nearest town. I then learned that this base was essentially non-operational, but with one runway maintained for the in and out flights of senior officers, and from which – using the Avro Anson 2-engine propeller planes which were maintained there – those officers on the base who had secured their 'wings' met the requirement for achieving so many hours per month of flying time, in case of an outbreak of hostilities.

Halton's main function, however, was essentially educational. Boys of sixteen upwards signed up for RAF careers involving an initial three years of training at Halton in their chosen field of technical services. At any one time there were upwards of 1500 of these apprentices divided into 'wings' and 'squadrons' for military purposes and engaged in their choice of technical training, involving both practical work and class work in maths, sciences and other studies. I was designated as an instructor in the latter area, incorporating some English language, history and geography, together with current international affairs and the history of the RAF. One's classroom teaching commitments totalled up to thirty hours per week, but there were also additional hours of responsibility for the apprentices' more military commitments, including parade ground practices, the imposition of treatment for those who broke RAF rules and in ensuring that the weekly church service was duly attended (whether C of E, non-Conformist or Catholic – each with their respective padres and a church on the base). Overall, the workload was by no means excessive and, indeed, the few traumatic occasions could be quickly mellowed by the quality of the officers' mess.

This was located in no less than a mansion that had been built in the mid-nineteenth century by the Rothschild family, as one of several other such homes along the Vale of Aylesbury, at the foot of the north side of the Chiltern Hills. And allegedly near enough each other so that they could communicate by semaphore! The accommodation, the food, the great hall and its balcony and the rooms set aside for the dining room, the splendid bar, the reading and the television rooms, all combined to provide a luxurious ambiance in which, moreover, the 'servants' (including both low-ranking Air Force personnel and civilian employees) were readily on call. Outside the house there were extensive gardens, a splendid croquet lawn, tennis courts and riding stables. My three years 'in residence' at RAF Halton provided a taste of 'upper class' living, the likes of which I have subsequently found on very few other occasions and even then only for very short periods!

An added bonus was the base's proximity to London with frequent train services from Wendover station on an extension of the London Metropolitan line. This was a couple of miles or so from Halton House for trains to Marylebone or Baker Street. Apart from sightseeing and social occasions in London town, I was also able to register for an evening course at the University of London. The subject was international relations (nicely fitting in with my requirement to teach the subject to the apprentices). The course extended over two academic years and demanded a great deal of homework both in reading the set books and in writing the required essays. Happily, all worked out well as I ended up with a post-graduate diploma in the subject – with distinction! I was also able to frequent evening French classes in Harrow-on-the-Hill (en route to London) and, in having done so, I registered for a two-week advanced course in the French University of Dijon, so adding further credentials for my post-RAF years!

A belated marriage

Throughout the first twenty-four years of my life, I had lived and worked in sexually mixed circumstances and situations. I was born into an extended family (the Odell/Randon mix) with a sister and half a dozen female cousins plus ten male cousins. Both the schools I attended from five to eighteen years old were for boy and girls, with segregation largely restricted to sporting-cum-physical training sessions. Additionally, at the grammar school there were male/female divides between woodwork and metalwork for the boys and 'domestic science' (cookery and all that) for the girls. However, from the age fourteen years upwards, compulsory (lunch-time) ballroom dancing lessons were imposed as a requirement. This led into a situation for the Class 5 year boys having to write a request to the girl of his choice that she become his partner at the school Christmas party! Such precocious requirements led, on balance, to an enhanced degree of antipathy between the sexes, rather than in the other direction.

At Birmingham University in the late forties and early fifties, female students were in a small minority, so that romances were rare. Within the

37. RAF Halton House for the officers – from the front

38. Rear view of the House

1954-58 – AS AN OFFICER OF THE QUEEN   57

39. Myself and four colleagues awaiting instructions!

40. Flying Officer Jean M. McKintosh in Princess Mary's RAF Nursing Service based at the RAF Halton hospital; and later to become my wife!

community, the only events to which nurses from the local hospital and a few other local girls were invited were the weekly Saturday evening 'hops' and, on a lesser scale, more formal dinner dances organised by members of various campus clubs and societies. Thus, over my six years at Birmingham the issue of possible courtship and marriage – let alone the unknown phenomenon of 'living together' outside matrimony – was of near-zero consideration!

On switching to a military function at Halton at the age of twenty-four, I found that many – even most – of my colleagues were in their early twenties after only three years at various universities, and that many of them were already married and, thus, lived off-base or in military housing quarters. For the in-house bachelors there was great interest in the 'pool' of Princess Mary Royal Air Force nursing sisters who staffed the adjacent RAF hospital and who by dint of Queen's Regulations were not, at that time, allowed to be married! Thus, there was a reciprocal interest between the two groups. Each Wednesday evening in the largest ante-room off Halton House's central Great Hall, and in the context of the 'rock'n'roll' era which swept the country, the Officers' Mess thus reverberated to the musical sounds of the time (no senior officers usually resided in the House!), accompanied by the consolidation of interests between the largely resident male air force officers with the female officers of the Princess Mary's RAF Nursing Service!

In February 1957, a newly-arrived, just-twenty-seven-year old nursing sister, Jean Mary McKintosh, joined the 'rock'n'roll' fray, and immediately (or soon thereafter) captivated my interest. And thus, together with a second meeting on the following Sunday evening at Halton's Trinity Church (the Church of Scotland's non-Conformist status), we initiated an inevitable process towards a quite-near-future matrimonial celebration. Not that all was quite straightforward, however, as Jean, on her giving notice to the Officer Commanding the RAF Halton nursing services of our engagement, was immediately posted from Halton to RAF Ely hospital for service in that rather remote location in East Anglia (160 cross-country kilometres from Halton, with no motorways en route!). Until the week before our mid-August wedding, when Jean terminated her short period in the RAF's nursing service, the only 'flying' that she did during the twenty or so weeks was between Ely and her home city of Liverpool, where the wedding arrangements for Saturday 17 August 1957 had to be made. In spite of the distant locations between Halton, Ely, Coalville and

Liverpool (with a total distance of 600 kilometres between them) most developments went smoothly, except for an illness to which Jean succumbed on a visit to Coalville in early August, that was thought initially to be the result of her nursing a poliomyelitis patient at Ely. But Dr Hamilton, the Coalville GP who had taken care of my health from birth to my departure to Birmingham, quickly diagnosed polyneuritis, so enabling plans for our wedding to proceed as scheduled.

Saturday 17 August was not brilliant weather-wise, but it was sufficiently warm and dry for the wedding service at the Aigburth Methodist Church in Liverpool, with which Jean's family had been involved for many decades. And at our request the RAF Chaplain from the Trinity Church at RAF Halton kindly came to assist in the ceremony. All elements of the ceremony were appropriately fulfilled, after which the sixty-plus guests joined us at Liverpool's Speke airport restaurant. Surprisingly, Mr McKintosh, the bride's father, accepted the provision of champagne and wine as part of the ceremony – in spite of his life-long abstinence from alcoholic beverages!

Thence, after a quick change by me from my formal Flight Lieutenant's uniform and Jean from her wedding dress, we departed from Liverpool in a hired car to the exhaust of which a long line of tin cans had been attached! Our destination for a few days' honeymoon was the small north Wales inland town of Bala. This choice was made from Jean's memories of her survival there over a two or three year period during World War II, so avoiding the aerial bombardment that Liverpool had suffered on being the port that had handled the intensity of incoming men, machinery, weaponry and provisions from across the Atlantic and other submarine infested seas in order to secure the UK's survival.

After three perfect sunny days in Bala we returned to Liverpool to pack our cases – and for Jean to secure her passport and her immigration visa from the US Consulate. On Thursday 22 August 1957 we boarded the 19,000 ton White Star liner, the MV *Britannic*, for our voyage to New York and arrived safely, in spite of a severe North Atlantic storm. This was in contrast with Jean's fortuitous escape from a liner she was registered to board as an evacuee from the UK in 1940, but which she was unable to do at the last minute, for family reasons. The liner was torpedoed and sunk, with a great loss of children's lives, on its first day out of Liverpool. Had she gone down with that ship then it is ninety-nine per cent likely that these memoirs would not have been written.

41. The Wedding Approaches: the best-man to my left

42. The bride and I – now married – leave the Methodist Church

43. *The two families gather: Odells to the left, McKintoshs to the right*

44. *The family plus other guests assemble prior to departure to the wedding feast*

A year in the United States, 1957/8

This opportunity arose from the success of the Coalville Rotary Club in late 1956 in sponsoring me for a Rotary International Foundation Fellowship in any other country in which Rotary Clubs were active. With the University of London Diploma in International Relations under my belt, I had decided to seek a place at a US academic institution in that field of study. The Institute which I favoured – and which was ready to accept me for a one-year Master's degree – was the Fletcher School of International Law and Diplomacy in Boston, run jointly by the two universities, Harvard and Tufts. With this acceptance and Coalville Rotary Club's support, I went through the selection process (along with a dozen or so other sponsored students from other UK towns and cities) and emerged as the proposed recipient for the 1957/58 award. I then proceeded to make all the necessary arrangements to get to the US between my departure from RAF Halton in August and the early-September 1957 opening of the Fletcher School's academic year.

A berth in a four-berth cabin in steerage class on the MV *Britannic* had long since been reserved for me by Rotary International with a defined mid-August departure date from Liverpool. Consternation arose, however, in the world of Rotary when I reported I was getting married in August and that my wife would accompany me to the United States where she had already been offered a senior nursing post in Boston's famous Children's Medical Centre. There was no precedent in the history of Rotary's International Fellowship programme for a Fellow to be accompanied by his or her spouse! After serious discussions over the propriety of my proposal, Rotary International finally accepted my argument that my wife would enhance the value of my appointment as, I argued, she could also be an 'ambassador' for improving international links, albeit in another part of the societal system and without any additional costs (of travel etc.) for Rotary International. And so the problem was solved: my wife could travel with me to Boston.

But another big 'but' had then emerged: namely that the MV *Britannic* was long since already fully booked! Jean's father, however, was in the shipping business in Liverpool, though not with Cunard/White Star line. But in Liverpool all such folk from the various shipping lines knew each other; so Mr McKintosh was able to speak from his job within the Blue Funnel Line to his colleagues in Cunard. Such an intervention led to an offer of a two-berth cabin on the *Britannic* for both the outward and the return journeys. Hence, on 22 August 1957 a taxi from Jean's parents' home in Liverpool dropped us at the MV *Britannic*'s berth on the Mersey docks! We were finally on our way to the US.

The trans-Atlantic crossing to New York via Cork in Ireland took eight to nine days. Unfortunately an extreme storm force wind, west of southern Ireland, inhibited life on board – most notably with respect to the gargantuan meals, to say nothing of the tax-free alcoholic drinks! After the storm, however, all was well with the combination of a peaceful sea and day-long sunshine.

New York's famous skyline finally hove into view, with the last couple of hours of the journey bringing us to the Cunard Company's berth on the west side of Manhattan Island. Unfortunately, a speedy disembarkation was not to be, as my US entry visa was assigned for special attention, given an indication of a required treatment arising from a problem with my lungs, on which the RAF Halton Hospital's x-rays had shown shadows arising from an infrequently named condition of sarcoidosis. US immigration officials, however, thought my problem might be tuberculosis. Thus, after docking, a two-hour delay intervened whilst the matter was cleared up and we then disembarked as the last two passengers to leave the ship. This was done in style with me in dark suit, homburg hat and a rolled umbrella – in the fashion of a typical English man overseas – and with Jean in her post-matrimonial outfit!

Belatedly we cleared customs and met Jean's relatives who were still awaiting us on the quay – Uncle Will, his wife and his daughter. We were then introduced to their 1957 Chevrolet of, by British standards, immense dimensions plus tail-fins and all! The first air-conditioned car in which we rode was a welcome blessing as the ambient temperature was not far short of 100°F (38°C). We were thus introduced to the affluence and other imposing features of the USA's largest city region in the 1950s – and to the generosity of Jean's relatives who were up to three generations' descended from English and Irish stock, and now living in the New Jersey town of Bergenfield, less than forty-five minutes' drive from downtown Manhattan. We became gradually attuned to the new US lifestyle, prior to our journey to Boston, Massachusetts. With all our baggage we were then taken in style to New York's famous Grand Central Station where we boarded the chosen train to take us northwards, by way of the coastal route along the shores of New England, to the city of Boston.

Here Rotary International instantly emerged in the form of the organisation's District Governor, Kenneth Faulkner, of Massachusetts and surrounding states. He was, indeed, awaiting us in the foyer of Boston South station, and almost immediately introduced us to a formidable Boston institution, a traffic jam through the road tunnel under the estuary of the Charles River, before finally bringing us to his home and family in the northern Boston suburb of Melrose.

The following day Jean and I began our search for an apartment in localities which were suitably positioned for both the Fletcher School and the Children's Medical Center, and, of course, at a price we could afford! Happily, success was achieved within forty-eight hours with a basically furnished first floor studio flat in the Brookline suburb of Boston, roughly midway between our respective work places. In order to make the apartment habitable, we quickly added necessary essentials such as bedclothes, kitchen equipment, china and cutlery and in doing so, established our first home as a married couple – though now virtually penniless after also paying the first two months rent! It was to be some weeks ahead before we were able to buy even a low-cost second hand Ford car, whereby we were able to cut down on the journey times taken by public transport from our apartment to and from the Fletcher School and the Children's Medical Center.

In the meantime, our respective working hours in the two institutions gradually became acceptable. This left us with time enough in the late afternoons and evening hours to familiarise ourselves with US late-hours' shopping facilities and to see something of the city of Boston, having 'sussed-out' the ordering of the city from the high look-out point just two blocks up to the top of the street in which our apartment was located. Down-town – as well as in the suburbs of Lexington and Concord – we became familiar with the beginnings of the rising against British occupation, together with Greater Boston's museums and art galleries – and with Symphony Hall, the home of the Boston Symphony Orchestra.

Once we had bought our 1953 Ford car – for about $300 – we were also able to explore Massachusetts' heritage and nature trails stretching from the coastal town of Ipswich to the north to the famous landing point of early immigrants of Plymouth to the south. Such travel was also a function of my responsibility as a Rotary Foundation Fellow: the need to accept what turned out to be an average of more than two invitations per week to speak at Rotary Club lunches and/or dinners, not only in Boston and its suburbs but also as far afield as Manchester in Vermont to the north,

London in Connecticut to the south and inland in Massachusetts almost as far as the town of Amherst. The massive difference between the short distances one could travel in the UK in the mid-1950s – given its non-existent of motorways – and the long distances it was possible to make along the open highways of New England was mightily impressive. These journeys opened our eyes to the possibilities ahead for seeing much more of North America after the end of the academic year in early June 1958: a prospect which was to enhance our feelings of separation from the rest of the world, in spite of the emergence at this time of the full force of the Cold War. We found that television and radio programmes were essentially local, but we were rescued from isolation by the Boston-published *Christian Science Monitor* from Mondays to Saturdays: and by the much weightier weekly Sunday edition of the *New York Times*.

Meanwhile, we were involved in socialising with neighbours in the apartment block, with colleagues of Jean on the staff at the Children's Medical Center and with fellow likewise-married students studying at the Fletcher School of International Law and Diplomacy. At the latter, lectures were given by prestigious academics and servants from the US establishment, so contributing to a significant widening of one's understanding of the relationship between the US and the rest of the world.

Within the framework of the Master's degree course, including international law, economics and politics plus history, the teaching staff presented knowledge and understanding *par excellence*. In the context of this, the approximately forty students – split about 50:50 between American and foreign backgrounds – were introduced and enthused by the depth and breadth of the teaching programme. This necessitated the proverbial nose-to-the-grindstone requirement in order to keep up with the pace of learning; together with a paid request that I accepted for teaching international affairs to undergraduate students in Tufts University, so securing the wherewithal required for visiting other parts of the US! Now, more than fifty years on, the recollections of the quality and depth of the degree course remain clear and positive, assisted by the Latin-language formal document dated 7 June 1958 setting out one's success in securing a *Magistri in Artibus*, accompanied by an official 'transcript of record'. The latter recorded a successful performance at a French examination on 4 October 1957 and in a final oral examination on 23 May 1958. This was then followed by the positive results from my submitted papers plus written examinations in the four subject areas: an A— and a B in international law;

two B+s in US foreign relations: two A— and B+ results in international economic relations and systems; an A grade in problems of international politics; and more specifically by my dissertation on the establishment and implications of the United Nations Special Agency; viz. The World Meteorological Organisation. A forerunner perhaps to fears for potential climate change?

Following the formal, open-air degree ceremony on 7 June 1958, and Jean's subsequent termination of her post at the Children's Medical Center the following week, we turned to the preparations for our final two months in the United States. We packed and dispatched unwanted household goods, books and clothes to the Cunard Line to be transported to Liverpool, followed all the necessary rules and requirements to ensure we could legally leave the United States without any remaining tax obligations and terminated our lease on the apartment. We were then able to depart from Boston on a lengthy jaunt in our much-aged Ford car across most of the continent, in the full knowledge by that time of Jean's pregnancy with an estimated delivery date in mid-December 1958!

Our itinerary across North America involved a total journey in excess of 10,000 kilometres. We visited numerous towns and cities and also passed through a range of environments which we encountered en route. Amongst these were the New England states and the rough Atlantic coastline and the St Lawrence estuary of New Brunswick. Then we switched to the north bank of the Saint Lawrence River in the Province of Quebec with visits to Montreal and Ottawa, to the Province of Ontario and specifically to the Province's capital, Toronto, prior to reaching Niagara Falls. Beyond that we travelled further north-west to the Sudbury copper-mining region and thence to Sault Ste Marie between Lake Superior and Lake Huron. This took us to a re-entry facility into the United States, but now in the mid-west state of Michigan and thence into the state of Wisconsin along the south bank of Lake Superior – on non-metalled roads as far as Duluth. Thereafter, we moved directly west through the flat-lands of Minnesota and North Dakota where the 'locals' treated us as almost long-lost cousins! Finally, we passed into Montana where during our overnight stay we were entertained in real 'western' style including beef steaks the size of our plates! Jean insisted that the volume of that night's meat was more than equal to our monthly ration during the 1939–45 period of the Second World War. Our hosts were astounded! Thereafter, we trailed up to Yellowstone Park amongst the spectacular peaks of the US Rockies, so ending our outward journey as lack of time inhibited our ability to reach the western coastal states of Washington, Oregon and California and, of course, the Pacific Ocean.

We turned back eastward back through the Rockies and then through the high plains of rural America par excellence, the bread-basket and meat-producing areas of the mid-West. Then on across the upper reaches of the Mississippi River which we crossed at Galena in Illinois, overnighting, we were told, in the very hotel room where General Grant had slept prior to winning the War of Independence! Without a further stop we continued on to Chicago and on to the heavily industrialised area east to Detroit. At the latter, then a thriving car-producing city, Jean's distant cousins entertained us in a magnificent house overlooking Lake St Clair and sorted out our lack of more than $5 on arrival with more than enough cash to see us through back to New York. This was hardly a burden on Jean's family members, the husband of which we were surprised to find was the senior fleet manager of General Motors Chevrolet company!

With more than 1000 kilometres still to go to New York we sped through parts of Ohio, Pennsylvania, Delaware and New Jersey, including a traverse across the Appalachian mountains, so returning, after nearly two months on the road, to Jean's relatives in Bergenfield, where a Thai fellow-student from the Fletcher School visited us to buy and take over our much-used Ford car for $100 (whereby he was helped on his way to become later the Ambassador of Thailand at the United Nations!). For Jean and me our ultimate ride in her uncle's car was the few miles to the Cunard Lines quay on the Manhattan waterfront where we re-embarked on the MV *Britannic*, thus bringing us back to Liverpool and to Jean's former home in mid-August 1958. The 'honeymoon year' was now over: Jean was pregnant; and I didn't have a job to go to. Return to reality was the order of the day!

The search for a career

I had to search for a career with a degree of urgency, given the progress of Jean's pregnancy and the fact that we had little money in any bank anywhere, in spite of our carefully controlled expenditures over the previous twelve months. On my first day back in the UK, I signed on at the Labour Exchange in Garston, Liverpool – and so became eligible for a very modest weekly unemployment payment!

Whilst in Boston I had responded to openings for jobs published in British newspapers and journals which were accessible at the university's library. My application to join the Foreign Office (in the relevant context of my studies of international law and diplomacy at the Fletcher School) had been perfunctorily dismissed with no suggestion whatsoever that I should undertake the relevant examination! My Coalville Grammar School, the University of Birmingham and Boston's Fletcher School backgrounds had clearly failed to impress the Foreign Office selection panel. But the Geography Departments of two universities, Liverpool and Birmingham, had already invited me for interviews on my return to the UK for lecturers' positions which appeared to fit my background of studies and publications. Indeed, my interview in Birmingham – my *alma mater* – was scheduled for a few days after returning to the UK and I went along with relatively high hopes, only to have them dashed as my field of study did not tie in precisely enough with the specific requirements of the lecturer.

Meanwhile, I had also made an application to join Shell International's Junior Management Course which was intended, the details of the advertisement said, for 'high-fliers'. Confident from my British B.A and Ph.D. and my American A.M. – and from my international experience over many years – I travelled to London for an interview and evaluation. This led to the offer of a position and what then seemed to be an attractive first year's salary of £1250 – plus a number of other benefits (e.g. a significant increase in salary if successful on the management course and then an entry to Shell's generous company pension fund). All this was, moreover, with the requirement that I accepted the offer within a matter of a few days, in order to be able to report for the opening of the course on Monday 2 September.

My interview for an appointment to the Geography Department of Liverpool University had, however, been scheduled for 6 September. Although Liverpool was a location which suited both Jean and me and given that the prospect for an appointment as a lecturer was very tempting, my choice, nevertheless, had to be for the bird-in-the-hand, rather than one- or two-in-the-bush! And so my fate – and that of Jean and our expected child – was sealed. Shell it had to be. We thus travelled to London and spent three nights with my cousin Ken (the best man at our wedding) and his family in Ashford, Middlesex. An intense few days of a searching for rented accommodation led to success, a ground floor flat with an inbuilt bathroom and an access to the large garden in the Thames-side suburb of Teddington in south-west London. The flat was, moreover, only a five minutes' walk from the Southern Region railway station from which there was a fifteen-minute service to Waterloo – and from there by the 'drain' (as it was then called) to the Bank underground station in the City. All, it seemed, had gone well for a potential lifetime career with one of the world's largest international oil companies. In this way my future began early in my twenty-eighth year, ten years on from my departure from Coalville, and now from one 'energetic life' to an opening offered by another, Shell International, an important subsidiary of the Royal Dutch/ Shell Company.

CHAPTER 4

1958–68: A Ten-Year UK Career; and our Evolution into a Family of Six

Into the world of Shell International

AS ALREADY SHOWN, I WAS born and grew up in the town of Coalville in a family with close links to the coal industry. Likewise, in my geographical, economic – and even geological – studies, my interest in 'natural' resources concentrated on coal, reflecting the commodity's importance in the UK where, as late as 1958, coal supplied well over 65 per cent of the country's energy requirements and even almost 50 per cent of the world's energy use. My exposure to oil products had been limited to paraffin for lights at home in the early 1930s before electricity was installed; to the lamps on railway stations and signaling equipment until the 1950s; and to the lamps on the many horse-drawn vehicles over my two first decades.

In joining Shell International I entered another – and almost an unknown – world. On a three-month course in late 1958 at Shell's Egham laboratories we were presented with the background to, and the development of, what was already in 1958 a world-wide industry, with the US and Canada way ahead of the rest of the industrialised world, but with the latter now rapidly expanding its use of, and dependence on, oil. In the decade starting in 1960 the average annual growth in oil production and use was no less than 7 per cent. The rapid learning process about the industry was comprehensive and formidable, extending from petroleum geology through crude oil production to refining, transportation and the marketing of products. The final part of the course was to be a visit to the more extensive Shell facilities in the Netherlands: the origin and home of Royal Dutch – ranging from the company's international HQ in Den Haag, through formidable laboratories in Rijswijk and Amsterdam and to Shell's massive refinery in the port of Rotterdam. Unfortunately, the timing of this visit coincided with the pending birth of our first child, successfully delivered at the world-famous Queen Charlotte's Children's Hospital in West London on 12 December 1958. From there wife and child were subsequently

45. Shell's new clan of potential managers, September 1958. I am seventh from the right at the rear!

brought home to Teddington in good time for Christmas and for a succession of family visitors from both Liverpool and Leicestershire, plus an American family, then currently in London, whom we had met in Boston through Jean's work at the Childrens Medical Centre. They, too, had recently also had their first child – also born in London, with only a few days' difference in the two boys' birth dates. Needless to say, this was quite a memorable Christmas!

Meanwhile, my employer had rostered me – following the end of the introductory course in Egham – to report for duty in Shell International's Economic Division, located in Gracechurch Street in the heart of the City of London. This involved a ten to eleven hour day away from home and the family, depending on the running time of the trains between Teddington and the City, via Waterloo and the 'Drain' and vice-versa; and, of course, on the degree of urgency for the completion of work under way in the office.

The total number of economists, administrators and secretaries was around fifty under the Divisional head of Geoffrey Chandler, ex-Cambridge University and the staff of the *Economist*. He was later to become a senior executive with Shell and also the President of the UK

Institute of Petroleum. He was demanding in the search for results on the issues which had to be tackled and was a stickler for the correct use of the English language. The section to which I was assigned embraced the politico-economic evaluation of, and prospects for, the countries of Latin America – from which there emerged a need for knowledge of Spanish, and of Portuguese in the case of Brazil. This involved registration at the London Institute for appropriate language classes some ten minutes walk up Bishopsgate for a few hours per week, plus private study at home. My introduction to Latin American countries greatly sharpened my interest in that part of the world (which was, some years later, to prove to be very important). The reports which I helped to produce were demanded by and subsequently delivered to Royal Dutch/Shell's London-based Regional Executives, from whom decisions could be made for evaluating investments by Shell in those relevant parts the world. Thus decisions were made that the company should diminish or even withdraw its participation in particular countries, given that by the late-1950s most of the countries had largely orientated their requirements for oil to be the work of state oil corporations: starting from Mexico, through to Chile and Argentina. Shell's locally-based staff in the various countries often expressed views on prospects which clashed with our submissions and so created insider in-fighting, prior to the Directors being informed on what best to do. The most severe conflict of interpretations related at that time to Brazil. Expatriate staff there were adamant that the politico-economic situation in Brazil necessitated a reduction – or even the cessation – of Shell's interests in the country. Our contrary advice was, however, soon justified by the emergence of Brazil as a major power in the developing world and by the discoveries in the country of large volumes of oil and gas, now long-since exploited in joint ventures between Petrobras and Shell (as well as with other international oil companies). Likewise, the prospects – or otherwise – for Shell's opportunities and involvement in other Latin American countries required evaluations and recommendations on a more or less continuing basis for which knowledge of the Spanish language became a must.

Additionally, there was a growing interest by Shell in the newly emerging role of the Soviet Union in Western Europe's now rapidly increasing demand for oil: a task which was allocated to the four of us in the group which hitherto had evaluated only Latin American affairs. And then, not much later, we were also given the responsibility for analysis of the affairs of the 'Communist world' extending to China, based on the deals for Shell products which had been made with 'Red China' as it emerged into world politics. Shell's agreements with that country raised the ire of the US (given its continuing attachment to the China of Chiang Kai-Shek) so that threats emerged against the company in terms of the American government's imposition of restraints on Shell's large US activities. Thus, another global interest for Shell's economic division was created – and, for me, an opportunity to put Fletcher School's learning to good use!

All these positive elements in working for Shell International (also including significant pay rises after one and then two years) should have indicated prospects for advancement up the promotional ladder by way of secondment to one or other of Shell's overseas empires. But there were offsets against these positive prospects, firstly in my realisation of the gross overstaffing of Shell's London offices coupled with its appointment of a US-based company which had repeatedly advised on the massive reduction of other companies' staff numbers. It seemed likely so to advise Shell in order to enhance the efficiency of Shell International's operations. Secondly, I had a feeling for the existence of a degree of apartheid between Oxbridge graduates and those from other universities. The former appeared to enjoy priority for promotion, so indicating the uncertainty of my future position in the company in the context not only of my non-Oxbridge status, but also my left-wing tendency in both national and international matters.

Hence, in the early part of my fourth year with Shell I handed in my resignation, to take up an offer to join the staff of the Geography Department at the internationally prestigious London School of Economics (LSE). This was achieved thanks to Professor Michael Wise, who had recently been appointed to the Chair in Geography at LSE and who had formerly been my tutor when I was an undergraduate in the University of Birmingham from 1948–51.

This alternative re-aroused my academic interests, particularly as I was offered a status and salary significantly higher than the norm for a first lectureship appointment. Even so, a reduced salary – compared with that at Shell – was a sombre prospect, given that our one-child family status had been doubled, with the birth of a daughter in June 1960 (eighteen months after our first child): and, moreover, at a time when we had recently moved from our flat in Teddington to a newly-built three-bedroomed house in the south-east London suburb of Orpington. In order to buy the house we had taken out a mortgage of about £2,500 from a bank which provided favourable terms for Shell employees – so this had to be re-negotiated. In addition there was, of course, one's loss from the generous Shell pension scheme together with a number of other bonuses – including Shell discounts from a number of designated shops and automatic membership of Shell's Lensbury Club in Teddington.

A return to academia

To set against all this, however, was the opportunity to join the ranks of academia – with all its attractions and possibilities. Thus, as from 1 October 1961 when I left Shell – and its world of employees who were looked after from 'the cradle to the grave' – I now faced the reality of an appointment to lecturing and research in my chosen fields of interest, European economic and social geography with special attention to natural resources (including oil) and to Latin America as a regional interest.

I was thus exposed immediately into a full whack of lecturing which required many hours per week of preparation from the starting line, together with tutorial responsibilities for up to ten undergraduates, and to active participation in both the Department's proceedings and in LSE's Council through which members of staff contributed to the School's development – at a period when student numbers were growing quickly at both undergraduate and graduate levels. Compared with the generally relaxed calm of Shell's Economic Division, LSE was bedlam for the thirty weeks or so of the three terms per year. Overall, the requirements were stimulating to the nth degree – and rewarding, in terms of daily contacts with the students and with one's academic colleagues, especially, as far as the latter were concerned, in the School's Senior Common Room and dining facilities, where issues of the moment were discussed and plans made to stimulate possible inter-departmental seminars and joint courses.

Meanwhile, as LSE was one of the many colleges of the University of London, there were also inter-collegiate courses to sustain. Even more significantly for the time element involved, all examinations were the responsibility of the University, leading to a complex set of requirements in both setting the exam papers and marking the students' efforts; and, thereafter, for the inter-collegiate examination boards' responsibilities for determining the grades to be awarded and then declared by Senate House. The complexities were formidable, yet somehow in each academic year all finally turned out well.

However, in the 1960s a university teacher's responsibilities and opportunities were very much broader than in earlier decades. This was partly because salaries were modest, so that with a family to provide for it was necessary to take on extra-mural activities – by teaching in the University of London's external studies' programmes both for diplomas and degrees, and also by marking the examination papers produced by the external students. Some of these were from within the UK, but there were many times more from overseas; in particular, from countries which had been – or, in some cases, from places which were still – within the British Empire (Commonwealth).

On top of all of the above challenges on the teaching side of one's career, there was also a requirement to undertake research on subjects of significance for advancing one's position in the hierarchy, with, of course, the appropriate publications of books, articles and papers. Thus I opted for work on the subjects of interest that had arisen from my years with Shell International (rather than following on from my Ph.D. thesis and papers based on that in the 1950s local economic and social geography). I embraced issues of, first, the economic and social geography of Latin America; and, second, the economic geographical aspects of international oil in particular and of energy in general.

A Latin American choice

Initially, it was this continent which secured most of my efforts; not least as the result of a flow of graduate students working on Latin American issues for their Ph.D.s under my supervision throughout the 1960s. All of them, I am pleased to record, were eventually successful. It was also a decade of rapid change in Latin America so that the Royal Institute for International Affairs (or Chatham House as it is more familiarly known) established a study programme on the continent's economic and political issues. As a member of the programme, I contributed to its deliberations as well as learning from other members on other issues. Because of this opportunity I also became a regular contributor to the BBC's World Service programmes to the continent, so establishing me as a so-called 'expert' on Latin American affairs, with a further opportunity which was thus secured for making contributions to journals and newspapers in both the UK and other countries.

Following the three-year period of my appointment at LSE, I was granted leave of absence in 1964 together with some financial assistance for a three-month visit to Latin America. In preparation for this venture I, together with the rest of the family, spent two months in the summer of 1963 in Fuengirola, a fishing village on Spain's Costa del Sol, in order to improve my command of the Spanish language. This I later found to have been a wise choice, given the nuances of the dialects throughout most of Latin America, compared with the Castilian orientation of the language in London's Spanish teaching institutes!

The visit to Latin America itself extended from mid-January to mid-April 1964, with the round-trip journey based on a set of more than twenty airline tickets embracing flights to New York, Puerto Rico, Trinidad, Caraças, Maraçaibo, Bogota, Cauca, Lima, La Paz, Arica, Santiago, Panama, Costa Rica, San Salvador, Guatemala, Mexico and Jamaica. Thus, I proceeded through a total of fourteen Latin American countries during the three-month period. In each country my interests were concerned with regional economic situations and policies; and on energy sector developments with special reference to the national oil industries, ranging from exploration and production activities to refining and products' distribution. Some of these involved lengthy journeys within the countries concerned – whenever possible by public overland transport, but often by plane, when distances and terrains inhibited surface travel.

The success of my venture was much enhanced by contacts which were made for me through UK Embassies, the British Council and Royal Dutch Shell's offices. Thus opportunities with universities, governments and companies' staff members, offered local knowledge and presentations of the issues involved, and also access to books, journals and reports on development plans, many of which I had in my archives until late 2010 when I gave all the literature to the Latin American Institute at Essex University, together with the several hundred now unusable colour slides taken of very many different locations. The whole exercise was of massive importance to my knowledge of the continent, and to my realisation of the great economic and social potential which lay in Latin America. In the context, however, of political and social situations and even conflicts which hindered, rather than helped, potential developments of energy prospects.

On returning to the UK, I was much more capable than hitherto on the presentation of my courses both on Latin American economic issues and on the geo-economic and political issues involving the international oil industry. In addition, the visit greatly enhanced my contribution to organisations concerned with Latin American affairs, ranging from the

University of London Institute for Latin American Studies through the Latin American research programme at Chatham House (the Royal Institute for International Affairs), to Canning House with its prime interest in UK/Latin American relationships and to the newly-formed academic Society for Latin American Studies. Needless to say, over the rest of 1964/5 I was invited – and willing – to speak to numerous meetings on Latin American issues; and was also able to write and publish a number of papers for both academic and trade journals, on aspects of the continent's situation and prospects. From all of this there emerged a challenge to write a jointly authored book, *Economies and Societies in Latin America*, with a colleague, Dr David Preston, who was more interested in the social side of Latin American development. The project took until 1973 to be finally published. Thereafter, the book served as an academic text for Latin American studies in many universities, both within the UK and in many other English speaking countries. A second edition followed in 1978. Thus, my Latin American interest extended over the whole period of my tenure at the LSE (to late-1968) and then in my early years at the Netherlands School of Economics in Rotterdam.

Oil and gas interests take over

Meanwhile, after my 1964 visit to Latin America, I returned to investigate a rapidly developing situation in the world's energy system. This was ultimately to generate the central academic interest for most of the rest of my working life, in effect to the first decade of the twenty-first century. It was, in essence, a follow-up to my time at Shell, through the rise in the importance of hydrocarbons from the local through to the global level. Indeed, this development had already pre-dated my visit to Latin America, as I had already within a year following my departure from Shell succeeded in completing the text of a 220 page book, *An Economic Geography of Oil*. This had four sections dealing first with the pattern of world oil supply; second, with the pattern of world oil demand; third, on refining, transport and distribution; and finally, with conclusions on the future of the oil industry and of its impact on economic development. In this effort I tried to pull together all the strings of the industry with which I had become familiar in my three years with Shell, in part as a result of the willingness of a number of my former Shell colleagues to take time to read and comment on the draft version, so that I could make any necessary changes.

On publication in 1963 the book was well-received as, indeed, it also generated an American version as well as several foreign language translations.

In particular, note was taken of my claims that the fears already expressed in the early 1960s of oil being a finite resource were without foundation. While the book did not exactly hit the headlines, it did set me up as a radio broadcaster and soon thereafter as a TV 'expert' on oil and gas affairs at both European and global levels. This recognition was further enhanced by my more modest publication in 1965 of a 15,000 world pamphlet published by the Fabian Society (the origin of which lay in the London School of Economics in the late nineteenth century). This was entitled *Oil: the New Commanding Height* and was centrally concerned with Britain's historic role in international oil initiatives – and with its rapidly increasing dependence since 1951 on oil for making the country tick. It was a development which had received little governmental attention, even though by 1965 oil already supplied 34 per cent of the country's energy needs, leading me to forecast that oil would be more important than coal by 1975 (and so it was)! The conclusion of my pamphlet was that oil – as already with coal, gas and electricity – should be controlled by the state, under the aegis of a National Oil Agency. This was, of course, of much interest to the contemporary Labour government so that I was called to meet the Parliamentary Secretary in the Ministry of Power and some of his colleagues for a discussion on my 'socialist policy for oil'.

This discussion was instrumental in leading to the establishment of a Labour Party Study Group Committee to consider energy policy which, of course, by 1966 incorporated the implications of the prospective exploitation of the UK's North Sea hydrocarbons potential. I was pleased to be able to accept an invitation to join that committee, the deliberations of which incorporated not only many of the suggestions made in my Fabian Society pamphlet, but also other ideas which I published in the meantime on the supply and price of natural gas from the British sector of the North Sea. One important example was a quarter-page article in *The Times* (on 8 December 1966) on how to calculate 'rational unit prices' for North Sea natural gas production. It followed on a 2000-word article in *New Society* (published as early as May 1966) on 'What will gas do to the East Coast of England' from the Humber estuary to the mouth of the Waveney in East Anglia).

Consequently upon those important developments, 1967 turned out to be a tumultuous year in many respects, first from the standpoint of the

46. *Our family completed with Nigel, Deborah, Mark and Susannah*

family which by then had become one with three children (Nigel Peter, December 1958; Deborah Grace, June 1960 and Mark John, June 1965), so requiring the use of a motor car for ease of movement not only locally around our house in Orpington, but also for visits to our families elsewhere in the country and for holidays in both the UK and Europe. This acquisition was then followed by the need for a larger house! The latter also reflected the anticipated arrival of a fourth child, given our decision to adopt a second daughter – Susannah Mary. She was presented to us at the age of two months following which the adoption proceeded successfully to be concluded in October 1967.

Somehow, in spite of my convoluted daily engagements from Mondays to Fridays – and often on Saturdays too – from the workload as outlined above, Jean managed to cope with the expanded family, and even to find time enough – plus that of a baby-sitter – to be able to join me in London for concerts, theatres and social gatherings. Meanwhile at LSE there were many invitations to make contacts with organisations and companies from which I sometimes secured an honorarium for advice which I gave to them. Not least was the assistance which I was asked to give on the proposed construction of a 'modern' shopping centre in Coalville – the town of my birth – and one of the market towns of Leicestershire which I had examined for its potential socio-economic development and prospects in my Ph.D. thesis dating back over a decade to 1954. Happily, my advice was positive and led to the first major development of a facility to enhance Coalville's retail trade since the 1920s!

Subsequently, however, I became involved with many other parties concerned in the early days (1965–7) of natural gas finds in the south North Sea (by BP, Shell, Exxon and especially the Gas Council, a public sector entity). These led to an *impasse* on the value of the potential gas supplies and hence on the price of the commodity, so inhibiting the badly-informed Ministry of Power's policy developments. Therefore Michael Posner, an economist at the University of Oxford, had already accepted an offer to become the Ministry's economic adviser. As his interests had previously been exclusively concerned with the economics of the coal and electricity industries, he asked me to join him in the Ministry with responsibility for natural gas and oil – on which, as demonstrated in my publications, I already had much interest and experience. After due consideration – and having sought LSE's agreement to allow me to take an indefinite period of sabbatical leave – I agreed to accept Michael's offer and prepared to go to work at the Ministry of Fuel and Power. But this was not to be, given that after a week or so of silence, Michael Posner asked to see me as a matter of urgency. This was to tell me that the Minister of Fuel and Power, Richard Marsh, had refused to agree to my appointment in any way whatsoever within his Ministry, a decision which was later shown to have been on ideological grounds, probably based on a radical reaction to that which I had published in the journal *New Society* in September 1967. This dealt with Marsh's decision severely to diminish the size of the UK's coal industry because he thought that nuclear-power based electricity production would be lower cost than coal-fired generation. His decision, however, failed to take into account the country's social costs in having to support the three thousand miners who were to be made instantly unemployed, together with thousands of workers in affiliated industries (most notably on the railways through their loss of coal movements from the mines to industry and the power stations). I was, it seems, much too far to the political left – over state ownership and all that – to be an acceptable policy maker/adviser to a right-wing politician, much, I recall at the time, to my regret and great disappointment. These feelings were, however, destined to be very short-lived for reasons which I set out below.

An opening to Europe

In a twist of fate and/or of fortune, however, I was more or less contemporaneously invited to consider taking up the vacant Chair in Economic and Social Geography at the Netherland School of Economics in Rotterdam, with the status of the appointment requiring that Queen Juliana of the Netherlands agreed to my taking the lifetime Chair (to the age of seventy) at a salary well near twice that of 1967 professorial appointments in the UK. In the context of Marsh's refusal to have me in his Ministry I accepted the post, contingent upon my family's agreement to a lock, stock and barrel move to the Netherlands. In the early weeks of 1968 these issues were all taken care of when my appointment in Rotterdam, as from the beginning of the next academic year (1 September, 1968), was confirmed. The Dutch newspaper with the largest circulation (*De Telegraaf*) immediately interviewed me in London and came out with the conclusion that such a professorial opening to a British academic in the Dutch university system was a first-time ever event! In this context, a rough ride for me on taking up my position seemed more than likely. This was a fear that did, indeed, turn out to be correct for at least the first decade of my academic career in Rotterdam!

The final half-year in London

Meanwhile, however, for the rest of the 1967/8 academic year in London it was essentially 'business as usual', with the continuation of my academic responsibilities for undergraduate teaching and graduate supervisions at LSE, for the extra-mural classes organised by the University of London, for visiting lectures at other UK universities and colleges and for the examination of students in various colleges of education around the country. Likewise, I continued with my research on Latin American economic geography, played an active role in the Society for Latin American Studies and got on with writing a book on the continent (but which was only completed jointly with a colleague in Leeds in 1972).

Alongside these purely academic efforts, however, I also tried to enhance still further my efforts to demonstrate the importance of the now rapidly emerging reserves of natural gas from the British southern sector of the North Sea (offshore the east coast from Yorkshire to Norfolk). In response to the Labour government's dalliance in stimulating gas exploitation (which I much criticised in the press and on the radio and TV), the parliamentary Labour Party set up a study group which I was invited to join. That creation in itself accelerated and enhanced actions by the Ministry of Fuel and Power. First, to expand the establishment of the UK's gas production and then to require the state-owned Gas Council to purchase the gas at a governmental-determined price and then transport it by its own pipelines for sale to potential users across most of the country. Meanwhile, the Labour Party's study group continued to pursue its examination of the prospects for the development of the offshore oil and gas industry and how they could best serve the country's energy needs. I continued to participate fully in these deliberations through to my departure from the UK in September 1968 and thereafter, as far as I was able to do so from Rotterdam, until the UK's change of government from Labour to Conservative in 1970.

Meanwhile, from the end of the LSE 1967/8 academic year in early July, our expanded family got ready for leaving its home in Orpington. Eventually, with our house already sold and our furniture en route to Rotterdam by 24 July, we headed northwards in our newly-acquired tax-free export-model Triumph estate car, first to holiday with Jean's parents in the Isle of Man until mid-August and then, for the remainder of our time in the UK, at my father and my sister's home in Coalville. From the latter location it was possible to tie up all the loose ends at the London School of Economics over the rest of the month. Our ultimate departure – with a very full carload – from Coalville to the East Anglian port of Harwich took us to the overnight boat scheduled to go to the Dutch port of the Hoek van Holland. We landed there at an early morning hour on 2 September. Unexpectedly, the immigration formalities were brief, so that following our clearance we drove away on the thirty-minute journey to our new home located in the up-market Rotterdam suburb of Kralingen, to a house bought by us with the help of a large, low-priced mortgage arranged for us by the governing body of the Nederlandse Economisch Hogeschool. The following day our two older children, Nigel aged 9 and three quarters and Deborah aged 8 and a quarter – went off to a Dutch Protestant primary school, located well within a ten minutes walk from our house.

Chapter 5

As Migrants to The Netherlands for Better or for Worse?

A S FAR AS MY FAMILY WAS concerned, our introductions to Dutch society and associated behavioural requirements in The Netherlands turned out to be less than traumatic. First and foremost, our house in Kralingen was near perfection. It provided not only easy access to the newly-located campus of the NEH, but likewise to a range of local shops and professional facilities (doctors, dentists etc.) and even to the city centre, either by cycle or by the frequent tram service from the top of Oudorpweg, as our street was named.

In spite of our going to Rotterdam knowing no more than a few pertinent words of Dutch, settling down in the much changed circumstances in the last four months of 1968 was exhilarating, rather than depressive. First, Nigel aged nine and Deborah aged eight settled down at the local Protestant primary school just one day after our arrival from the UK. Within a matter of weeks they were Dutch speaking – and playing out in the road with the neighbours' children. Later in the year, under the guidance of our immediate neighbours they were introduced to Sinta Claus and his presents, plus the festivities and delicacies which came with him early in December.

Our two younger children (Mark, aged only just over three years on arrival in Rotterdam and Susannah, only a little over one year old) were taken care of by Elly van Put, a sixteen or seventeen-year-old Rotterdammer, already with two years experience in looking after families following her education and training at the Rotterdam Huishoudelijke School. She came to work for us, within a month of our arrival, for five and a half days each week. This made it possible for Jean not only to put our new home in order – with the repair and decoration work that was required from local tradespeople – but also to shop around for necessary furniture and fittings from the local and city centre shops, in spite of some language problems from time to time!

Indeed, there was only one really unpleasant incident, when on my absence in India, my wife was leaving our home in Oudorpweg to go

47. Our arrival in Rotterdam at Oudorpweg 9 in early September 1968

shopping with our four children in the car. Jean was then immediately ordered to stop by an official dressed in what seemed to be a uniform borrowed from the wartime German SS. He also chose to act as a member of that organisation, challenging the validity of Jean's use of a motor car with English number plates: and then forcing her, plus all four children, immediately to follow his vehicle to the car control and taxation office on the far side of the city. This happened in spite of the fact that the Dutch embassy in London had, prior to our departure from the UK, informed us that there was a year of grace between our arrival date in the Netherlands and a requirement for the car to be registered and taxed under Dutch law! The procedures which were now immediately demanded took much time and even more bureaucracy before the necessary changes were completed. Jean, on mentioning this episode to the wife of the NEH's Rector Magnificus (a near neighbour and with children of much the same ages as ours), successfully secured a reprieve. The Rector was then a lawyer of distinction in the country and he chose forcibly to express his concern over

48. The family in Rotterdam in the mid-1970s

the incident to the appropriate government authority – the equivalent of the UK's Home Office. He speedily reported back to us that he had secured an assurance that procedures would be changed!

Meanwhile, Jean registered for attendance at a *Talenpracticum* (a language school in English) to enable her to master the Dutch language. This she did with significant success, probably consequent upon her previous linguistic experience as a ten-year-old girl evacuated from Liverpool in 1940 to Bala in North Wales, where the only school was Welsh speaking! After only eighteen months there she passed the 'scholarship' exams in Welsh for entry to a Welsh speaking grammar school. This precedent proved to be of importance to her in her studies and pronunciation of the Dutch language.

For me, the early days in Rotterdam (from 2 September 1968) were taken up by the required formalities in registering the family as immigrants to the country. Thus, appropriate ID cards (to be carried at all times and available for production when requested by police and for proof of identity) were issued through our registration in the Stadhuis as residents of Rotterdam. Visits to the relevant banks for agreement on the matter of mortgage payments and for the opening of current accounts were also required. All of this was greatly speeded up with the help of the NEH's administrative staff. A formal introductory *tête à tête* with the Chairman of the Board of Governors of the School was also fulfilled. After all this I presented myself to the Rector Magnificus and the Dean of the Faculty of Economics and, at last, to the Department of Economic and Social Geography of which I had been appointed the Head – with a rather formidable title: De Hoogleerde Heer Professor Dr. Peter R. Odell! All of the proceedings were somewhat difficult for me to sort out as the Hogeschool had, in the summer of 1968, been moved from its original buildings, close to the centre of Rotterdam, to the much more spacious site and more extensive buildings on what was then the eastern edge of Rotterdam – albeit only a fifteen-minute or so tram ride to the centre of the city.

Two weeks after arrival in Rotterdam, on Monday 16 September, the official opening of the academic year and the installation of the Rector of the NEH took place in the newly opened auditorium, seating upwards of 1,500 persons. With the Rector's entry, preceded by the *pedel* carrying his staff, there then followed the cortège of the professoriat, with each professor in a black toga (made of satin and fur) from the shoulders to the floor, topped with a white *beff* around the neck and a flat black cap on the head, as etiquette required. The London School of Economics and Political Science, with nothing by way of such formalities, melted into insignificance!

Just two days later, on the basis of a programme that had been defined prior to my arrival, I was listed to give my first lecture – necessarily of course in English and with what visual aids I could immediately locate. The standard fifty-minute lecture, on the principles of economic geography, was given in a lecture hall packed with upwards of two hundred students. Happily, I survived the near-to-an-hour's ordeal with, I am pleased to record, a very positive response from most of the students. Thereafter, 'with my feet now under the table', I was now able to adjust to the formalities of the Dutch university system – in terms of lecturing (though not yet in the Dutch language) and through contacts with the students following the process of oral, rather than written, examinations. I also participated in the proceedings of the Economic Faculty's Council and in the meetings of the Senate of the NEH. There was also a requirement to attend the Congregation for degree ceremonies. All the professorial staff wore full regalia as described above, whilst the almost entirely male graduates appeared in morning dress with black ties and tails!

I gradually made contact with relevant national organisations such as the Dutch Royal Geographical Society and a state-required national professorial group consisting of the professors of geography from all the universities in the country. I was invited and accepted to give a number of invitation lectures in other universities around the country and even in the Flemish-speaking region of Belgium. All of these commitments, however, were interwoven with two-day visits to London where I continued, as agreed, with my responsibilities as the supervisor to graduate students at LSE working on their Ph.D. theses.

Meanwhile, however, I had been invited to represent the Royal Dutch Geographical Society (KNGS) at the 1968 conference of the International Geographical Union to be held in New Delhi, India in November. For the visit I was sufficiently well funded by the NEH to cover all the costs involved. The previous meeting of the IGU had been in London in 1964 (in which I was also modestly involved), so I was able to anticipate the nature of the event. A series of meetings and seminars in the cities of New Delhi, Patna, Calcutta and Durgapur added considerably to my knowledge of India as the itinerary was totally different from that of my visit in 1953. The latter was almost entirely in the rural south of that vast country while this 1968 visit introduced me to the large and very heavily populated and industrial-orientated northern areas, with their massive resources of coal and iron ore, amongst other minerals, so that their mining, their transportation and their use formed the basis for India's emerging industrial revolution, albeit with technology which was mainly of nineteenth and early twentieth centuries' origin.

As a consequence of the above, however, and of the very noticeable low levels of per capita income, the visit was a depressing one, with an impact on me that persisted long after my return to Rotterdam just a few days before the Christmas of 1968.

During my month's absence from Rotterdam, little had changed in the university (NEH) – in which the first semester had come to an end – except for the appearance of significant piles of paper on my desk relating to in-house affairs which I needed to know. Meanwhile, as a family we had decided to stay in Rotterdam over the Christmas/New Year period with, of course, the children all at home so that there was time enough to sort things out, in terms of 'life in Rotterdam'; and to acclimatise ourselves to somewhat colder winter conditions than those of London.

Given the traumas of 1968, my output of publications during the year was relatively modest and, moreover, with a weighting to Latin America rather than to the oil and gas industry. I did, however, make a significant contribution to an important book by Professor Edith Penrose on *The Large International Firm in Developing Countries*: namely a chapter on 'The Oil Industry in Latin America'. I likewise contributed a chapter on 'Oil and Politics in Latin America' in a comprehensive handbook on the continent and, yet more specifically, a chapter in a Middle East issue of the *Journal of Contemporary History*. My eighteen-page article was fortuitously entitled 'The Significance of Oil', helping the establishment of my understanding of the global industry. In the *Geographical Journal*, I contributed a review article on 'The British Gas Industry' with emphasis on the impending expansion of the industry to the production and use of natural gas at the expense of both coal and oil. More specifically on Latin America, the *Journal of Common Market Studies* carried my twenty-page article on 'Economic Integration and Spatial Patterns of Economic and Societal Geography', on the basis of which I was committed to contribute to a newly introduced study programme on *Ruimtelijk Economie* (Spatial Economics) in the NEH's economic faculty.

1969, however, turned out to be significantly different from earlier years, with little by way of publications as I spent most of my time in getting to grips with the Dutch system of university teaching together with the preparation of my inaugural lecture (known as a *rede* in Dutch) to be delivered in the Aula in April, in the presence of my professorial colleagues and with an open invitation to all other members of staff and to all students, to say nothing of the public's right to be there – and, as I found out as the ceremony began, also that of the media! The following days' press, TV and radio generated headlines and lengthy columns on my apparently controversial presentation. My *rede* had, it seemed, generally been seen as an attack on the policies already put in place by the Dutch government for the exploitation of the massive Groningen natural gas field: the 'life-saver' of the Dutch economy in the aftermath of its costly 1953 floods and in financing the massive construction efforts in the Rhine delta to ensure that such a phenomenon could not be repeated.

My lecture was entitled 'The Economic Geography of Energy Resources: a Case Study of Natural Gas in Europe'. This was seemingly low key, but it was not so in the context of The Netherlands as a unique European gas-rich nation in 1969. Nor, in particular, given that the potential riches of natural gas were half-owned by the State and the other half jointly by Royal Dutch/Shell and Exxon (or Esso as it was then named). Between them, they had conjured up an exploitative regime which was duopolistic and highly profitable and, of course, a potential monopolistic supplier to most of a still largely energy-scarce Europe – with agreements to pipeline supplies at prices which were related to oil prices in Belgium, France, West Germany, Luxembourg, Switzerland and Italy. Plans had also been drawn up for Dutch gas to be pipe-lined and sold to the UK, but this was not to be, as gas discoveries in the British sector of the south North Sea had by 1969 been found to be exploitable at very low costs, so undermining the much higher Dutch gas prices!

At the time, I seriously thought that I was to be declared *persona non grata* because my inaugural lecture had opened up potential negative consequences for the finances of the Dutch government and on the profitability of the Royal Dutch company in which the Dutch Queen was the largest shareholder! I had no idea as to what exchanges arose between the governors of the NEH and the various Dutch Ministries of State with direct interests in Groningen gas, but I have no doubt that my academic colleagues argued for 'academic freedom of speech' and for my 'legal rights' following the Royal Assent given for my appointment. I thus remained at my appointed post as Professor of Economic and Social Geography and proceeded with my teaching and research responsibilities, as required, and, in general, on an acceptable base as shown from both my professorial colleagues and the students whom I taught. Moreover, having broached a subject in my inaugural lecture of great importance to the Dutch economy and to enhanced government funding for social welfare, I became useful to the media for interpreting changes that were being made in the exploitation of sales of Groningen gas. Strangely, very few members of the Dutch academic world appeared to offer their views on the issues at stake!

Having thus overcome the trials and consequences of my inaugural lecture, I was able to stretch my wings in a modest way to a number of contacts in other parts of The Netherlands, most notably to the European Institute in Amsterdam as a guest lecturer; and also to make visits to lecture in other foreign countries (Belgium, Switzerland, Austria and Germany) and, of course, to the UK for purposes of advising my Ph.D. students working on Latin America at the LSE; and also because of my continuing membership of the British Labour Party's North Sea Oil and Gas Committee.

In spite of the above foreign issues, my integration into various Dutch systems gradually emerged – with more effect after my several months' stint at a *Talenpracticum* in the small town of Vught in the eastern part of the country. This was run in a convent by the Sisters who covered a wide range of language learning, including Dutch for foreigners. This was intense and worthwhile with out-of-hours practice in the household to which I was allocated as a guest: in my case to the widow of a high court judge. She insisted that all communication must be made in the Dutch language: a procedure which was not limited only to help with syntax and pronunciation but also to achieve familiarity with Dutch protocol. On completion of the two- to three-month course I was able to operate much more effectively than hitherto!

In our Rotterdam family world, we gradually adapted well to Dutch habits and ways of doing things. Our two older children had settled down well at school so that by mid-year in 1969 they were fully integrated, and our two younger children were assisted by Elly to become competent in the Dutch language – and also in Dutch childhood manners. Jean, given her early command of the Dutch language, was able to get out and about and able to talk to the schoolteachers concerning our older children's progress. She was also welcomed into the circle of the wives of the university's professors (very few of them had jobs of their own) and in the NEH choir. More generally, socialising in the neighbourhood and with colleagues built up gradually. Simultaneously we were introduced to the Scots Church in Rotterdam, then recently rebuilt in a city location following its destruction on its original site nearer the river (dating back to the seventeenth century), by the bombing of the city prior to its invasion from Germany in 1940.

Overall, by the end of 1969 I think it is reasonable to claim that we had 'our feet under the table' in a city which had recovered from its wartime/post war depression, which had achieved the status of Europe's largest port, and which was still in the throes of yet further expansion.

Thereafter, from 1970 to 1977 we enjoyed and participated in the dynamic developments of Rotterdam in general and, in equal parts, in both Dutch and British Commonwealth organisations, with the latter owing its success to the large number of English employees in Unilever and in the port and its activities. We achieved much satisfaction from the location and first-class attributes of our family house in Kralingen.

Meanwhile, my professorial appointment had now become one in the Faculty of Economics of Erasmus University Rotterdam (the birth place of Erasmus) which had been created from the amalgamation of the NEH and the Medical Faculty in the locality of Hoboken (in downtown Rotterdam). A number of other faculties, philosophy, history and sociology, were also designated – but there was no development into the sciences or technology. The early 1970s was thus a time of consolidation in the Economic Geography Institute of the university, involving an expansion of staff for both teaching and research in the context of the new doctoral programme in spatial (plus regional) economics. This in turn stimulated my efforts to complete the manuscript of my book on the economic geography of Latin America. The book was eventually published early in 1973 and proved to be successful in sales and use.

Meanwhile, my previously completed manuscript of *Oil and World Power* had been published as a Pelican Original by Penguin Books in 1970 in what turned out to be a very propitious time for such a book, with rising oil prices and the awakening of the Organisation of Petroleum Exporting Countries (OPEC) to a power potential which was evolving from the rapid expansion of global oil use. The book itself was very successful, running to seven sequential English editions – through to 1986 – and to translations into thirteen or more languages, with total sales well in excess of 100,000. These developments, along with the interest stimulated by my inaugural lecture on natural gas in Europe, generated a parallel expansion in the EGI of energy studies and a rapidly growing number of invitations by the media (newspapers, journals, radio and television) and by interested organisations to explain the fundamental changes in oil and gas production and use which were under way.

From a multitude of articles and papers which were written and/or presented in 1971 and 1972, two stand out. The first, a paper published in *New Society* (11 February 1971), defined the emergence of a cartel between the United States government, the major international oil companies and OPEC, to the detriment of customers worldwide. The second was a presentation to a Norwegian oil company (on 15 November 1972) in which I suggested that North-west European oil and gas prospects were capable of fundamentally changing the global distribution of power in the oil and gas industries over the next 10–15 years. Norway was much impressed!

Over these years the EGI at Erasmus University was virtually swamped by requests to explain the future prospects for the world of energy. Amongst these demands on my time, two such requests stood out. The first was by KLM, on behalf of the world's airlines, as to the prospects for the future prices of aviation fuels. After meetings and discussions in Amsterdam and Geneva, this culminated in a round-the-world journey to and from the annual meeting of IATA in Auckland, New Zealand in November 1973,

49. *Shell UK's Sea Oil and Gas Exploitation Team invites me to dine with them in Aberdeen prior to taking me on a visit to Shetland; and from there on a round-trip by helicopter to and from the company's massive Brent oil and gas field*

with many stopovers to brief particular participants. The second was an invitation to me by a leading Edinburgh financial entity, Ivory and Sime, to present each month the rapidly changing prospects for the UK's North Sea developments. The global range of assembled financiers seemed to take my views as a basis for their decision-taking on investments in the international oil industry, in general, and on North-west European offshore prospects in particular.

Further diversification for me emerged over the weeks and months to come from requests for lectures from both within the Netherlands and from many other European countries, with special interest in oil and gas supply prospects. This was accompanied by an invitation to join the board of a company with Anglo/Dutch interests in enhancing the efficiency of energy use through 'Total Energy' systems capable of serving individual industries, offices, hospitals, swimming pools with on-site generated steam (heat) and electricity. Unhappily, the company did not become a very successful venture, given the hostility of the powerful monopolies of the state-owned gas and electricity suppliers to such developments.

1974, 1975, 1976 and the first half of 1977 were equally – if not even more – responsible for years of severe pressures on my time and capabilities. In each of these years there were about 150 days (out of about 250 'working' days) when I had commitments outside the University. One such ongoing commitment was to the leading Dutch newspaper (the equivalent of *The Times* or the *Guardian*), the *Nieuwe Rotterdamse Courant* (NRC) for which I wrote thirty articles of 2000+ words, each on many different aspects of the international and European oil issues, between late-1973 and mid-1976 – plus a few more between then and the second oil price shock in 1979/81! Many of the rest of my commitments were in countries other than The Netherlands, involving ten or more countries each year. Most of these foreign visits (including those to the UK) were for lectures on energy matters at universities and other professional institutions, but there were a number of extra-special visits (see photograph no. 50 on page 102).

In January 1975 BBC television invited me to do the 'Controversy' programme to be filmed in the Faraday lecture theatre of the Royal Society. On this occasion, I presented a three-hour defence of the hypothesis that 'North Sea Oil is a Bonanza for Britain'. The steeply tiered seating for some three hundred people – mainly employees of various oil companies – was a formidable environment, made even more so by my opponents, two high-powered executives of Shell and BP (Peter Baxendale of Shell and Mr Bexxon of BP), plus hundreds of invited participants from the oil industry! After editing, the BBC 2 programme ran for almost ninety minutes and was well received as portraying the potential positive prospect for the UK's future. It was, indeed, a video which I have since occasionally viewed to lift my spirits!

Just a few days later I was en route, by KLM 1st class, from Schiphol to Curaçao at the request of the government of the Nederlandse Antillen to give advice on its policies on the refineries of Shell and Esso – and also on the possibility of offshore exploration for oil and gas. Needless to say, in the particularly cold 1975 North-west European winter, eight days in the Caribbean with Jean was a very acceptable proposition. This was followed two weeks later by a four-day visit to Norway in February 1975 to a high-powered international seminar on North-west Europe's prospects for oil and gas exploration and exploitation. By then my colleague Kenneth E. Rosing and I had recently completed an attempt to simulate the North Sea's development and exploitation for up to sixty years from 1969. The model also showed a mean possibility that 75 per cent of Western Europe's oil demands by the end of the twentieth century could be secured from the North Sea. Our analyses greatly exceeded the values of the data then provided by governments and oil companies on oil expectations and estimates for North Sea oil production. Our study was thus received with unjustified scepticism. Its content has, however, subsequently proved to be more nearly correct than all other published data of the time.

Later in 1975 I was invited to give the prestigious annual Stamp Memorial Lecture to be delivered before the University of London Trustees and senior academic staff in Senate House. In the lecture, given before an audience of three hundred or so attendees, I made a longer than one-hour presentation indicating the ways and means whereby the challenges and opportunities for the Western European energy economy could be met through the exploitation of the continent's offshore oil and gas reserves. Having thus set a reasoned base in 1975 from which to look more intensively and extensively at international energy matters in general, and European oil and gas prospects in particular, the scene was then firmly established for our further work over the rest of the decade to be continued – and eventually widely accepted.

In the context of the impact of the first oil price shock, the eight-fold increase in oil prices in the 1970–74 period was maintained. 1976, 1977 and years thereafter continued to sustain requests for both articles and lectures – as well as for updates and new editions of my Penguin book, *Oil and World Power* (2nd Edition, 1972; 3rd, 1974; 4th, 1975; 5th, 1979; Reprint, 1980; 6th, 1981; 7th, 1983; 8th, 1986). These editions were accompanied by the publication of a book written jointly with Dr Luis Valenilla in Venezuela in 1977, *The Pressures of Oil: a Strategy for Economic Revival* (Harper and Row Ltd, London, 1978); and, at the end of the decade, by yet another book, this time jointly authored by Dr K. Rosing, *The Future of Oil: a Simulation Study of the Inter-relationships of Resources, Reserves and Use, 1980–2080* (Kogan Page Ltd, London and the Nicols Publishing Company, New York in 1980, with a second edition in 1983).

By this time, after the second oil price shock caused by the revolution in Iran, the proliferation of my books, papers and articles for press publications were becoming overpowering. I will thus desist from yet more details of my interpretation of the world of oil for the period hitherto examined, except to draw attention to a more recent compilation of my work during that period, viz. *Oil and Gas: Crises and Controversies, 1961– 2000, Volume 1, Global Issues* (2001) and *Volume 2, Europe's Entanglement*

(2002) published by Multi-Science Publishing Company, Brentwood with a total of 1,160 pages and including twenty-six chapters of work which I had first published in the 1970s!

Meanwhile, however, late in the 1970s there were family reasons for a re-think of our adaptation to life in Rotterdam. Our two older children had progressed well through the primary school system and had been followed by the two younger ones, Mark and Susannah, through both kindergarten (from 4 to 6 years old) and then into the same primary school as their older siblings. All had thus seemed 'hunky-dorey' for the first eight years in Rotterdam. Indeed, Nigel and Deborah had done so well at primary school that they were recommended for progress to the Marnix Gymnasium in Rotterdam (the equivalent of a selective traditional English grammar school, but with links to the Dutch Protestant Church). Nigel's progress through his first and second years appeared satisfactory and he had no adverse comments about the school. This was not, however, destined to last as he 'failed' an exam at the end of his second year and was not permitted to proceed further at the school. The 'failure' however, was only on the Dutch language examination for which his grade was 'only 5.5' rather than the required minimum mark of 6.0. My protestations to the Rector – based on Nigel's pass-marks in all other subjects in general and on his 9.5 mark in English in particular, so that there was room for compensation to be made – came to nothing! Indeed, the Rector said that Nigel had to leave the school immediately and transfer to a lower level HAVO School (on a par with a secondary school modern in the UK and with little hope from any HAVO for meeting Dutch university entrance standards). This left the British School in Den Haag as the only local option, involving high costs for the school fees and a time-consuming journey each day to and from Den Haag. This was impracticable, so that Jean and I were obliged to make a decision for Nigel to go to a boarding school back in the UK, with a late choice of Colston's School in Bristol: much, I think in retrospect, to his chagrin – and my unhappiness!

Deborah, meantime, stayed on at the Marnix Gymnasium for another year but with little enthusiasm so that we had to take a further decision for her to go to boarding school in England. After her failing to be accepted at Marlborough School, we made the choice of a girl's school in Runton, Norfolk, in fairly close proximity to the home of my Aunty Ethel – my father's youngest sister – so that she could keep an eye on our daughter. Again, there was no great enthusiasm about this chosen school, especially when the headmaster, whose background in science subjects was a prime reason for our choice of school, almost immediately left his post and was replaced by a headmistress without any academic qualifications!

By this time the English public school fees and travel costs between Rotterdam and Bristol and Norfolk began to tell on my finances, in spite of significant children's allowances from the Dutch state for children of civil servants (my status in the Dutch university system) who were being educated away from home. Thus, in late 1976, Jean and I decided that the upcoming tenth year qualification of my academic years in the Netherlands should be taken in large part in the UK, where we would establish a new home base for the family. The choice made for this base was deliberately close to the UK port of Harwich, with its twice-daily ferry service to and from the Hoek van Holland. In the summer of 1977 we moved to a newly-purchased, large Edwardian house in Ipswich, very close to the public school for boys in the town to which we had already sent our eleven-year-old son Mark in January of that year as a boarder in the junior section of the school.

Thus, by September 1977 all six of us in the extended family were temporarily back in the UK. Nigel almost immediately went off to the University of Hull for a 4-year BA course in European and Language Studies (the latter being German and Dutch) during which period one year was well spent at the University of Osnabrück in Lower Saxony. Meanwhile, Deborah had left Runton Hill School with enough success in GCSE examinations to qualify for the Ipswich School 6th form, which for the first time in its several hundred years' existence accepted girls! Mark, of course, left the Ipswich junior school boarding house in July and became a day-boy. Susie, now a ten-year-old, switched from the Calvinistic primary school in Rotterdam and joined the St Matthew's Church of England school in the final year class. Jean, of course, was enormously busy settling anew into our Edwardian house in which many repairs and much redecoration had to be done. These were eventually completed, albeit over more than one year, by the autumn of 1978. By this time Jean was also fit and well and able to accept two other pupils from Ipswich School – one boy and one girl – as lodgers in our eight-bedroomed house, with plenty of space for homework and indoor games (such as billiards and table tennis). She was also able to re-establish the tennis court in a very large garden. As for myself, in my sabbatical year I was 'in' and 'out' very frequently as my research and contacts elsewhere had to be undertaken. This is shown in Chapter 6.

CHAPTER 6

Mid 1977 to Early 1978 – A Sabbatical Intermission; with Hard Work and Multiple Failures

By late August 1977 our 'new' home in Ipswich was just about habitable – in spite of the extensive repairs and maintenance which were under way – so that all the family, except for me, had become re-based in the UK. My proposed sabbatical 'year' (in reality about eighteen months) was now delayed for a month or so whilst I completed my Erasmus University duties, partly in Rotterdam for the required needs of a new academic year. I was then required for my professional presentation at a UK public enquiry in Whitehaven in Cumbria concerning the Windscale nuclear power plant expansion; and then at an eight-day International Geographical Union meeting in cities which I had not previously visited, viz. Kraków and Warsaw in Poland. For the first time at such an Eastern European meeting there were clear signs from the Polish participants of the existence of difficulties for the country's Communist government and indications of a possible near-future change of fundamental importance.

During my sabbatical, I had also arranged for visits to Iran, Canada and Venezuela, as well as accepting the offer of a post as a Special Adviser to the Rt. Hon. Tony Benn, then the UK's Secretary of State for Fuel and Power. This offer emerged from the advice of Lord Balogh, a respected academic economist and a member of the House of Lords where he held an appointment as the deputy to the Energy Minister in that part of the UK's Labour government. I shall return later in this chapter to my experience as a Special Adviser for more than two years.

Meanwhile, my invitation to make a two to three weeks' planned visit to Iran to lecture on the international energy situation and to study Iran's oil, gas and nuclear power prospects did not materialise, given the rapidly emerging revolutionary situation against the Shah's regime. This development was somewhat ironic, given that it was the success of that revolution which led to the second world oil price shock. In the overthrow of the old regime Iranian crude oil almost disappeared from the market and so led to oil price increases that far exceeded those of the first oil crisis. The consequential downturn in the global economy eventually produced a 20 per cent downturn in global oil demand – and led to a more than 50 per cent fall in oil prices from a designated peak of $36 per barrel in 1980 to a low of about $14 in 1986.

It was in these circumstances that two important developments in my career come into play: first, my appointment as a Special Adviser to Tony Benn over UK oil policy; and second, my co-operation with a Venezuelan oil expert, Dr Luis Valenilla, in writing a book, *The Pressures of Oil*. For this latter purpose I spent a period of a month or so in Venezuela; mostly at the Caribbean beach house of the joint author. The house was large and luxurious (with a staff of servants in both the house and the garden), located high up on the mountain-side behind Venezuela's narrow coastal strip, so giving a perfect view out over the southern Caribbean Sea. It was above this location that Air France's daily flight between Paris and Caracas, served by the newly-developed Concorde airliner, approached its destination and made its subsequent departure from the Venezuelan airport. In spite of Concorde's daily diversion, we still managed to achieve the successful conclusion of our draft manuscript on *The Pressures of Oil* which I subsequently then made ready for Harper and Row's production of the 200-page book. Prior to that, however, I had revisited Curaçao for further discussions with, and to give further advice to, the Nederlandse Antillen government, concerning its limited payments from the significantly highly profitable operations of the Shell and Exxon's refineries in Curaçao and Aruba respectively. From Curaçao I went on to New York in December to give a number of lectures at Colombia University on international oil affairs.

On my return to the UK in December there were just two hectic weeks before the Christmas of 1977. This very short period involved liaison with Ministers and civil servants in the UK's fuel and power department, presentations over the international oil situation in Edinburgh and Rotterdam, meetings with fellow directors of TELS Ltd (Total Energy Leasing Systems), lectures to be given at LSE; and last, but by no means least, to hold discussions with the publishers, Harper and Row, over the progress of our book, *The Pressures of Oil*, which was scheduled for publication in mid-1978. Quite a fortnight on which to look back!

Following on from these multiple obligations in 1977, the subsequent first Christmas/New Year period back in England since that of 1967 was a welcome respite – notwithstanding the still incomplete repairs and decorations of our house on Constitution Hill after the six-month period since the house was purchased. For Mark and Susannah, our two younger children, this was their first belated experience of a traditional English Christmas – and they then had to wait for over a month into February 1978 before there was any snow. In early February it fell with a vengeance – even to the extent that drifts of snow on the roads and railways isolated Ipswich from the rest of the country for several days! Luckily, I had decided to leave my work in London on Friday in time to catch the last train which managed to get to Ipswich.

Thereafter, in the rest of the first two months of 1978, I was principally concerned with just two main tasks: first, the completion of the final text of *The Pressures of Oil* – requiring long telephone calls with Luis Vallenilla in Caracas and the express mailing of the texts (given the absence of internet facilities at that time!) in the hope for their early arrival! Happily, all was completed before the end-February deadline and the manuscript was delivered on time. Secondly, my most important task was my work as a special adviser to Tony Benn. This was an appointment, I found out later, which had been strongly opposed by his senior civil servants and by ex-oil industry personnel who had been recruited by the government to make the allocation to oil companies of prospective oil and gas rich blocks of acreage in the UK's offshore waters. Nevertheless, I was eventually allowed to contribute to evaluating the results of successful finds of oil and gas prior to the allocation of production licences, together with advice on the approvals needed for the laying of underwater pipelines to bring the oil and gas produced from offshore fields to terminals at various places on the east coasts of England and Scotland. The government's fundamentals for these objectives – which had already been established over the period from 1967 for gas and from 1973 for oil – gave highly favourable agreements to the exploration and production companies through to the late 1970s.

The post-1973 Labour governments of Wilson and Callaghan (along with the preceding Conservative governments) had failed to recognise the immense significance of the oil and gas wealth of the UK's continental shelf – given the fivefold increase in the price of oil between 1970 and 1974 and in the light of the emerging even higher values for the oil by 1978, as a result of the Iranian revolutionaries' success in bringing out the foreign oil companies' workers on an indefinite strike. Though this event enabled North Sea oil to be sold at much higher prices, so boosting the profits of the British National Oil Corporation (BNOC), it also secured the right to buy about half of the oil companies' production at prices which were much lower than those at which oil could be sold in the markets. In essence, the Labour government was thus either unable or unwilling to make any radical changes to the way in which the country's offshore oil and gas was exploited or left unexploited!

Tony Benn, the Secretary of State, and Lord Balogh, the Minister for Fuel and Power in the House of Lords, had both quizzed me over these issues in some previous years, in the aftermath of the 'recommendations of the Labour Party's investigation into North Sea issues'. They now asked me to investigate the validity of the existing legislation for the exploitation of the country's wealth, and to present alternative options for securing a more substantial element of state involvement and control in the now rapidly emerging much larger prospects for long-term production than the oil companies had chosen to reveal and activate.

My response to these requests emerged from a number of studies on North Sea oil and gas that I and my colleagues had undertaken at Erasmus University in Rotterdam earlier in the 1970s. The most important of these were a 1975 monograph on *The North Sea Oil Province: an Attempt to Simulate its Development and Exploitation 1969–2029* and a subsequent publication in 1977 with the title *The Optimal Development of the North Sea's Oil Fields; a Study in Divergent Government and Company Interests and their Reconciliation*. Both of these monographs were published by Kogan Page in London. Given their radical nature – from both the geological/geo-physical and the politico-economic standpoints – there was much discussion within the industry and in the media (including radio and TV presentations in many European countries) over my work for, and advice to, Tony Benn. Nevertheless, in spite of the oil companies' attempts to 'rubbish' our work, Tony Benn and Tommy Balogh, as well as Dr Mabon, Tony Benn's number two, remained convinced that we had successfully rejected the validity of the companies' hostility. It was in this context that I willingly went to work with modest recompense over the fifteen-month period from January 1978. Nevertheless, I still had to face negative views from many officials in the Ministry, as well as having to put up with delays in gaining access to the oil companies' representations on their exploration and exploitation activities. The procrastination by some thirty companies left me without complete access to the necessary data for over nine months – by which time my initial twelve-month contract with the Ministry was well-nigh over. It was, however, then extended month by month through to March 1979.

50. Lecturing on the UK's Developing Offshore Oil and Gas Production and Potential

By sheer coincidence, the day in March 1979, when the civil service head of the Department of Energy finally and reluctantly agreed to accept my Report under the title *The Exploitation of Britain's Offshore Oil Resources* (following a number of changes which I was required to make to drafts over the previous two months), turned out to be the very same day on which the Labour government was defeated in the House of Commons and was thus obliged to call an election!

The latter produced a subsequent fundamental change of government; with a requirement that all papers and studies generated by the previous government be declared unusable by the successor Ministers. Thus, unhappily, my study received no consideration for subsequent policy making. The Report, *per se*, was simply given to, and filed by, the Library of the Houses of Parliament. As such, its availability was only to parliamentarians – and to judge from the very few MPs who contacted me about it, it received very little attention! It thus seemed as though my eighteen-months' work had been very much in vain! All, however, was not lost, as Kogan Page Ltd – which had published my monographs in 1975 and 1977 – approached the Controller of Her Majesty's Stationery Office for permission to publish my report under the title *British Oil Policy: a*

Radical Alternative. Surprisingly perhaps, permission so to do was given and it was put on the market by the publishers early in 1980. Given its radical content, it created significant media attention – and sold many hundreds of copies, not only in the UK, but also in other countries with offshore hydrocarbons resources. Thirty years later I continue to think that my recommendations in the Report for public/private partnerships which would successfully enhance the level of offshore oil and gas exploitation seemed, in part, at least to influence Norway's subsequent creation of Statoil. The intent for the latter's manner of working was that together with the private companies there would be a successfully secure basis on which the search for and development of the country's offshore oil and gas went ahead. No such manner of development emerged in the UK under the post-1979 Conservative governments of Mrs Thatcher.

On the contrary, one of her first major actions as Prime Minister was to eliminate the British National Oil Corporation (BNOC) by selling off its interests at modest prices to private sector oil companies. The latter, paradoxically, were almost simultaneously subjected to much higher taxes on their offshore oil and gas activities so that they, of course, subsequently retreated from some of their earlier commitments to find and produce oil and gas. Thus, the UK's output of oil declined year by year from 1986 to 1990 and that of natural gas from 1987 to 1990. This decline occurred in spite of the known high volume of accessible reserves of 7,900 million barrels of oil, but at a time when the price of oil on the international market fell year by year – to an ultimate low of $14 per barrel in 1986. For the UK, no longer with any effective governmental control over the oil companies' decisions on their exploration and exploitation activities, my earlier expectations for an oil and gas bonanza were severely undermined.

Meanwhile, with my sabbatical eighteen months or so having come to an end, I went back to Rotterdam for an undetermined future. First, however, I must record my hopes and expectations that a combination of my physical return to the UK, together with the reality of oil (and gas) as the country's new commanding height, would have presented many opportunities for my expertise and enthusiasm to secure me a relevant – and, perhaps, a highly remunerative – career prospect. Indeed, three prospective openings had emerged during my period of service to the now entitled Department of Energy.

First, a vacancy occurred in the government's obligation to appoint a director to the Board of British Petroleum PLC . I duly approached Tony

Benn for his consideration as to the suitability of my appointment to the post on the grounds of my familiarity with the knowledge of the international oil industry, of which BP was one of the so-called 'Seven Sisters'. In fact, I heard nothing more of my possible appointment – not even of the possible fears by BP that I knew too much about the industry! It then emerged that the person who had been appointed to this part-time directorship of such an important entity for the UK's future was someone who knew little or nothing about the oil industry, viz. the head of the Post Office Workers' Union! Hardly, I think, an appointment which was likely to keep BP under control.

Secondly, in light of the central conclusions of my Report that state intervention was a necessary component for the successful and ongoing exploitation of the UK's offshore oil and gas resources, I thought that I would at least be suitable to fill a vacancy in the senior management of the British National Oil Corporation. I thus also made such a suggestion to Tony Benn to this effect, within the context of the procedure due for such appointments by the relevant part of the Labour government. This, however, also came to nothing, due, I suspect, to the opposition of the then chairman of the BNOC, Lord Kearton, with whom I had had a number of confrontations in high-level meetings called by the Secretary of State for setting out the way ahead for the expansion of BNOC's activities. In particular, I had proposed that BNOC should expand its North Sea exploration and production activities by moving into the industry's downstream sector. This could have started with the purchase of a refinery in the port of Rotterdam (where refining and petrochemical activities were dominant in Europe), which had been built and operated by a major US oil company, Gulf Oil. This company had, however, failed to cope with the rapidly changing international oil situation and markets – and had thus decided to exit from its European-based activities. Instead of the refinery becoming a part of BNOC's activities, as I had argued it should, it was instead eventually sold to the Kuwaiti national oil company – and remains so to the present time!

Third, there was a suggestion by a number of Edinburgh financiers, to whose companies I had offered many analyses and much advice over the years on both the global and the British oil and gas prospects. They argued that I should be invited to launch a Centre for Energy Research at one or other of Edinburgh's two universities, given the highly favourable emerging prospects for Scotland as a major oil country. The formalities of my 'sponsors' thus went to work with the necessary financial offers and to persuade the Prime Minister's office – through a visit, including myself, to No. 10 Downing Street – to support the proposal in the interests of Edinburgh for such a university-based development in Scotland. Unhappily, neither of the universities' Vice-Chancellors, nor the Prime Minister's office, were persuaded to accept the proposition.

Given these three 'statutory' failures and the accompanying lack of any success elsewhere in finding an appropriate appointment to one of the then large-growing number of oil and oil related companies in the City of London and in Edinburgh which were now taking interests in the UK's rapidly expanding oil and gas interests, I thus decided to stay on with my professorial post at Erasmus University in Rotterdam, and then seek to launch a Centre for International Energy Studies in the University's Faculty of Economics. My 'leftist political tendencies' had, it seemed, eliminated all other options!

CHAPTER 7

Fifteen More Very Energetic Years in Rotterdam, 1978–92

WITH MY SABBATICAL YEAR COMING to an end at the beginning of the 1978/9 Dutch academic year, my family's newly-found home and its speedy readjustment to the Ipswich way of life enabled me to return to Rotterdam in August 1978: in good time, that is, to evolve a new set of necessary teaching and research obligations within the Economic Geography Institute. I did, however, return with a degree of trepidation, given my hundred per cent loss of hair (*alopecia universalis*) in my period away from Erasmus University – a development which, it seems, happened because of difficulties and stress which I had experienced on traversing a thousand metre high, knife-edge ridge in the Andorran Pyrenees during a walking holiday in the Principality! Or perhaps from my failure to secure any one of three high level posts in the UK's oil and gas exploitation?

Fortunately, in Rotterdam neither my colleagues nor the students I taught treated me with other than courtesy – and interest – in the cause of my misfortune. There was also one other problem which had to be overcome: how I could cope with looking after myself – and our Rotterdam house which we had not sold on leaving the city a year previously, in order to keep open the option of a family return. As this did not happen I had to settle down to necessary housekeeping – and to preparing and cooking my own meals! Fortunately, neighbours and friends – in both the neighbourhood and elsewhere in Rotterdam – helped me to survive! Nevertheless, it was about another five years – by when it became clear that there would be no family return to Rotterdam – before Jean and I decided that our house in Rotterdam should be sold. This decision produced a significant capital gain on the original 1968 purchase price. In place of the house, we purchased and moved into a more manageable three-room apartment in a block of flats located alongside the university campus.

Meanwhile, of course, Jean and three of our children (excluding Nigel who was studying German in Osnabrück as part of his chosen course at the University of Hull), plus two lodgers from Ipswich School (which was short of accommodation for its pupils) were getting used to life at our Ipswich house. Though not, I should add, without some help from me during the long weekends that I managed to secure at the Hill by using the Hoek van Holland/Harwich night ferries for my fortnightly visits! For each of my visits Jean would have drawn up a list of repairs and replacements etc. that awaited my 'expertise' – to say nothing of the family's financial affairs which usually also needed attention! In no year, prior to my taking an early retirement from my position in the university at the end of 1991, was I in the UK for more than ninety days – that is, within the annual time period that the Inland Revenue allowed for UK citizens working overseas before imposing taxes on their income. Over this period of fifteen years both Jean and I remained formally resident in the Netherlands and were thus liable to Dutch income and wealth taxes and were also eligible for the Dutch government's generous children's allowances. Given their ages and the fact that they were living away from my house in Rotterdam, each child was counted three times – so giving us a temporary twelve-child family claim to children's allowances!

Socially, we continued to attend and support the Scots Church in Rotterdam and to support the Rotterdam Branches of the Commonwealth Club and the Anglo/Dutch Society. We also joined in a number of Dutch events and facilities in the Kralingen community. One set, however, of previous contacts in the Netherlands that had been important disappeared from our diaries: invitations that had hitherto been received year by year to 1977 from a number of foreign countries' embassies and consulates – perhaps because we were not able to respond to the mailed invitations from them in 1977/8. These were all sent to our Rotterdam address and we were thus unable to reply! These consequential absences from such 'jollies' did, however, leave more time to spend on a whole host of invitations and opportunities from elsewhere, mainly to present and advise on the complications of the emerging international energy systems in the aftermath of the revolution in Iran in 1979/81.

Before proceeding to list such obligations I must, however, point out a fundamental change in my position in Erasmus University. In 1968 I had been appointed to the Chair of Economic and Social Geography through to my seventieth birthday, with a requirement from me over the whole period to teach and undertake research on the subject. But my sabbatical year had persuaded me of my need to switch to energy studies – both economic and political and at the global level. In 1980, I therefore offered my resignation from my Erasmus Chair in Geography to Queen

51. The staff of my Geographical Institute in 1980: on my resignation

Beatrix – as required by Dutch procedures. This was duly accepted. Simultaneously, I took up the University's designation of a special Chair in International Energy Studies in the Economic Faculty, together with an Institutional entity: the Erasmus University Centre for International Energy Studies (described as EURICES). Thus began a decade during which period my academic and other efforts were almost entirely concentrated on energy issues: with Rotterdam as the 'working base' and elsewhere in the world, as and when required, for enhancing my understandings of global energy systems.

In the absence of my earlier responsibilities for the EGI (the Economic Geography Institute) and for the teaching programme in those studies, plus a contribution to the Economic Faculty's spatial and regional economics programme, I was in a much more flexible position for achieving the objective of sustaining an already reputable Rotterdam centre for analysing local, European and global energy issues in the 1970s. In 1980/1, in the immediate aftermath of the Iranian Revolution which had upset the equilibrium of the international energy – and especially the oil – markets, the work of the Erasmus Centre for Energy Studies remained soundly-based, so that we were able to analyse the longer-term consequences for Europe and, indeed, much of the rest of the world.

Subsequently, more than one hundred EURICES Papers were written over the twelve-year period to the end of 1991. Most of these were for presentation to meetings in many different countries and, thereafter, accepted in relevant energy and/or economic and geographical journals. There was thus a continuing outflow of pertinent literature over the decade. In addition, I – alone or sometimes with a colleague (or colleagues) – published a number of books: *British Oil Policy: a Radical Alternative* in 1980; *The Future of Oil: a Simulation Study on the Inter-relationships of Resources, Reserves and Use, 1980–2080* (with Ken Rosing) in 1980; *Oil and World Power*, 6th Edition in 1981; *Energie: Geen Probleem?* (with J.A. van Reijn) in 1981; *Oil and World Power*, 7th Edition in 1983; *The Future of Oil*, 2nd Edition (with K.E. Rosing) in 1983; and finally *Oil and World Power*, 8th edition in 1986.

Concurrently, and also after 1986 there were, in addition, major contributions by EURICES to conferences and seminars of relevant interest to regional and/or global energy issues. Some of the examples of these were *The Maritime Dimension of Oil and Gas Resources* (Eds. R.P. Barston and P. Birnie) in 1980; *The Electricity Sector and Energy Policy* (Ed. C. Sweet) in 1980; *Energy Policies in the EEC and their Impact on the 3rd World* (Ed. C. Stevens) in 1981; *International Energy Issues: the Next 10 Years* (Ed. P. Tempest) in 1981; *Oil and Gas Potential in Developing Countries* (United Nations) in 1982; *World Oil Energy Potential* (Eds. Y. Elizar and E. Saltpeter) in 1982; *Institutional and Economic Constraints on the Utilisation of Natural Gas Resources* (Eds. C. Delahage and M. Grenon) in 1983; *The Oil and Gas Resources of the 3rd World Importing Countries* (United Nations, 1984); *Energy* (The Social Science Encyclopedia, 1985); *Institutional Constraints on the Development of the West European Gas Market* (Ed. P. Stevens), 1986; *The Changing Structure of the Oil Industry in the Caribbean* (Ed. H.E. Chin), 1986; *Prospects for the West European Energy Markets* (John Hopkins University), 1989; *Draining the World of Energy* (Eds. R.J. Johnston and P.J. Taylor), 1989; *Continuing Long-Term Hydrocarbons' Dominance of World Energy Markets: an Economic and Societal Necessity* (Pergamon Press) in 1990; and *West European Energy Markets in the 1990's* (Estonian Academy of Sciences) in 1990.

Overall, the formidable above-listed commitments, together with many other invitations which I accepted for presentations and lectures in forty or so countries around the world, totalled about seven hundred over the

52. Reflections on my Energy Institute's future

decade. Together with the books previously listed and all other contributions, a decade of my writing appears to have constituted some 10,000 to 15,000 pages of text. 'Midnight oil' was a self-evident element in my endeavours!

This, however, is indicative of only part of my academic story. In addition there were many other ways and means in the 1980s of contributing to the literature and/or understandings on the world's global energy situation. Some of these were related to other parts of academia. These included appointments to temporary and/or part-time posts; viz. as a part-time visiting professor on European energy issues for a period of five years at the College of Europe in Brugge; as a visiting professor in resources geography from 1988 (to 2000) at the London School of Economics; to a visiting lectureship at Clingendael for several years in Den Haag (the equivalent of Chatham House in London); as a Killam visiting scholar in 1987 for one semester to teach energy economics in the Department of Economics in the University of Calgary; and a like appointment, albeit of shorter duration, at the University of Toronto. I also went as a visiting lecturer to the University College of Curaçao in the Dutch Antilles; to lecture at several universities in the United States including Stanford, Houston, Washington, New York, Harvard and MIT in Boston; and likewise at many educational establishments in Europe, including every single one in the Netherlands, to institutions in Oslo, Bergen, Stavanger, Trondheim and Bodô in Norway, to both French and Flemish universities in Belgium, to most universities in Scotland, to Cork and Dublin in Ireland, to some twenty-five universities in England; to Köln, Nuremberg and München in Germany; to many Swedish and Danish academic institutions; and ultimately to the east of the Iron Curtain in Warsaw and Kraków in Poland and ultimately to Tallinn in Estonia and Kaunas in Lithuania, both still incorporated in the Soviet Union. Outside Europe and North America, I also made visits to universities in Caracas, Rio de Janeiro and Mexico in Latin America: to India, Pakistan, Singapore and China in Asia and to a dozen or so institutions in Australia and New Zealand.

Meanwhile, back in Europe there was a real highlight still remaining very memorably: the opportunity of a month's stay as a scholar-in-residence at the Rockefeller Study Centre in Bellagio on Lake Como in Italy – in a magnificent building (in which Jean and I were lodged in a bedroom previously used by John F. Kennedy on his visit to the Centre), with its fabulous wines and meals; and in providing extensive grounds in which to walk and think – all of which enabled one to look northwards to the upper end of Lake Como in an autumn season of near perfect weather (making the concentration on revising my 8th revision of *Oil and World Power* very difficult)!

After this experience subsequent invitations to seminar centres were very much down-market in terms of creative comfort, if not in the value of the proceedings! It was, perhaps, the British Foreign Office's Ditchley Park's Centre for in-depth analyses of international issues in 1985 that took second place status to Bellagio, in terms not only of the hospitality offered and enjoyed for a long weekend, but also in the context of an intensive programme of discussion on international oil/energy issues which I was subsequently asked to evaluate. The conclusions in my report, however, turned out to be much too radical, given that it was built around my view at the time (in 1985) that the oil price would soon collapse – an anathema to oil dependent countries (such as the UK at that time) and, of course, to energy companies. Thus, my report was pigeon-holed. Just a few months later, the price collapse did occur but there were no apologies from those who insisted that this would not happen: particularly, the Chairman of the National Coal Board!

In other conference/seminar circumstances in the 1980s – both in academia and in industry/political circles – I did, indeed, encounter a great deal of scepticism over the views and ideas which I presented. But these were pressures which I comprehensively and continuously declined to accept: with significant justification, as events increasingly emerged in ways which I had forecast. The clearest manifestation of the justification of my views arose though a decision of the International Institute for Applied Systems' Analysis (IIASA) in Vienna – an East/West late cold-war entity, jointly sponsored by the US and the USSR – to seek forecasts from energy-sector modellers in many countries on the future development of oil supply/demand and prices through to 2000. From the 1981 highest price level for oil (as a result of the second oil price shock) we (EURICES) forecast a 50 per cent fall in the near future – correctly, as the five years to 1986 showed. Thereafter, prices made only a slow recovery so that by 2000 the most likely price we foresaw was, in real terms, still under half of that in 1981. Accompanying this price level for oil we also forecast an early decline in oil production and use to 1985; and thereafter a relatively slow rate of recovery, at an annual average rate of only just over 2 per cent until 2000. I correctly sustained these forecasts through to the end of the twentieth century – and was basically proved correct!

In the context of such correct expectations, EURICES went from strength to strength as an Institute which made reliable forecasts of the price of oil and on the likely evolution of the volume of demand: and hence on oil production around the world. This aspect of oil's future prospects was set out – though not exclusively – in half of the ten or so of EURICES Working Papers per year, most of which were requested for publication in many of the journals which were centrally concerned on oil/energy supplies and uses.

As already shown above, many of our papers produced encouraged requests from institutions *et al* in most countries of Western Europe, plus the US, Canada, Mexico, Nederlands Antilles, Venezuela, India and Pakistan – and a number of other countries in the Levant and the Middle East.

Enough, however, of my academic role in these halcyon days – some 'rewards' from which were not to emerge until the 1990s. Meanwhile, I became very heavily concerned with, and committed to, non-academic work in the field of energy in general, and of oil and gas in particular. This involvement with governments' energy problems, opportunities and difficulties for over twenty-five years was prolonged, albeit less intensively than in the 1970s, with the evolution of natural gas and oil exploration and exploitation in north-west Europe, especially in the Netherlands, the UK and Norway.

Additionally, I took on time-consuming evaluations over a variety of political issues. The most elevated – and demanding – was my appointment as a specialist witness in the International Court of Justice's hearings for oil companies which were fighting United States' claims for compensation (measured in terms of hundreds of millions of US dollars), arising from Libya's and Iran's nationalisation; and/or the confiscation of American oil companies' activities in the two countries. Each of the hearings by the Court went on for years before decisions were made, during which periods, as a specialist witness, I was required to prepare documentation which attempted to justify the actions of the country involved. The formality of International Court of Justice was intense – and formidable in respect of the cross-examinations pursued by the other parties' lawyers. Such cross-examinations, however, were intellectually challenging, stimulating and rewarding in terms of the successes I achieved in defeating the opponents' efforts to prove that my arguments were defective. Fortunately, the International Court of Justice was located in Den Haag; only a forty-minute train or bus journey from my home in Rotterdam so that the use of my time was not overwhelmed.

Second in rank order for both the challenges and the protracted nature of judicial proceedings, was my appointment as a specialist witness by the US Internal Revenue Service. I was asked to show that several major US-based oil companies (most notably Exxon and Philips) had underpaid the US taxes due from them on the profits which they had earned from their exploitation of oil fields in the Norwegian sector of the North Sea. The preparation for the extensive documentation and appropriate arguments which had to be put together by specified dates was largely home-based work, but this spilled over from time to time into discussions with the Revenue Services' lawyers in their offices in Washington DC. The tax courts were also located there, so that required appearances in the proceedings also necessitated many North Atlantic return flights between Amsterdam and Washington.

Given my familiarity with North Sea developments – and an extensive knowledge of the costs and prices of the oil exploited – I largely succeeded in supplying a case for the Internal Revenue Service lawyers, but, unhappily, the latter made little progress in persuading the judges of the validity of their case – given the formidable array of lawyers which the oil companies had retained to have their cases argued! I have subsequently been given to understand that the companies eventually escaped from most, or even all, of the additional taxes sought. I think, however, that my arguments could have almost carried the day had the Internal Revenue sharpened up its ability to use them. Indeed, I was flattered by the commendation made to me in a private conversation with Exxon's top lawyer, following his lengthy cross-examination of my claims and arguments: first, he said it had been his most strenuous examination ever in his efforts to undermine the opponent's arguments; and second, that it had been an exhilarating in-court experience! I concurred with him!

Beyond that, following omissions by the Internal Revenue lawyers relating to my situation in the Court, I was subpeoned by the judge late on a Friday afternoon to reappear on the witness stand immediately after the weekend break. In a situation in which I was scheduled to be back in Rotterdam for important and unchangeable commitments, it took a dash through Washington that Friday evening to find a notary who would commit himself to producing a document which legally confirmed my commitments elsewhere! The judge just in time accepted my claim – so that I could then dash to Washington's major airport to catch the overnight plane to Amsterdam; but only after I accepted the Judge's order that I would be back in court on the Monday of the next week but one.

I kept to this latter requirement and undertook another trans-Atlantic round trip, Washington/Amsterdam/Washington, only to find in reaching the Washington courtroom on the Monday, as stipulated, that other events between the parties (the US Internal Revenue service and the relevant US oil companies) had intervened. Thus after only a few minutes in the witness box, I was 'stood down' as an irrelevancy to the further proceedings! That same evening I was on the KLM flight back to Amsterdam.

Thereafter, I was for several more years sought out for advice on matters concerning oil disputes and natural gas transport arrangements – but only one such occasion necessitated my cross-examination, at the Paris Arbitration Tribunal on a company's excess profits on its oil sales. There were, however, also some energy related developments in the UK which involved hearings at legally constituted inquiries into the validity of locations selected for installations of oil and nuclear facilities. The first of these was Shell's application to build and use an offshore/onshore oil terminal and associated pipelines on the coast of Anglesey from which imported crude oil would then be transported to the company's refinery located almost 160 kilometres away between Liverpool and Manchester. I was asked by the Town and Country Planning Association (TCPA) to offer economic evidence against this development, on the grounds of its likely near-future uneconomic location, as the UK's imminent production of North Sea oil became available to substitute crude oil imported from Africa and the Middle East. Though my extensive and formidable evidence was rejected by the Inspector in his decision to allow Shell to go ahead with the project, the physical facilities subsequently built were barely operational before my forecast of the uneconomic nature of the venture because of North Sea oil was proved correct, so that the company's facilities were soon closed down – at a significant loss of the investment costs.

The same happened on my conclusion of the inherently uneconomic nature of a proposed new facility for enhancing the productivity of a nuclear material processing plant at Windscale in Cumbria. On this occasion the Inspector severely limited the argument of my case to well under one hour and then blithely went ahead, without serious consideration, to allow the nuclear facility's development to be built. The eventual costs of enhanced investments much exceeded those indicated to be required by the nuclear industry which eventually only just managed to complete the plant's construction years after it should have been ready. Even since then the nuclear authority has never been able to use it effectively and profitably. It is thus now being demolished, albeit slowly given its dangerous nuclear basis.

These two failures turned out, however, to be relatively low-key compared with the state-owned Central Electricity Generating Board's decision to proceed with its plan for an advanced nuclear power station on the Suffolk Coast just north of Aldeburgh, alongside an earlier much smaller nuclear facility. Again I produced copious evidence to show that a nuclear power station would be an inherently non-economic facility, in the context of alternative electricity production from the UK's own oil and natural gas – already, long since, known to be producible from the country's prolific and accessible offshore hydrocarbon wealth. Nevertheless, in spite of the evidence against the potential success of the development which both I and others advanced, the Inspector still recommended that permission to proceed with the projected 2000 megawatt nuclear power station should be given. By the time it was built and operating, it failed, as I had advised, to operate economically so that some years later (in 1989) the government sold it off to a private company for a fraction of its original cost, adding to an already significant additional public debt – which, of course, had to be covered by means of higher taxes. The Sizewell nuclear plant's subsequent so-called 'success' in making nuclear electricity profitable was thus already, in part, the result of subsidies from the public purse – which have yet to be further enhanced by virtue of the still-to-be expected high costs to the public purse when the nuclear power station eventually has to be decommissioned!

This succinct overview of my twelve years from 1980 to 1991 as the Professor of International Energy Studies at Erasmus University has attempted to demonstrate the breadth and depth of my responsibilities and to indicate the broad front on which I attempted to make a contribution to the knowledge of my chosen subject. Much of it was undertaken in the context of the relatively generous professorial salary of Erasmus University – and of the allowances which were made for covering the costs of visits to enhance the reputation of the university in many other such institutions around much of the world. But there were sometimes also honoraria from the institutions which I visited and then strove to present high quality lectures and seminars.

There were also other institutions – both public and private – which offered financial rewards for advice which was given. The best paying bodies were usually the lawyers who had responsibilities for successfully challenging the validity of the claims made against their clients – with payments negotiated and agreed on an hourly, daily or weekly basis. Many of these payments were devoted to the establishment of life insurance policies and/or market investments whereby future financial needs – of myself or my family – could be established. The Dutch government (responsible for almost all of the country's universities' costs) eventually laid down the maximum percentage addition to one's salary which a university professor could secure from external clients. This restraint was, however, relatively generous, so that no deductions had to be made from the payments I received as a full-time employee. Nevertheless, higher-rate income tax of up to 50 per cent necessarily had to be paid as required by the Ministry of Finance.

This also applied to paid work for ongoing extra-mural activities, in my case for my role as a Director and/or shareholder in companies that sought my services. There were two such entities, TELS Ltd and Energy Advice Ltd, both registered in the UK. The former had been launched in the 1970s but it subsequently turned out to be unsustainable in reducing "on site" costs of producing electricity and heat. It was thus wound up in 1980, shortly after my return to Rotterdam. The then very limited cash resources that remained were used to launch Energy Advice Ltd, on the basis of which several governments' energy ministries and various state-owned and private companies operating in the energy sector chose to use my expertise.

There were three major 'clients'. First, there was the government of Curaçao (in the Caribbean) which sought assistance in its dealings with the Royal Dutch/Shell Company's operational activities in refining and oil storage facilities and also in its attempts to secure enhanced tax payments. The importance of the Company in the small Curaçao economy had for many decades overawed and even replaced the government's responsibilities. Now, in the changing international oil system, given the rise of OPEC and of many nationalisations of the private sector oil companies, the Curaçao government sought – partially on my advice – to challenge the power of Shell. As an ultimate result of the challenge the government bought the refinery and its other facilities for just $1, so resolving both the taxation and the physical problems for the company and the state! Subsequently – but still involving my involvement through Energy Advice Ltd – the refinery etc. was leased to the state oil company of Venezuela. This situation remains. Inevitably, however, my advice on the necessary procedural arrangements has long since gone, following my somewhat controversial comments in 1986 on Curaçao's doubtful long-term benefits from Venezuela's lease and operational responsibilities for the island's oil facilities.

Second, there was a long-standing commitment for Energy Advice Ltd to provide both short- and long-term forecasts of volume and price developments in the international oil market to AGI Petroli, the Italian state-owned oil company. At one extreme, these responsibilities involved quarterly presentations on the future months' and years' price prospects for both crude oil and oil products: and at the other extreme, the production of an annual survey of the behaviour and performance of the world's top twenty global oil corporations. Additionally, AGIP requested information and advice on specific issues most likely to affect costs and prices, very often with only a two to three day deadline for the efforts which were expected from me.

Third, Air Products Inc., one of the world's most important producers of a range of gases produced for industrial and medical purposes, also sought my views on the oil and natural gas supply and market prospects at both international and various national levels. Apart from the many contacts at local levels in the Netherlands, Belgium and the UK, I was often invited to meet with the senior executives *et al* of the company, located both at its headquarters in the US and also 'on the ground' in Switzerland. My visits to present ideas to their international meetings took me and my wife to a winter gathering in the formidable eastern Swiss ski resort of Flims, on the one hand, and to the headquarters of the parent company in Pennsylvania and in Michigan, on the other. All such meetings provoked high-level discussions on the global oil and natural gas situations.

Apart from these principal 'clients' – with the latter two seeking my advice right through to, and even beyond, my leaving EURICES at the end of 1991 – there were many other entities involved in seeking my views on the oil and gas industries' situations and prospects. Ivory and Sime, then a leading Edinburgh financial house, continued to request my views each month on the international and the British oil and gas markets. Likewise, with the Norwegian oil tankers' association in Oslo which asked me over several years to report on developments affecting their interests in global movements of oil, as did the International Energy Agency in Paris and the Energy Secretariat of the European Commission in Brussels; while the United Nations energy division in New York commissioned me to prepare a lengthy report on oil and gas potential in the countries of the developing world – and then did nothing with my suggestions!

Overall, the above mentioned and many other non-academic energy sector research activities on the requirements of international, governmental and private sector organisations, coupled with the teaching, writing and research analyses within the framework of Erasmus University's International Centre for Energy Studies from late 1979 to the end of 1991 (when I formally chose to take an early retirement), took me to the high point of my career in my 24 years and 4 months as a professor in the Dutch university system. I think that what I did achieve was more than worthwhile, not only for my own satisfaction, but also as a positive element in helping to put Erasmus University's Economic Faculty on the map, through a widely-achieved academic recognition of the quality of the work on the geographical and the political economics which had been undertaken in Rotterdam and then published and presented around much of the world.

I eventually gave my *afscheid collega* (farewell lecture) on 11 April 1991 in the main auditorium of the University – with but only a modest-sized congregation of Faculty colleagues, given a much more important presentation in Den Haag on the same day and time on recommended governmental changes to the country's economic policy which had severely curbed growth over the previous three years or so. Perhaps, needless to say, my farewell lecture entitled 'Global and Regional Energy Supplies: Recent Fictions and Fallacies Revisited' was as controversial as my 1969 inaugural lecture, but this time with an emphasis on the unfortunate propensity of policies around the world, in general, and in Europe, in particular, 'to follow interpretations of the nature of energy resources and of the appropriate or inappropriate processes of their exploitation . . . so that efforts are made to achieve efficient ways of meeting the energy demands of our economies and societies were secured.' The Dutch media highlighted my arguments, but its presentations secured only modest reactions from elsewhere, in marked contrast to the reactions generated twenty-three years earlier to my inaugural lecture! Nevertheless, the text of my farewell lecture was published with only minor changes in a subsequent issue of *Energy Policy* (Vol. 20, No. 4, pp. 248–286) from which arguments then followed through into the 1990s. In this latter decade many aspects of my conclusions came to fruition.

In purely academic terms I think that my work on the global and regional energy sectors in the economic, political and geographical circumstances of the 1970s and 1980s was treated internationally with respect, but I was disappointed – to put it mildly – by the absence of any recognition by the Economic Faculty and the Governors of Erasmus University of the twenty-four years of my commitment to enhance the university's academic status. On the contrary, on my retirement the Faculty decided to close down the International Energy Institute in favour of the establishment of a unit with the parochial task of enhancing the city of Rotterdam's function as a transportation centre – with funds largely supplied by the city's port! Subsequent events in the global energy system – with its important implications for the well-being of Rotterdam as a city and of a role that the University's Centre for Energy Studies could have played in evaluating the international situation, could not be pursued, to the detriment not only of the Economic Faculty but also of the University as a whole!

This situation led to my not being presented with an 'Erasmus Medal' by the university, contrary to the normal practice for professors of long-standing on their retirement. And neither, it seems, was the Queen advised by the University that I might justifiably be awarded even the lowest-ranking designation in her Honours List! Perhaps it was my forays against the repeatedly inept energy-orientated units of the Dutch Ministry of Economic Affairs, together with my challenges not only on the policies of the Royal Dutch Shell petroleum company's policies in the Netherlands itself (over Groningen gas developments), but also in the Nederland Antilles (over its refining and transportation policies) and over Shell's policies in South Africa in the years of apartheid and over Southern Rhodesia, that led to my non-recognition? Happily, such decisions did not affect my pension rights, arising from my 24.625 years (finely calculated by the appropriate Dutch Ministry) as an employee of the State!

Following the termination of my post in the university on 31 December 1991 and my subsequent *afscheid collega*, I was given some leeway for a continuing presence in the university. This was in order, first, to wind up the Centre for International Energy Studies; second, to continue with my responsibilities as the 'promoter' of students' working for their doctorates; and, third, to have access when required to facilities which were necessary for the preparation of academic and other papers for publication or presentation. Overall, from January to October 1992 I managed to give

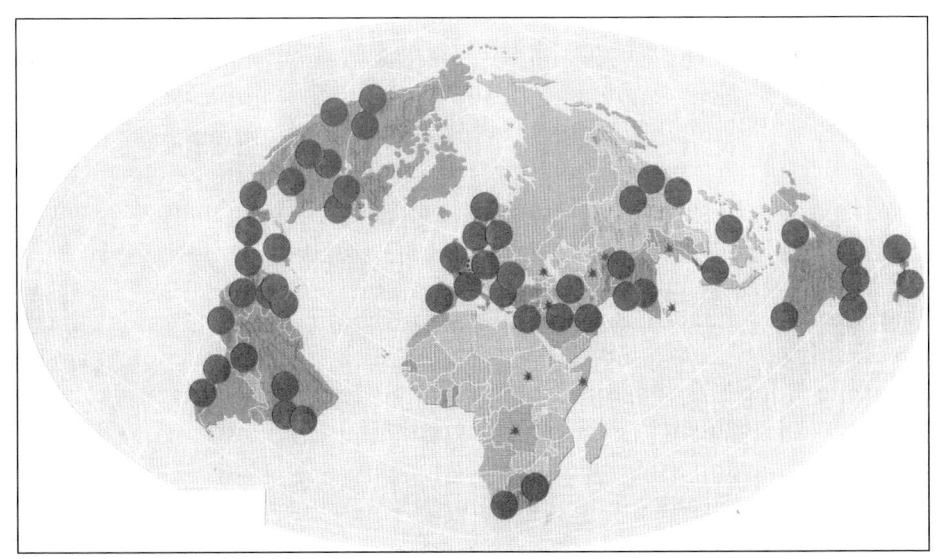

53. The author's international visits to different countries and regions around the world

more than one hundred lectures, to attend many conferences and seminar presentations, and to publish nine more papers!

On 4 October 1992, following the formalities of a cessation of residence in Rotterdam and with our goods and chattels already on their way to the UK from our flat in Kralingen, Jean and I sailed on the night boat from the Hoek van Holland with our Saab 95 loaded to the gunnels with our remaining 'clobber'. On 5 October 1992 I registered at the Ipswich office of the Inland Revenue as a resident in the UK. This was initially as a 'guest' in the house of our family – then formally owned jointly by our four children: Nigel, Deborah, Mark and Susannah. But the ownership was soon changed to Jean and me. Our children used the sale of their assets to spread their wings into houses of their own, in whole or in part!

Chapter 8

From 1992 to 2000: On Rejoining my Family in Ipswich and a Formidable Range of Activities

The formalities on 5 October 1992 associated with my returning to live in the UK were modest, given the rest of the family's residence here since 1977. Our house in Ipswich was long since registered in the names of Nigel, Deborah, Mark and Susannah, so I simply moved in with some accompanying furnishings from Rotterdam, plus the more considerable elements of my books and archives. Our flat in Rotterdam remained furnished and available for visits as required by the university's demands on my time, and was also used on many occasions in the four subsequent years for family visits to the Netherlands. Indeed, because Jean and I were the flat's owners we remained registered as *inwoners* in Rotterdam, whilst I also continued to receive 75 per cent of my salary as a 'dormant' member of the university's staff until my sixty-fifth birthday on 1 July 1995. Then I reached pensionable age with a much diminished monthly income based on close to twenty-five years service to the University. Just over one year later in October 1996 we sold the flat and formally signed ourselves out of Rotterdam with state pensions which for both Jean and me were based on our nearly twenty-eight years of payments to the Dutch state's pension fund. This was also the signing-off date for payments at source of Dutch taxes (though details of the sums involved were forwarded from the Dutch to the UK tax authorities!). Happily, the efficiency and the modestly-generous Dutch pension and social services, plus the internationality of the Dutch banks that handled our financial transactions, have since served us exceedingly well.

Jean's and my permanent establishment at the 'Hill' – coupled with the coming-of-age of all our four children – necessarily required a reallocation of the earlier established family assets, the children's ownership of the house. This proved to be a somewhat complex change but, nevertheless, each of them secured in cash or kind one-quarter of the value of the house on the Hill. Deborah was given cash to invest in a house on

54. Our Edwardian house – now 108 years old

55. The garden of the house

56. Our 'pied à terre' in Islington, London

the other side of Christchurch Park which she and Steve, her partner, had purchased as their home. Nigel and Mark were each given a 25 per cent interest in the maisonette in Islington, London, N1, which I had bought in 1982. And Susannah was given a cottage in Hemingstone in return for her loss of one-quarter of the value of the Hill which she had held.

Jean and I had accumulated 'wealth' from both cash payments and from some investments made in stocks and shares, partly in the UK and partly in the Netherlands. In 1987, we felt that these funds were superfluous to our needs, so each of us created a Discretionary Settlement in favour of our four children – and, in the event of their deaths, in favour of their children too. Over the next few years other provisions were made as appropriate, but this time 'bare trusts' were also launched specifically for our grandchildren with annual payments for their respective benefits to be passed on to each one of them on reaching the age of eighteen. Thereafter, Jean and I have continued with our relatively parsimonious life-style – and with taking further tax-free investment opportunities – so as to ensure financial security over the rest of our lives. Hopefully, there will in the fullness of time still be remaining considerable assets to be passed on to our succeeding generations.

On other counts and scores over our eighteen years to date back in the UK, there have been events, opportunities and commitments which remain to be related, albeit briefly. First – and foremost – we have now gone through the fiftieth anniversary of our wedding (on 17 August 1957). This was celebrated on two successive Saturdays: the first at home in Ipswich with some fifty or more friends and relatives; and a week later at the Lansdowne Club in Berkeley Square, London with just under forty guests. Just before those occasions, we had also decided to buy a top-floor apartment in a traditional Swiss chalet in the lower (1500m) levels of the Alps, with the idea of spending half the year there, from early March through to the end of May and then from September through to early December. Over the six months or so lying between Switzerland's winter and summer seasons our renting of the property was to be an attractive option. For those six months of each year our intention was to be back in Ipswich, or on visits Nigel and family in Australia. Unhappily, the purchase of the Swiss chalet fell through very quickly as a result of serious medical problems which were diagnosed with Jean's eyes. We had to remain UK-bound and so cancelled our purchase of the property. And then we tried to secure the refund of the not insignificant deposit which we had made to the builders; eventually, after a legal battle we were fifty per cent successful, but still much out-of-pocket!

Preceding these very recent family events there have also been other aspects to our pensionable years. First, there was the continuation of my teaching interests on international energy issues as a visiting Professor at the London School of Economics, together with designated visiting chairs at the Universities of Cambridge and Plymouth. I much enjoyed lecturing on my energy orientated interests, only occasionally in Cambridge and Plymouth but on a more or less permanent schedule at the LSE. At the latter I was first back to my 1960s' work in the Department of Geography on resources issues to undergraduate students; and then I switched to the Department of International Affairs to give an MA course on the geopolitics and geo-economics of the energy industries, with special attention to oil and natural gas. These latter commitments continued for the nine years to 2000 when I reached my fortieth year as a university teacher. Those latter nine years turned out to be amongst the most stimulating and rewarding of my teaching career, given, on the one hand, the complexity of the issues involved and, on the other, the dedicated interest of the students in every one of the many years of classes. The course for most students constituted 25 per cent of their total teaching opportunities, whilst

> The
> International Association for Energy Economics
>
> Presents to
>
> # Peter R. Odell
>
> The 1991 Award for Outstanding Contributions
> to the Profession of Energy Economics
> and to its Literature
>
> $\dfrac{I\ A}{E\ E}$
>
> May, 1992　　　　　　　　　　　　　　　　Ulf Hansen
> Tours, France　　　　　　　　　　　　　　　President

57. My 1991 IAEE award, presented in May 1992

their written examination in the subject was 20 per cent of the total load required to secure a Master's degree.

Moreover, the thirty or so students each year came from a wide range of national backgrounds from around the world, such that they brought with them contrasting and varied contributions to the subjects which collectively helped constitute the contents of the course. Over the years I always felt a high degree of satisfaction with my teaching – reflected in both the exam results achieved by the students (with only a very small numbers of failures), and in their generally very positive views on the content of my course work and my successful presentations, as indicated in formal feed-back views on my efforts. I have since become aware that a significant number of the students whom I taught went on to higher degrees and/or to jobs involving international energy issues. Now looking back to 2000, I am sorry that I gave up those teaching responsibilities and opportunities, given that events in the energy world post-2001 have become yet more interesting and more intensively complicated.

58. Presentation of my award at the 1993 Annual Meeting by the President of the Royal Scottish Geographical Society

My long-lived academic work on international energy issues in the 1990s produced two unexpected, but rewarding, events. The first was in May 1992 in Tours in France where the annual international meeting of the International Association of Energy Economists was being held. At this meeting I was presented with the Association's 1991 annual award for 'Outstanding Contributions to the Profession of Energy Economics and its Literature'. This was surprisingly presented with appropriate decorum by the Association's President, followed by my acknowledgement of the award in the context of my interpretation of the then current – and prospective – situation for future international energy systems. Unhappily, due to what I now think was the unwillingness on the part of the then-editor of the IAEE's *Journal* to publish my somewhat controversial speech – the content of which he did not like – my acknowledgement speech was never published!

The second event was just over a year later (in October 1993) at the Annual Meeting in Glasgow of the Royal Scottish Geographical Society. On that occasion I was presented with the Society's Centenary Medal for my research and publications on the exploitation and development of the

UK's offshore oil and gas resources since the mid-1960s. This was done at the Geographical Society's dinner in Glasgow's magnificent City Hall and chaired by the then President of the RSGS. On this occasion no more than the formalities of the presentation of the Medal were required, but there was a somewhat quaint occurrence: viz. that it was BP which had sponsored the dinner and thus had its logo as a back-drop to all the photographs which were taken, including the Society's President making the presentation to me. Perhaps this could have been a kind of BP 'apology' to me for its earlier savage attacks on our research on North Sea oil and gas, given that it demonstrated the company's underestimate of the production potential of BP's North Sea Forties Field! Subsequently, however, in 1994, at a conference in Aberdeen for all the parties with an interest in the North Sea's oil and gas, the head of BP, then John Browne (later to be honoured by the Queen to the status of Lord Browne), expressed apologies for his company's earlier actions against me (see Chapter 5). I formally – and immediately – accepted the apology made, but did remind Lord Browne that his company's actions in attacking our work in Rotterdam in the 1970s had led indirectly to the refusals of our requests to the European Commission to find adequate funding for us to determine the North Sea's potential oil and gas wealth! A feature which has still not been effectively evaluated.

Following the above events in the early 1990s, the intensity of my work in the field of international energy studies slackened quite markedly as I used much of the seventh decade of my life to re-establish myself as a 'useful' British citizen, in Ipswich and London. The latter was largely formulated by my increasingly important teaching responsibilities at the London School of Economics and by my active membership of a number of London-based institutions ranging from the Commonwealth Club in Northumberland Avenue; to visits to and attachments at the Royal Institute of International Affairs, of which I had been a member since 1960; to fellowships of the Royal Society of Arts, the Institute of Petroleum, the British Association of Energy Economics and the Royal Geographical Society/Institute of British Geographers. With the availability of our *pied à terre* in Islington for overnight stays in London, it was possible to attend meetings and to take advantage of library facilities and so on in these institutions, as well as arranging meetings in London with ex-Rotterdam friends who had also returned to live in the south-east of England.

Nevertheless, Ipswich had become the home-base of most of the family so I was able to follow up contacts and activities which had emerged from Jean having become ensconced in the town since the late 1970s. Indeed, this family home base had already enabled me to pursue developments in both the town and the county: initially, by my involvement as an adviser to the Town and Country Planning Association in its objections to the building of Sizewell B nuclear power station on the coast of Suffolk; and thereafter in the context of a radical change in the UK's political system with the breakaway of senior members of the Labour Party to form the Social Democratic Party – of which I became a member from day one of its creation in 1981. Thereafter, I was involved with the new political party at both the local and the national levels: in the former for electioneering and in the latter as a member of the Party's Energy Committee concerned with the UK's oil and gas prospects and with the country's nuclear power developments.

In the immediate aftermath of a formal alliance between the SDP and the Liberal party, I was persuaded to stand in 1989 as the candidate of the

59. My attempt to become a Euro MP

Alliance for election to the Eastern England constituency of the European Parliament. That year was, however, something of a political disaster for the Alliance, though I did rather better than most other SDP candidates across the country in my securing sufficient votes to save my deposit (in that I had more than 5 per cent of the total votes cast)!

Jean, meanwhile, had already been active in local politics with the Ipswich Liberal Party for which she often stood as a candidate in both the Suffolk County and the Ipswich Borough elections. With the merger of the Liberal and SDP parties, with the new name of the Liberal Democratic Party, the two of us were able to put on a united front in which Jean kept up her efforts to become elected locally, whilst I became involved in the Lib/Dem Eastern Region organisation stretching across six counties (Essex, Suffolk, Norfolk, Cambridge, Bedford and Hertford). This culminated in the early 1990s with my election to the deputy Chairmanship of both the Regional and the County organisations. This post, however, lasted for a very short period of time following what seemed to me to be the creation of a breakaway group centred on Cambridge and which had succeeded, against party rules, in fixing the choice of a candidate for the next election to the European Parliament!

I therefore resigned from my office and from the party and turned instead to become an active member and later the Chairman of the Ipswich Society – devoted to matters which were important for enhancing the status of the town. At that time in the early 1990s the county town was still attempting to recover from its earlier failure to secure its nomination as one of the 1960s' 'expanding towns' to which London was to send its 'surplus populations and industries'. This failure, coupled with the contemporary decline in the town's industrial and service activities, made Ipswich's post-1974 role as the county town for the whole of Suffolk to be of limited significance.

Thus, in my close to eight years as Chairman of the Ipswich Society there were a succession of issues concerning the future of the town which required attention and commitments for which much time was taken, and from the use of which little success was only infrequently achieved. Given these circumstances I eventually decided that my time was being wasted and so I gave up my considerable commitments to the Society and to Ipswich in 2000, bowing out on the basis of a critique of Ipswich's failure on both economic and social grounds in the second half of the twentieth century, following its loss of status in not being chosen to become an 'expanded town' by the Labour government of the 1960s.

In the period 1992–2000 when my attention had been largely orientated to local affairs, the continuation of my work and interest in international energy affairs had been somewhat constrained. On the commercial front, as a director of Energy Advice Ltd and as the company's principal forecaster of future developments in the international oil and gas industries, I continued with earlier commitments to AGIP and also accepted further interesting invitations to advise the Midland Electricity Board, the German Dresdner and other associated Banks, the Finnish oil industry, the German Energy Ministry, the US Air Products gas company and the Irish Peat Board amongst others.

Unhappily, I was obliged to resign from Energy Advice Ltd given my inability to participate in – let alone to control – the company's financial affairs. This gave rise to acrimony with the ex-Shell colleague whom I had invited jointly to run the company with me way back in the 1980s. He and I turned out to be incompatible in our interests and procedures and I had inappropriately allowed him to control the company's finances. I thus chose to make my own way on a personal, rather than a company, basis. With

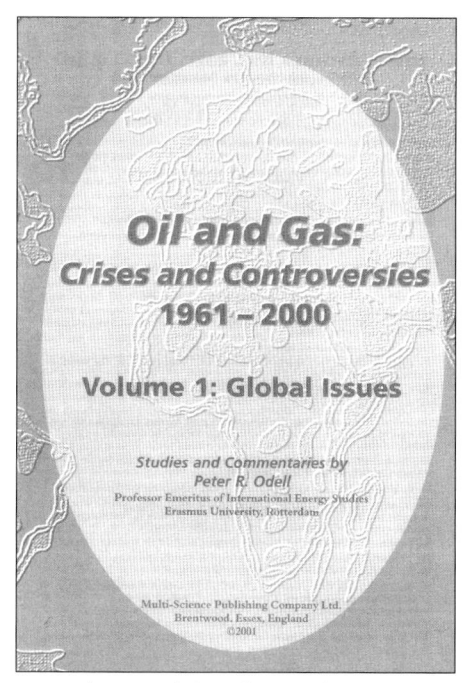

60. *Volume 1 of the collection of my important global articles and lectures*

61. *Volume 2: Europe's Energy Entanglement*

the success which I had already achieved through my internationally recognised knowledge of the world's oil and gas industries, I was able to continue to pursue my perambulations on examinations and advice for most countries of mainland Europe and to the United States, Canada, Hong Kong, China, Malaysia and Australia.

In this context, given the now long-lived continuity of my role as an 'energy expert' with a long record of achieving successes in forecasting developments, I concluded that a collection of my most important articles and lectures over the last four decades of the twentieth century would constitute an informative and long-lived record for future students and policy makers. The Multi-Science Publishing Company in Brentwood, Essex agreed to my proposal to put together a two-volume work under the title *Oil and Gas: Crises and Controversies, 1961–2000*. Volume 1, entitled *Global Issues*, was published in February 2001 with a total of almost 500 pages for the twenty-five chapters – with 58 Figures and 37 Tables, plus a thirteen-page Foreword setting out the background to the contents of the book. I have now concluded that an abbreviated version of that Foreword is worthy of recording in this book – as follows:

> 'The "global issues" which have concerned me extend way back over time and widely over space. My forebears over three generations from the mid-nineteenth century worked in the mining and associated transport industries in the Nottinghamshire and Leicestershire coalfields, thus assuring me of the genes and/or the social influences which caused energy to run in my blood. Their arduous and ill-paid work did little more than keep proverbial body and soul together, but they could well lay claim to an importance for their work in respect of the country's economic development and strength. But they also recognised that education was the only possible means whereby succeeding generations could escape from the constraints imposed by the social system within which their lives had been lived. This was to be my privilege.
>
> By the time I had passed through the portal of a lengthy period of exposure to secondary and higher education from 1941 to 1958, there were already clear signs of the beginning of coal's terminal decline as a source of energy so that my choice of the oil industry as my work environment was "a natural successor". Though my career with Shell International was limited to only a little over three

years, it was long enough for me to familiarise myself with the language of the oil industry and to achieve some "feel" for the factors that made it tick. My mentors over that period – notably Geoffrey Chandler and Napier Collyns and my other colleagues in the Company's London-based economic division – ensured my understanding of the oil industry's critical variables: to the extent that my earliest contributions on oil and gas in the early 1960s as an academic at the London School of Economics were soundly based on the realities of the global oil and gas industry at that time.

Over my seven years at LSE I was also privileged to know and to work with the outstanding UK economist with a central interest in international oil developments; namely, Professor Edith Penrose, whose experience and knowledge of the Middle East and of the role of the major international oil corporations in that area was formidable. The rigour and effectiveness of her work was a major stimulus to my own efforts to interpret the then rapidly evolving and expanding international oil industry. In particular, the fortnightly seminars on international oil which we jointly organised each year from the mid-60s (when it was, indeed, the only academically-orientated British University study programme on the subject), opened up many issues that had long remained undiscussed: at the very time, coincidentally, when the companies were turning their attention to the North Sea on which, therefore, I was well-placed to comment and advise.

An invitation in late 1967 by Michael Posner (an Oxford don who had been appointed in that year as the economic adviser to the Ministry of Fuel and Power) asked me to join him to work on the government's policy on oil and gas. Unhappily, this did not materialise because of opposition from the civil servants to the appointment of an informed outsider who was known to have views on the North Sea which were contrary to those previously evolved within the Ministry under the earlier Conservative administration. Instead, I decided to accept an alternative invitation to take up a professorial appointment at the Netherlands School of Economics in Rotterdam, then the epicentre of Europe's rapidly expanding downstream oil industry and of trading in crude oil and oil products on the so-called "Rotterdam Market". Moreover, the Dutch natural gas industry, based on the giant Groningen gasfield, was just emerging as a massive new source of European energy.

Thus, the atmosphere in Rotterdam was highly conducive to oil and gas studies. Indeed, as events unfolded over the decade from 1968, it was the perfect place to be from which to examine, record and interpret the fundamental changes in the international oil and gas industry. These ranged from the re-establishment of an ordered oil market in the aftermath of the 1967 Arab/Israeli conflict, then to the first oil price shock of 1973/4; followed by the subsequent wholesale nationalisation of the major upstream assets of the international oil corporations in the countries which collectively formed the Organisation of Petroleum Exporting Countries. Then on to the second oil price shock of 1979/81 with its subsequent adverse ramifications for the international oil industry; and finally to the restructuring of the European energy sector arising from the rapid growth of indigenous oil and gas production from the North Sea.

Throughout this exhilarating period, marked by the series of fundamental changes in my field of academic interest, the challenges to keeping pace with emerging events, burgeoning information and of the need to understand and interpret changing developments were collectively very formidable. Yet the Rotterdam School of Economics (soon to become part of Erasmus University – the first "new" university in The Netherlands for many decades) provided an environment in which such work could be done, on the basis of the financial resources which were made available in generous measure. In large part, these were a result of the state's huge revenue windfalls at that time as a result of its 50 per cent interest in the production of very low-cost Groningen gas. In institutional terms this eventually led to the establishment within the University's Faculty of Economics of a Centre for International Energy Studies (known as EURICES), to which I was appointed the first Director in 1982.

During the whole of this challenging period Dr Ken Rosing was my "right-hand man" in the many studies which were undertaken. Had he lived, I would have extended my full acknowledgement of his massive contribution to the work involved, with particular reference to the statistical and mathematical inputs which he made in a number of major research projects.

A succession of numerous other assistants, students and academic visitors helped to create the opportunities for expanding the range of international energy studies undertaken, not only on oil and gas, but also relating to coal and nuclear power. An expanding range of national, European and international contacts in both academia and in government and industry also helped to stimulate and broaden the range of topics put under examination. This diversity of interests is reflected in the range of papers etc., dating from the mid-1970s to the early 1990s, which have been included in the "Global Issues" volume.

Following my retirement from Erasmus University in 1992, I resumed my earlier academic links in London (by this time the global centre for the international oil business) at the London School of Economics, where I was asked to teach a course on the International Political Economy of Energy in the M.Sc. programme developed by Professor Susan Strange on the Politics of the World Economy. This not only attracted an annual flow of students from many parts of the world – whereby my need to keep up with the subject was required – but it also enabled me to continue to make contributions on international oil and gas issues. Indeed, five of the chapters in "Global Issues" emerge from the stimulus given by my latter-day academic activities, with the final contribution dating from 2000, so extending the range of publications constituting this book to a period of almost forty years.

The first part of my book is concerned with the physical and economic attributes of oil and gas resources, reserves and supply – with emphases on "how much" and "where". The world's leading oil petroleum economist for many years, Professor M.A. Adelman of the Massachusetts Institution of Technology, has characterised the issue of the world's ultimate resources of oil (and gas) as being "unknown, unknowable and unimportant." He is, of course, right in his view on the impossibility of "knowing" the world's prospective ultimate volumes of oil and gas and he is also right in theory over the unimportance of estimating how much there will ultimately prove to be. But he was ill-advised not to recognise the need for economists and other social scientists to discuss the issue in a world in which fears of the near-future exhaustion of oil resources have been so widely – and so adamantly – expressed by a succession of earth scientists. The latter's fears of oil scarcity date back even to the early part of the twentieth century and often led to costly and inappropriate policies and expenditures by governments anxious to mitigate the perceived dangers.

Thus, much of my work has been devoted to that issue. In the early 1960s global oil consumption was little more than 1000 million tons per year and the great oil wealth of the Middle East was only just being revealed. Nevertheless, even then a coming scarcity of oil was already held out to be a danger by some of the major oil corporations – and by the US government!

By 1970 oil use had doubled so that, in spite of the massive discoveries of oil wealth over the preceding decade, the voices indicating a world running out of oil were even more robust – including further contributions in this vein by some of the major oil corporations themselves. At that time, therefore, I thought it necessary carefully to rebut the pessimistic and over-simplistic view of the future of oil. Subsequently, based on a thorough and integrated examination of the range of probabilities for volumes of ultimately recoverable resources, for annual additions to reserves and for annual rates of use, it became possible to present the evolution of the world's oil prospects for a 100-year period.

In the early 1980s, however, the price of oil in the market escalated to record high levels as a result of political factors. This development not only led to a decrease in oil use, but it also stimulated large volumes of production and the establishment of significant reserves in hitherto unexpected places, most notably beneath the offshore waters around many of the world's continents. As a result, expressions of fears for oil scarcity were more or less silenced, though not before those fears had severely damaged not only the industry, but also the global economy. My valedictory lecture at Erasmus University in 1991 drew attention to the range of energy sector fictions and fallacies that had been propagated and to the difficulties that these had posed for economies and societies around the world.

Yet it was not very long before the misconceptions and misunderstandings over the future of oil and gas re-surfaced – but this time with the added component of fears for global warming and climate change as a result of the increasing use of carbon fuels. This new claim for a near-future scarcity of oil and gas is as much as ever at variance with the real-world prospects. Moreover, the important alternative hypotheses on the origin and nature of hydrocarbons – abiogenically as well as biogenically – are introduced as pointing to a prospect for a potentially even longer-term availability of more than adequate supplies to match even optimistic views on the development of oil and gas demand in the twenty-first century.

Other parts of "Global Issues" are devoted to the geography of world oil and gas supplies. They examine the importance of the location of markets to decisions on the exploitation of newly discovered and technically accessible reserves. Dating from research done in the early 1980s, the impact of the changed relations between OPEC and the rest of the world on supplies from outside the OPEC countries are presented. First, the OECD set of countries and then that of the Third World, show how the major international oil corporations had hitherto been either reluctant or unable to explore for oil, let alone to exploit known reserves.

Aspects of global oil developments after more than the 1980s decade of high prices for oil and gas are then compared with the previous long period of low prices for most of the first seventy years of the twentieth century. This update not only confirmed the existence of much greater oil resources in more countries than previously suggested by the oil corporations, but also indicated a rapid and extensive rapprochement between the governments and companies concerned, giving evidence of a "revealed mutuality" of interests between the parties.

The book's concern then turns to the economic and political inputs to global oil and gas industry developments since the early 1960s. The mid-1960s saw the organisation and structure of the industry after almost a half-century of effective control over the system exercised by the major multi-national oil companies. There are also concerns specific to oil developments in the Middle East following a decade and a half of concentration of international upstream investment in that small part of the petroliferous world as a result of which it became by far the single most important region for oil production and, even more so, for exports of the commodity. In contrast, the relationships between the international oil corporations and the highly nationalistic countries of Latin America at the time of acrimony over state/foreign private oil company relationships are discussed and show in a number of case studies how the political confrontation between the parties inhibited the effective development of oil exploration and exploitation across the continent.

These are followed by my contemporaneous interpretations of the revolution in the world of oil from 1971 to 1986, a period when revolutions encompassed many aspects of the political economy of oil. First, a shift in power relationships between the producing countries, on the one hand, and the international oil corporations, on the other. Second, a consequential dramatic – eventually a ten-fold – increase in the real price of oil. Third, important spin-off impacts on the global economic situation and prospects. Fourth, misinterpretations of the realities of the changes under way and of their long-term significance. Fifth, the eventual emergence of competitive markets in crude oil and oil products, compared with the previous "ordered" markets, as organised by the international oil companies. And last, but by no means least, a diminution in the role of, and the prospects for, oil use in the emerging global economy. These chapters synthesise the conflicting strands in the set of dramatic events.

There is then one chapter which was prepared as a contribution to the book published to mark the opening of the Maritime Museum in Rotterdam in 1986 on the century of maritime oil transport. This is a particularly important aspect of the political economy of oil throughout most of the industry's history, given the geographical separation of supply and demand on a very grand scale: in terms of both the volumes involved and the distances over which most of it had to be shipped, with a requirement for continuity of supply no matter what physical or political restraints arose.

Finally, the last few chapters incorporate my attempts to interpret the evolution of the global oil system, in terms of both challenges and responses, over the fifteen years since 1986. They suggest the evolution of a partial recovery of the international oil industry from the days of confusion and little hope in the aftermath of six years of declining demand from 1979 to 1985. At the end of that period there were not only fears for the well-being of the western system, given the pressures to which the oil shocks had subjected it, but also concerns for the security of oil supplies from both the physical and political standpoints. And there were also questions as to the possible impact that the redistribution of power in the oil system could have had on relations between the power blocs of the US and the USSR (prior to the latter's demise in 1991), and between the oil exporters (notably in the Middle East) and the importers over most of the rest of the world.

The continuity and still-growing complexity of the issues necessarily meant that the book could not conclude with a set of rationally argued and well-defined conclusions as to present status of the global oil and gas system, let alone with forecasts as to how the politics and economics of the industry will develop. I hope that it does, nevertheless, show that the oil and gas systems have a long-term future (despite the fears for global warming from the increasing use of hydrocarbon fuels). Finally, it exposes the set of inter-related issues from which the future structure of this long-since globalised industry will emerge.

The thirty-four selected contributions presented in this book have been chosen from a much larger number which I published during my continuing forty years' study of the global oil industry. All the opinions and interpretations as originally expressed have been maintained so as to show how things appeared to be at the time, rather then reinterpreted with the benefit of hindsight.

I hope that the end result is not only readable, but that it will also be enlightening with respect to an understanding of the sometimes tumultuous and always interesting years of global oil and gas in the second half of the twentieth century.'

Volume 2, *Oil and Gas: Crises and Controversies, 1961–2000*, was published just over a year later with even more pages of text (625) and entitled *Europe's Entanglement* with thirty-three chapters – incorporating 54 Figures and 51 Tables – and a ten page Foreword. An attenuated version of this is presented below:

'My choice of Europe as the region for exclusive attention in this second Volume of my papers and commentaries reflects my almost full-time residence and employment over the forty years since 1961 in the United Kingdom and the Netherlands; and my familiarity with the continent as a whole through continuing observation and evaluation of energy-important events and, more specifically, through my participation in numerous conferences and seminars on energy issues across Europe and by liaison and cooperation with colleagues concerned with energy studies in virtually every other country of the continent.

For the first thirty years from 1961 Europe was divided by an "iron curtain" separating western Europe from the countries to the east lying within the sphere of influence – and control – of the Soviet Union. Under these political conditions not only were contacts with the latter group of countries severely circumscribed, but those nations' developments so reflected the requirements of Soviet-style central planning that their energy sectors came to bear little resemblance to those which were emerging in the rest of the continent. Pan-European studies thus became difficult and inappropriate. Hence the studies and commentaries dating from before 1990 are almost exclusively concerned with the western part of the continent.

Since 1990 the political and economic barriers have been broken down. Nevertheless, integration by the east European countries into the rest of Europe has necessarily proceeded relatively slowly (except for East Germany) so that the "weight" of the commentaries and analyses on the oil and gas sectors of the economies of that part of Europe still remains relatively modest. Moreover, the boundary of Europe, as far as the geographical scope of this book is concerned, has continued to exclude the territories of the former Soviet Union. Indeed, these enter the analyses only as an energy-supplying region external to Europe, in a like manner – and in competition with – the oil and gas supplying regions of North Africa and the Middle East. Turkey is also specifically excluded, in spite of its political and military links with Europe, in that its role vis à vis energy is essentially as a transit country, not only for oil and gas from the Gulf countries, but also from the Caspian basin. This role has placed Turkey in a very special sort of contemporary energy relationship with Europe; and one, moreover, that seems likely to become steadily more important over the next two decades.

Historically, the content of this volume is determined by the time-span of the author's contribution to European energy studies, from the early 1960s to 2002. Given the particular "personalised" start-point – which does not happen to coincide with a break-point in the extended evolutionary process of the European energy economy – it seems appropriate that I should first briefly set out my knowledge and understanding of the relevant pre-1945 antecedents.

a. Pre-1945 Components

These date as far back as the late eighteenth century, since when there has been a slow evolution of Europe's traditional coal-based energy system. Dependence on indigenously-mined coal remained of the essence throughout the period during which people and industry became concentrated on Europe's coalfields. Even the late nineteenth century introduction of electricity made only slow headway in industrial and residential applications. It was, indeed, only in a few locations with advantageous geographical conditions for the exploitation of low-cost hydro-power that the pre-1920s' use of electricity became the basis for the location of some energy intensive industries and was also cheap enough to secure its widespread use in the commercial and residential sectors.

Elsewhere, most of non-urban Europe remained beyond the local electricity supply networks through the 1930s and even into the post-World War II period. Meanwhile, coal continued to dominate the supply of primary energy – such that in 1937 oil still supplied only 7 per cent of total energy used in Europe and natural gas, under 0.5 per cent. Countries and regions without coal (or hydro-electricity) remained energy-poor with little industrialisation and low living standards.

b. The post-1945 Period

In western Europe post-World War II recovery and economic rehabilitation was predicated on the basis of an "energy-mix" input as before 1939, but with an anticipated eventual addition of nuclear power. Significantly, the first two European integration treaties, the European Coal and Steel Community and the European Atomic Energy Community, pre-dated the Treaty of Rome which created the European Union. The earlier Treaties were specifically concerned with coal (plus steel) and with atomic power. In 1952, coal still provided 90 and 95 per cent, respectively, of the UK's and Western Germany's primary energy – and all but 13 per cent of Europe's total energy demand.

Very considerable efforts – and investments – were made

between 1945 and 1955 to resuscitate and stimulate indigenous coal production. Eventually, the industry just about recovered to its pre-1939 size. Nevertheless, increasing depletion costs, resulting from the need to exploit geologically more difficult coal resources and rapidly rising real labour costs in a labour-intensive industry in the context of full employment, quickly led thereafter to the dethroning of coal in what was becoming a rapidly expanding Western European energy market. Oil rapidly substituted its use in most sectors of the economy.

Concurrently, the other main thrust in the energy sector, the growth of electricity, was resumed. Networks of supply were expanded and intensified so that virtually the whole of the region's population – except in the remotest areas – secured access to electricity. Its range and intensity of use was steadily expanded in the commercial, industrial and even the agricultural sectors. By the early 1960s, after three-quarters of a century of development, electricity finally became the norm across the whole of western Europe, not only for lighting, but also for power and even heating applications.

Meanwhile, in Eastern Europe, the adoption of Soviet-style central planning, requiring the maximum possible exploitation of indigenous energy resources and the adaptation of forced industrialisation, also brought rapid, but contrasting, changes in this region's energy situation. On the supply side, this involved the expansion of deep carboniferous coal, brown coal and lignite production and of what little indigenous oil there was to exploit (most notably in Romania). In marked contrast with the post-1955 decline in indigenous energy production in western Europe, east European energy output rose to almost 200 million tons oil equivalent by 1960; that is to 135 per cent of that of 1937. Imports, mainly of Soviet coal and oil, did also increase, but they were complementary to national energy production, rather than at the expense of indigenous resources' exploitation, as was the case for Western Europe.

The contents of this volume thus present a selection of my post-1961 contributions to the analysis of Europe's evolving energy sector. These are ordered in four Sections, each dealing with a particular theme. Section I is concerned with the concurrent explosion of energy demand and the diversification of supply. First and foremost, oil effected its takeover of western Europe's supply of energy and thus became a new commanding height in the continent's political economy. With its powerful corporate structure and its access to very low cost external supplies, the oil industry was able successfully to offer energy at significantly lower costs to consumers, so subordinating the severe social consequences of the demise of coal and the political risks of dependence on imported oil to purely economic considerations.

Falling real oil prices – and, later, those of gas too – not only overwhelmed coal as a competitor, but also constrained the ability of indigenous nuclear power to achieve the expansion that had been anticipated. The belated recognition of the dangers of a 65+ per cent imported oil dependence came too late to save Europe from the adverse consequences of the oil supply and price shocks of the early 1970s. The crisis conditions that oil-dependence thus generated for Europe's continued development were, however, ultimately avoided: albeit only by the fortuitous success by the oil industry in discovering and developing unexpected and well-nigh unbelievable volumes of indigenous resources of north-west Europe. In the historical context of preceding discoveries of a large number of small oilfields in the countries located around the North Sea that had proved to be of little significance (except for their contribution to Germany's oil needs in World War Two), the discovery of the Slochteren gasfield in the northern part of the Netherlands in 1959 was initially little more than casually presented in public. It is worthy of note that within Shell, the company responsible for the discovery, it was talked about with bated breath, such were the in-house unconfirmed reports of the size of its potentially producible reserves. A paper concerned essentially with the phenomenon was published in 1969, ten years on from the Slochteren discovery which by this time had been renamed the Groningen gasfield – appropriately so, given that the reservoir was now known to underlie the whole of the north-east part of the Dutch province of that name. This presented the exploitation of this mega-giant gasfield as the most significant development in the post-1945 history of the European energy sector. Subsequent papers offer periodic reviews of its importance, not only because of its designation as the largest gasfield in the world outside the Soviet Union, but also because it was the geological indicator for the existence of a world-rated hydrocarbons province stretching northwards for almost 1000 kilometres under the North Sea. Thus, there are time-series of studies and commentaries on the oil and gas prospects of this massive European hydrocarbons province over the remaining decades of the century: I have also speculated on the implications therefrom for the prospects for the European energy sector for up to 60 years in the future!

These show that my interpretations of the future of Europe's hydrocarbons were sometimes overly optimistic, especially vis à vis the ability and/or willingness of national and European Community energy policy makers to take decisions which would have maximised the contributions of this new world-standard hydrocarbons province to the continent's oil and gas supplies. In due course, however, subsequent events demonstrate that such optimism was, indeed, largely justified. This is eventually shown in two of my papers which offer retrospectives on the first thirty-plus years of the exploitation of north-west European oil and gas, together with views on the province's continuing future prospects in the early twenty-first century.

I have then enhanced my attention to the evolution of natural gas as Europe's third major energy source: and to its marketing in the context of oligopolistic, monopsonistic and other governmental/corporate constraints on its use. It also challenges the fifteen year long period from the mid-1970s when there were widely held "beliefs" that gas was either a "scarce resource" − contrary to the evidence of its ready availability from both indigenous and external sources − or an indigenous energy source which was too "noble" to use in applications as mundane as steam-raising facilities for power stations and energy intensive industry.

Happily, after some necessarily gloomy presentations, there are subsequent re-appraisals of the prospects for natural gas. These show that my earlier predictions of natural gas as Europe's most important future energy source became very generally recognised in industry circles, even if not yet fully so amongst national and Euro-governmental energy policy makers. Their full "conversion" soon, however, simply became a matter of time!

Finally, I have stressed the deep concern emerging from a mélange of European energy sector politics, policies and structures. Some of my papers recall the "crisis" outlook for Europe's politico-economic prospects arising from foreign oil's domination of our energy supply, and stressed the need at that time to implement measures to enhance efficiency in energy use and the effective development of indigenous oil and gas resources. Then the attitude of the oil industry to the creation of an integrated and freely trading Europe is examined. This shows how the international oil companies – almost exclusively responsible for Europe's oil supply, refining, distribution and marketing – had, in effect, already created European-wide integrated operational systems which were far ahead of the inter-governmental agreements for economic integration. Aspects of British policies towards oil and of Dutch attitudes to the exploitation of its low-cost gas are then presented. They highlight the institutional constraints on indigenous oil and gas exploitation.

Eventually, in my concluding papers, the implications of some very important political developments, including the demise of the Soviet Union and the loss of its control over the countries of Eastern Europe, are considered, as is also the rise of the now dominant ideology of the need for energy markets' liberalisation.

By the end of the twentieth century, a combination of demand, supply and structural elements in the oil and gas dominated energy economy of Europe did, I argue, lead to a level of energy security which it would have been impossible to contemplate in the dark days of the Cold War and of dependence on oil imported from OPEC member countries, especially those in the Middle East. Europe's own growing oil and gas resources and the still increasing levels of production from them, combined with ready access to sea-borne oil from various world regions and to some 70 per cent of the world's resources of natural gas through emerging pipeline systems, provide sound foundations for the continuation of a European oil and gas-based economy for well into the second quarter of the twenty-first century – and possibly well beyond that. In this respect Europe is in a more favourable long-term position than either of its rival groupings of industrialised nations in the Americas and the Western Pacific Rim.

As in Volume 1 of my book, the selection of 35 contributions in this volume have been made from a much larger number of studies and commentaries which I published over the past forty years. A greater range and/or depth of description and analyses can be achieved by reference to my other publications – and to those of others – which have been examined. Except where severe editing has been required to limit the length of individual chapters, the contributions as presented here are much as they were in their original publications. All my opinions and interpretations have been maintained so as to show how prospects appeared to be at the time of writing, rather than indulging in the re-interpretation of events and their significance with the benefit of hindsight. Forecasts, in particular, remain as they were made, so indicating failures – as with the too optimistic view which I took as to the speed with which the countries concerned would allow their gas and oil resources to be developed; as well as achieving successes in terms of the long-term future of gas in Europe.

Finally, I would wish to acknowledge my debts to the many academic colleagues and research students and to the even greater number of governments' officials, oil and gas companies' employees and to those working in consultancies directly or indirectly concerned with European energy issues. Their contributions to my understanding and knowledge of European oil and gas matters have been very significant. We didn't always see eye to eye on issues of importance, but our discussions were invariably of utility. A number of companies and institutions concerned with oil and gas in Europe generously contributed towards the costs involved in undertaking the compilation of studies for this volume. I gratefully acknowledge their help, but all have requested anonymity. None of them placed any requirements on what I might include in – or exclude from – the contents.'

This late twentieth century return with a vengeance to my lifetime field of interest snapped me out of the Ipswichian mode to which I had orientated myself in the 1990s. I resigned as the Chairman of the Ipswich Society early in 2000, broke contacts which I had established in the town and opted out of further contributions to its long-term plans for rehabilitation. This followed carping and inappropriate criticisms of my presented and published contribution to the Society's Year-2000 Ipswich Symposium on the town's prospects.

Instead, Jean and I migrated to London where our maisonette in Islington had been vacated by both Nigel (who had emigrated to Australia with his wife and child) and Mark (who had set himself up in an Islington town house with a wife and child). We took up residence in the maisonette on 15 August 2000, with no definitive plans as to how long we might stay there. From my point of view – but not that of Jean – it seemed that we were back in clover. Then in my seventies, my intention was to make good use of a London home and as many of the city's facilities as it was possible to enjoy.

CHAPTER 9

Back to Life in London after 32 Years

AFTER ALMOST TEN YEARS of a tranquil environment in the house and garden of Constitution Hill in Ipswich, the maisonette in Compton Road, Islington, London N1 was in another world in which tranquility was restricted to a few hours between midnight and 4:00 a.m. Early morning flights into Heathrow became familiar and were followed up by the 6:00 a.m. start of commuter traffic which thereafter was more or less maintained for the rest of the day! Surprisingly, perhaps, acclimatisation was achieved as, in a real sense, one became part of the urban scene. The slightly-larger-than-a-handkerchief-sized garden and the prolific growth rate of a eucalyptus and a wild cherry tree were positive elements in daily life; as was the continual passage of pedestrians in the streets outside and the privacy of our second, third and fourth first floor rooms from all sides of the property.

This positive *in situ* situation was, moreover, complemented by easy and ready access to public services, shops, cafés and restaurants and, most of all, to public transport facilities – particularly to buses which ran in all directions from bus-stops which were within a short walk of the house. This facility was most notable following the Mayor of London's introduction of the congestion charge for vehicles going to the centre of the City of London and the West End. The North London train services to the east (to Stratford, City airport and Woolwich) and to the west (to Hampstead, Kew and Richmond) were poorly operated but, nevertheless, still eminently useful to many locations such as Hampstead Heath, Kew Gardens and the Public Record Office (renamed the National Archives) in a magnificent building and with excellent built-in services for locating historic documentation. Meanwhile, the Victoria underground line whisked one to Oxford Circus in less than fifteen minutes as well as to closer destinations (for example, Kings Cross, St Pancras and Euston) and then on to Victoria and beyond with connections to services from most of London's other mainline stations and to Heathrow. Overall, Compton Road was and is a near-perfect location for an active and varied lifestyle. Long may it continue as a place for two very senior citizens (with free access to almost all public transport services): and with a council tax that was less than that for our house on Constitution Hill in Ipswich!

The relocation to London transformed my pre-2000 period of only a limited continuation of my academic interests, in the aftermath of the termination of my Chair at Erasmus University. LSE was now only a short bus-ride to Holborn so that I was able to enhance my post-graduate teaching commitments there, and also able to follow the students through much more intensively at other relevant centres with interests in energy matters, such as Chatham House (the Royal Institute for International Affairs), the Institute of Petroleum (later reconfigured as the Energy Institute) and, perhaps most significantly, the House of Commons Department of Trade and Industry Committee to which I was invited to become a specialist adviser on the UK's energy security issues. Here my advice was largely rejected, but it was included in the Report as *An Alternative Analysis* under the title, 'The UK Gas Industry in the Long Term: and the Liberalisation of European Markets'.

There was also the benefit of proximity to the media in a period of growing interest and increasing concerns for energy matters, so I received not infrequent telephone calls for comments on emerging events for the major newspapers and also requests – usually at very short notice – to participate in programmes for BBC radio and TV, and also for foreign broadcasters and correspondents.

It was under this set of changed circumstances that I hastened the completion of my *Oil and Gas Crises and Controversies* books so that they were published much earlier (in 2001 and 2002) than I had previously anticipated. And then, having cleared these from my obligations, I was able to follow up with a book on *Carbon Fuels in the 21st Century*.

First and foremost in my decision to write yet another book was the immediate access to the libraries and the national archives, from which data and ideas for the book could be accessed. In the book I determined to write on the inevitability of the continuing production and use of carbon fuels in the twenty-first century, in spite of contemporary claims for the need to reduce their contribution to overall energy needs in order to secure the stabilisation of global CO_2 emissions. The book was also intended to set out my arguments proving that the growing claims for short-term limitations of oil and natural gas resources – and hence of their use – were without foundation.

Thus, the data and the arguments for the book to be entitled *Why Carbon Fuels will Dominate the 21st Century's Global Energy Economy* were assembled,

62. *My book on the future of carbon fuels, published in 2004*

sorted and written within a year – and again published by the Multi-Science Publishing Company Ltd within a few months in February 2004. This book was, however, a relatively modest effort with only 110 pages of text, plus a comprehensive bibliography of over twenty pages listing almost five hundred entries. Unhappily the publisher's price tag of £39 and no exposure of the book in retail outlets either here in the UK or in the US made sales relatively dismal – measured in hundreds, rather than thousands, over the following few years. It is, however, still in print as I write my memoirs in 2010. Over these six years since 2004, however, the world's energy markets have been much changed so that an updated version of the text currently seems highly unlikely! Nevertheless, I still maintain the validity of the book's title and of much of its content – in spite of the six times increase in the price of oil (and of somewhat lower price rises for the other carbon fuels) since the book's publication.

In order to demonstrate my faith in these prognostications, herewith is an abbreviated presentation of the Preface and the Postscript of the book.

I do not think that I will now – or at any time in the rest of my lifetime – need to change my mind on the issues presented to any significant degree:

> 'Realism over the critical issues of energy supply and use in the twenty-first century's economies and societies has become a very scarce commodity. This has emerged from a combination of three widely presented, but controversial, hypotheses: first, that there is an inherent scarcity in the world's endowment of energy resources; second, that a rapid onset of global warming and climatic change will be a consequence of anthropogenically derived CO_2 emissions into the atmosphere; and third, that a set of geopolitical constraints will inevitably inhibit the production of, and trade in, energy. Individually, each of these beliefs implies a relatively near-future requirement for moderating the current degree of dependence on carbon fuels; while, collectively, the three concerns not only enhance, but also accelerate, a perceived need for a comprehensive switch to the use of alternative energy sources. The objective of this study is, however, to demonstrate that the moves to economies and societies wholly or largely free from dependence on carbon energy are, in the real world, incapable of being achieved.
>
> The greater part of the book is thus dedicated to showing that for most of the twenty-first century energy demand limitations will be so significant that little or no pressure will be brought to bear on the relatively plentiful and profitable-to-produce flows of coal, oil and natural gas. Indeed, continuity in the slowly increasing supply of carbon energy – based on a modest depletion of the world's generous coal resource base and on the exploitation of about three-quarters of the world's currently conservatively estimated remaining 5000 billion barrels of oil – will be achieved, albeit in part as a result of an accelerating substitution of coal and oil products by natural gas, so creating a successful evolution of the markets for carbon fuels for at least the first half of the century. Thereafter, plentiful natural gas resources – partly conventional, but more significantly, unconventional – can readily sustain an increasing percentage of the total potential energy supply required until the very last decade of the twenty-first century. In so doing, the world's natural gas industry will, by 2100, be more than five times its size in 2000.

Over the Twenty-first century as a whole a total of some 1660×10^9 tons oil equivalent of carbon energy will be produced and used, compared with a cumulative total in the twentieth century of just under 500×10^9 tons. This more than threefold increase in the use of carbon energy in the present century reflects not only the bountiful nature of the world's endowment of carbon energy fuels, but also the willingness of the nations which are rich in coal, oil and/or natural gas to accept the depletion of their "natural" resources in return for the economic growth which it generates for the countries concerned and the rising incomes it secures for their populations.

It also indicates the managerial and technological achievements which can be anticipated through the multitude of global, regional and local entities responsible for the extraction, the transportation and the processing of the world's energy resources. The fundamental mutuality of the interests of the very many parties already involved in such activities – albeit with temporary disturbances between them arising from economic and/or political difficulties (as over the past hundred years) – will virtually ensure supply continuity at the levels required by demand developments. In this set of defined circumstances for the exploitation of carbon energies, the concept of "resource wars" becomes invalid as such phenomena are likely only in the context of a terminal scarcity of coal, oil and/or natural gas. This study demonstrates that such scarcity is excludable, except on a local or regional scale from time to time, for the twenty-first century.

Neither is the carbon-energy production industry a serious or even relevant phenomenon with respect to the issues of global warming and climate change, except under the close to unthinkable circumstances of very large scale and long-continuing releases of methane (natural gas) to the atmosphere from the production and transportation infrastructure of the gas industry. This could occur only in the context of the generally expected markets for gas failing to materialise, so that the companies and other entities involved had neither the will, nor any commercial motivation, to inhibit such a development.

Ironically, the only possible cause of such an occurrence would be a rapid and low-cost expansion of renewable energy sources so that the "bottom" traumatically drops out of the natural gas markets. In reality, neither the speed of constructing renewable energy production plants (windmills, solar power installations, tidal or wave power driven generators, biomass-fuelled electricity production and motor vehicle use, etc.), nor the inability of such plants competitively to produce alternative (renewable) power can extensively challenge electricity made from gas – or, indeed, from coal or oil. It is, indeed, precisely these negative attributes of most renewable energy production which make its expansion, at a rate whereby renewables meet all the *incremental* demands for energy in the twenty-first century, quite impossible.

This inability has already been effectively demonstrated in the world's richest and most technologically orientated countries since 1990, the base year from which the Kyoto Treaty required the use of carbon fuels, and hence the volumes of their CO_2 emissions to be reduced. Instead, their collective use of 7,000 million tons of oil equivalent in 1990 (from a mélange of oil, gas and coal) increased to 10,000 million tons by 2008. In marked contrast with this 42 per cent rise in carbon energy use over 18 years, their use of renewables increased only marginally by 175 million tons oil equivalent with an additional 160 mtoe accounted for by nuclear power – a pseudo-renewable energy source. Meanwhile the supply of nuclear electricity has now temporarily peaked, given that the small number of new stations currently under construction or planned is failing to replace the output of the stations which are being decommissioned in the relatively short term.

To date the status of other non-renewable energy producers (except for hydro-power) remains that of an "infant industry": an industry, that is, which is incapable of sustaining growth without either a continuing input of state subsidies to reduce production costs, or the willingness of consumers to pay a premium price – over that for carbon energy – for so-called "green" energy. Thus, even for the world's already "well-energised" economies and societies – still more than 85 per cent dependent on carbon fuels and with half of the remaining 15 per cent derived from a nuclear power industry in decline – there are no realistic prospects at all for the incremental demand for energy to be totally met from renewables, let alone for them being capable of substituting the countries' existing use of carbon energy!

Unless, that is, the governments of these countries stipulate *and* require an energy market which is so transformed. The supply disruptions and the populist protests against the burdens of both additional capital and running costs which would consequently emerge make such a radical policy well-nigh impossible. Such a change is thus an extremely unlikely development in the overall energy economies of these countries, in general; while, in particular, it is an impossible change for the near-exclusively carbon-fuelled transportation sector of their economies. Over 50 per cent of global oil use and about 22 per cent of energy use are already concentrated in this single sector – and the percentages are still increasing.

Thus, in spite of the rich world's countries' so-called Kyoto Treaty "commitments" to reduce CO_2 emissions, future progress towards the achievements required remains highly improbable. At best, progress in the rate of reducing emissions will be slow until 2020, but there is some hope thereafter of more rapid progress. This will most likely be associated with an increasingly large-scale sequestration of CO_2 captured from the combustion of carbon fuels. The technological developments, the effective management and the falling real costs of sequestration will make this a more acceptable and a financially less costly way of achieving emissions' reduction targets, compared with that which could be achieved from constraints on carbon fuels' use, given the consequential adverse effects of such constraints on economic growth and on public opinion. Offsetting the costs of sequestration will, moreover, directly motivate attempts to enhance energy use efficiency and will also stimulate changes in economic and societal structures designed to reduce energy requirements. Albeit with a decade or more's delay, one may also reasonably expect similar developments in the until recently centrally planned economies of the former Soviet Union and Eastern Europe.

The above sets of countries – with only one-fifth of the world's present population – currently account for almost two-thirds of global energy use. But, a combination of their relatively low rates of population growth and their ability to achieve higher efficiencies in energy use will continue to reduce their share of the world's use of energy, and in due course could eventually lead to the stabilisation of their CO_2 emissions. Such progress will, moreover, be accompanied by the sequestration of their CO_2 emissions on an increasing scale.

Under those emerging circumstances the world's developing countries – already with 80 per cent of the world's population and with the percentage still growing – will play a rising relative role in both global energy use and in CO_2 emissions. Indeed, as in most other attributes related to the process of development, these countries "need" to use increasing amounts of energy, which, on an average per capita basis, is only one-eighth of that in the rich counties of the world. This "natural" phenomenon of rising per capita energy inputs to the world's developing countries' economic and social advancement is, however, largely only possible by the countries' increasing their use of low-cost carbon fuels. The alternative renewable sources of energy are – to an even greater extent than in the developed countries – simply too-high cost, except in niche markets largely unrelated to industrialisation, urbanisation and motorisation.

Thus, the future global energy needs of the developing world will inevitably be low-cost coal, oil and natural gas – albeit increasingly used at the higher efficiencies already achieved in the rich world – in contrast to the generally higher capital-cost renewables such as are now under development in the OECD countries with subsidies from both international organisations such as the International Energy Agency and the European Commission, and from national governments. Given that the significant benefits – of higher per capita incomes, enhanced standards of social welfare and significant spatial mobility that have steadily and cumulatively accrued over the many decades from the late eighteenth century to the present day for the populations in the countries early to industrialise and urbanise – arose, in large part, from the high level of the availability of, and access to, energy sources at low prices. Similar opportunities that are now opening up to the world's other countries and to their rapidly growing populations cannot be denied to them, unless, that is, it is done in the context of subsidies from the "north" to the "south" which fully offset the higher costs – both financial and temporal – which the production and use of renewable energies involve.

Meanwhile, demographic trends will locate the overwhelming percentage of the increased three billion or more people expected to inhabit the earth by 2050 in the currently developing world. All of these should expect, as a matter of course, to have access to enhanced supplies of energy in general, and to electricity in particular, together with the estimated present close-to-two billion people in the developing world who are still without access to domestic electricity.

This necessary – rather than simply desirable – completion of access to electricity for all the world's householders is a more realistic and positive form of sustainability than that which OECD policymakers present as their top priority: the achievement of global sustainability through the containment – and the relatively near-future reduction – of CO_2 emissions to the globe's atmosphere so that their hypothesised fears for global warming and climatic change can be eliminated. Quite apart from continuing doubts over these hypothesised links and the potential developments in the relatively near future of technologies which can significantly reduce and eventually eliminate the growth in atmospheric CO_2 at a cost well below that of changing from carbon fuels to renewables, there can be neither economic nor ethical justification for actions which delay or even obstruct the poor world's needs for sufficiency of energy to secure development and enhanced living standards. Most of the people concerned live in, or will be born into, countries that can only achieve such improvements through the exploitation of coal, oil and/or natural gas.

Thus, instead of the high profile demands of the supporters of the Kyoto Treaty (and its possible successor organisation) through heavy-handed and urgent pressures to secure the substitution of carbon fuels around the world by the direct and indirect use of solar power, this study firmly relegates the enhancement of the presently low percentage contribution of renewable energies to the total energy supply to the second half of the twenty-first century. Renewables, it is predicted, will by 2050 still contribute no more than 20 per cent of total global energy supply (compared with a little over 10 per cent in 2000 – excluding non-commercial collected biomass in the world's poorer countries). Such a close to 100 per cent enhancement of renewable energy's importance by the mid twenty-first century can be defined as an organic growth rate, rather than one forced through by policies which require fundamental societal changes and the denial of the use of low-cost carbon fuels. The additional use of renewables will, thus, be concentrated mainly in those countries which are severely constrained, or even completely devoid, of exploitable indigenous sources of carbon energy, so that renewables' exploitation is an imperative for their advancement. Examples of such countries are Belgium, the Czech Republic, France, Sweden, Germany and Belarus in Europe; Chile, Paraguay and Uruguay in the Americas; Japan, the Philippines, South Korea and Turkey in Asia and a number of countries in sub-Saharan Africa. For these countries, near future enhanced security of energy supply, rather than concern for long-term climate change possibilities, is of the essence.

Post-2050, however, following a potential peak of global oil production and in the context of a possible reduction in the currently expected growth rate of the natural gas industry, there will be a market-orientated widening of interest in renewables, especially in the rising number of countries in which indigenous carbon fuels become relatively scarce and more expensive. As a result, renewables could, by 2080, account for about 30 per cent of global energy use; and for over 40 per cent by 2100. Nevertheless, even then carbon fuels will collectively still be the more important component in energy supply. But by then the world will have become emphatically marked by significant regional and country-by-country variations as a function of highly significant geographical variations both in the availability of carbon fuels and of renewables. Cumulatively over the century, renewables will supply just under 30 per cent of the total energy used.

This predicated division of the twenty-first century global energy market between carbon fuels and renewables, in a world in which the population has stabilised at about nine billion of which the overwhelming majority are linked into gas and electricity systems, represents in large part a continuation of the organisation of the energy sector in a way that has already become the norm in the world's richer countries. With the indicated fourfold increase in annual energy use over the century, but with an increase of only about 50 per cent in the world's population, average per capita use of energy will increase by 2.3 times. This generalised statistic does, however, conceal a wide range of changing per capita energy use variations across the world, from close to zero or even negative increases in the world's already energy intensive counties (the current OECD countries minus Mexico, plus the formerly centrally planned economies of the 1950–90 Soviet bloc), to multi-fold increases in energy use per head in the populations of today's poorest underdeveloped countries. In almost all cases, however, the efficiency of energy use in terms of the GDP generated by a unit of energy input will certainly have increased, and will also have reduced the rate of growth in greenhouse gas emissions.

Nevertheless, the indicated inevitability of continuing increases in the production and use of carbon energy sources seem likely to cause consternation in the ranks of the believers in a causal link between CO_2 emissions from the combustion of such fuels and global warming/climate change. For those pessimists who visualise only adverse results from such developments, this study's conclusions incorporate only two saving graces: first, that only a three-fold increase in carbon energy use is indicated, compared with a more than five-fold increase predicated by the IPCC's basic scenario; and, second, that the forecast relatively strong increase for natural gas in the mix of carbon energy sources serves to reduce CO_2 emissions by at least 10 per cent from what they would have been, had the year 2000 division of the carbon energy market remained the same in the twenty-first century.

The conclusions of this study for CO_2 emissions in 2100 are thus indicated at 2.35 times their 2000 level: self-evidently an "unsustainable" proposition for the global warming lobbyists. Given a widely-held acceptance of the latter's claims and warnings, then the only way out of the impasse created by the inevitability – and the economic and social desirability – of increased carbon energy use, as argued here, lies in an immediate start to the implementation of measures to sequestrate the CO_2 produced by combustion. The costs of this procedure will, given the difficulties ranging from the technological to the political which remain to be resolved, necessarily increase the costs – and hence the price – of carbon energy: but this price impact on users will have a positive feed-back effect on the rate of enhancement in the efficiency of carbon energy use and will thus, in due course, serve to reduce the rate of growth in the demand for energy.

Under these circumstances the volume of carbon energy required over the century could turn out to be significantly lower than this study suggests, while its share of the total energy market would be below the 70 per cent calculated. Nevertheless, the twenty-first century energy economy will remain dominated by carbon fuels, albeit with much of their supply and use orientated to environmentally more friendly modes of production and transformation: most notably in natural gas's potential use for the production of hydrogen, initially for inputs to fuel cells, costs permitting; and, later, for the direct use of the hydrogen in both static and mobile outlets.'

In the convolution – as set out in detail above – during the early years of the twenty-first century, my location in London was of immense significance. This has already been shown above concerning the 'end-game' of my academic career. There were, however, also other aspects to our lives between mid-2000 and 2005 which were important. The first was one in which Jean, rather than I, set the scene: in making an active contribution to the Liberal Democrat Party's assault on the Labour Party's previously long-held domination of Islington Borough Council, and in an attempt to secure the election of the Lib/Dem candidate for Islington South in the 2002 general election. Electioneering required a good deal of foot-slogging and negotiating many steps both down to basements and up to flats and maisonettes on higher floors. There were also social occasions ranging from events in the Town Hall to other members' houses and/or gardens – all of which implied fund-raising for election expenses!

The high points of our Islington sojourn were, however, a function of what London has always been said to offer, including the multitude of musical offerings in the Barbican, with the top-ranking London Symphony Orchestra and a mélange of visiting orchestras from the rest of Europe, the Americas and the rest of the world. For at least part of each year we could visit the Royal Albert Hall for a selection from the promenade concerts. Other classical musical performances ranged across a number of other locations, such as St Luke's converted church in the City, St Paul's Cathedral and the Festival Hall on the South Bank (albeit in a restrained way, given its then being *hors de combat* for purposes of renovation but fortunately offset by the newly opened Cadogan Hall close by Sloane

Square). In total in our five years at Compton Road we frequented well in excess of one hundred musical performances in many different parts of London.

Likewise with theatres: beginning with the semi-professional performances at the local Tower Theatre which was literally less than a stone's throw from Compton Road on the other side of Canonbury Palace – until, alas, it prematurely closed after three seasons as the result of the solicitor failing to act for the theatre company so as to secure an extension to the lease of the facilities to the Theatre group. Just a little further afield – less than fifteen minutes' walk – we were able to take immediate advantage of the refurbished Almeida Theatre. This is small and unprepossing, but it enjoys the highest accolades for most of its memorable performances, usually with internationally known actors and actresses on the programme. Beyond Islington there were, of course, other theatres within a short bus or underground train ride. These included the theatres in the Barbican and the National Theatre on the South Bank, all with relatively modest ticket prices, for actors and presentations which served up high-quality performances. And beyond that, metaphorically, there was also the West End with its plethora of theatres – albeit with far too many devoted to so-called 'musicals' (depending on provincial coach-companies' clientele). Inordinately high prices for evening performances restricted the number of our attendances, but there were almost always the under-supported matinees (usually Wednesday and Saturday). Then one could usually be sure of 'the best seat in the house' for a much reduced price for senior citizens by calling on the theatre in the hour or so before the time of 'curtain up'. As with our frequent visits to classical music concerts, so during our time in London we also indulged in other 100 or so theatrical attendances.

Thirdly, there was the prolific London art world in which to participate, largely accessible on the basis of our membership of the National Art Fund and of the Friends of the Royal Society of Arts; plus, of course, the extensive 'no charge for entry' facility to all such nationally owned facilities. Thus, from the RSA to the National Gallery – with its recent expansions – and from Tate Britain/Tate Modern to the Wallace Collection, there was almost always an exhibition worth seeing. There were, moreover, other galleries which periodically offered upmarket presentations, such as the Dulwich Gallery in south-east London, the City of London Galleries in Canary Wharf and in the Guildhall, the East London Gallery in Shoreditch, Soames House in Lincolns Inn Field, National Trust and English Heritage houses in various parts of greater London, the Hayward Gallery on the South Bank and, to round off the world of art, the very prolific art dealers' galleries mainly in London's West End. In total there were more than enough events to justify more than an average two visits per week throughout the whole of our residence in London from 2000 to 2005. In addition there were annual displays by the art world in locations which stretched from Alexandra Palace to the Islington Business Centre and to the displays in a number of upmarket London hotels such as the Grosvenor and the Carlton. Generally speaking, moreover, we frequented events to which there was free entry on the production of a postal-delivered 'invitation' to attend!

On our visits to this plethora of London art display facilities we occasionally succumbed to purchases from the world of art which attracted our attention, ranging from a painting at the 2003 Royal Academy Summer Exhibition of the Aztec calendar (to supplement the bronze version which we had bought for a song many decades ago in Mexico itself) to a small watercolour of an Indian market scene, presented in the Claridge Hotel's annual art display. Other purchases from the world of art were the specially produced books on the international artists whose work was on display. These have added considerably to our 'library'; it was difficult to find space enough on our bookshelves but they are now hopefully resting for appraisal by our succeeding generation!

Thus, so very much for the wide range of indoor London opportunities come rain or shine and cold snaps or heatwaves. But, these were – and still are – not the only sets of things to do. There was also a broad range of outdoor places to visit and enjoy. Two such places stand head and shoulders above all else: Hampstead Heath and Kew Gardens, both of which are well served by public transport from Islington's Highbury Corner. To the former one takes the 271 bus up to Highgate Village and a second bus from there to the northern entry to Hampstead Heath and to Kenmore House. From the magnificent view over much of London from just inside the northern gates of the Heath, the north/south downhill routes on the heath lead one to a choice of two railway stations (Hampstead Heath and Gospel Oak), both on the North London line with a twenty-minute service back to Highbury and Islington station in a little over fifteen minutes. Overall, the Heath provided a very enjoyable morning or afternoon in the open air, with a more or less fumeless environment!

Secondly are the wide open-air spaces of Kew Gardens – from Islington a 35-minute North London rail line journey to the Kew Garden station and then a few minutes' walk to the entrance of the Gardens – with free entry on production of an annual Friends of Kew Gardens' membership card. Though the Gardens do not cover anything like as much ground as Hampstead Heath, a visit is very much an all-day excursion to some – but never all – of the many various sections of the gardens: ranging from the Victorian hot-houses to the hectares of trees and plants and the various buildings which constitute the rest of the beautifully kept facilities. With one's choice for a particular visit resulting from the specific function of the season involved!

Beyond these world-famous elements of London's open-air life there are many other places to visit. Regent's Park – plus the zoo if accompanied by children – is an extensive and variable place with the acres of rose gardens in the summer months being the best part to see. Then there are the walks around the City and along the Thames and its adjunct canal facilities. Given six or seven evening walks, stretching from Deptford in the east to Paddington and beyond in the west under the guidance of a member of the Bishopsgate Institute, we secured views of places that we would not otherwise have found; and likewise were introduced to specific buildings – most notably of seventeenth and eighteenth century churches. Each summer evening's walk ended up at one of London's many, many taverns for drink and/or food, so rounding off the day close to a convenient bus route or an underground station for an easy journey back to Islington.

Within the large east to west extent of interesting Thameside walks there was the newly extended and improved South Bank pedestrian facilities between London Bridge and Waterloo Bridge. First, it offered changing views over the city on the North Bank and second, it proceeded along a route with character and with several relics of buildings before arriving at the National Theatre and Waterloo Bridge. Wide spaces are available to the many thousands of patrons in this area of great interest. It also passed by the frontage of the Tate Modern, previously a coal-fired power station, and by the south end of the pedestrianised Millennium Bridge with its view of St Paul's Cathedral back on its north side location. This South Bank pathway became one of our favourite walks, easily reachable by any number of buses running south from Islington.

Thus, somewhat amazingly in my view as a resident of London, outdoor facilities and opportunities well-nigh equalled the city's indoor attributes. Overall, five years was much too short a period in which to come to know London. Sooner, however, than expected, back to Ipswich became a

BACK TO LIFE IN LONDON: AFTER 32 YEARS   163

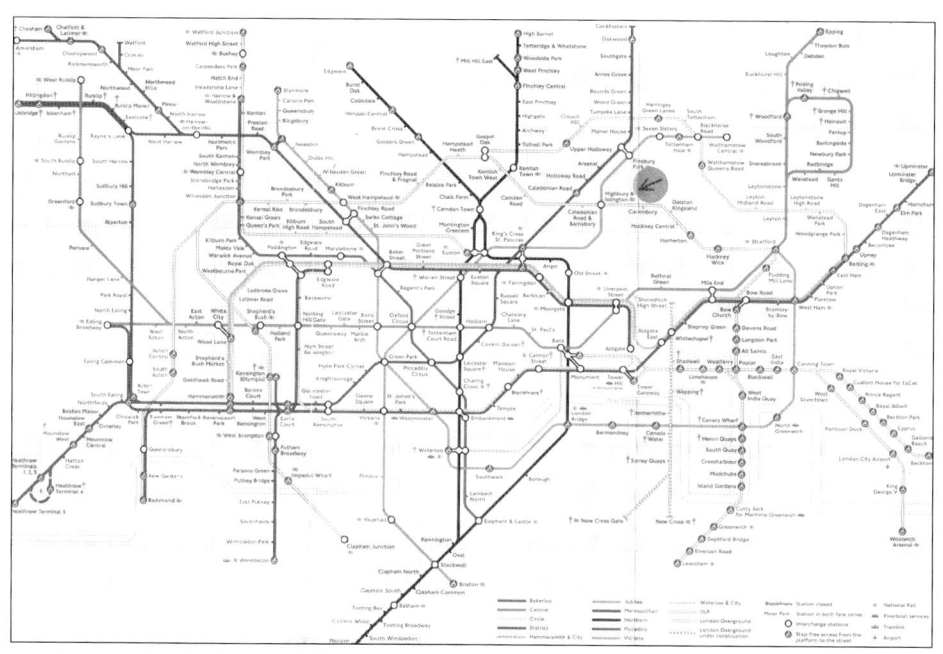

63. The London Underground showing the location of Highbury and Islington on the Victoria and North London lines

requirement for family reasons: the decision by Mark to leave his wife on grounds of incompatibility and thus necessarily move into the pied à terre in Compton Road, so as to be able to continue his job at the *Financial Times*. The impact of this event was somewhat traumatic; ranging from the costs of running the household to the regular incursion of our two grand-daughters – Robin and Lucy – as part of the sharing process between the parents in what was a maisonette of limited space. Within a few months, Mark found a new partner who on her return from a visit to Australia had nowhere to go except to Compton Road. This 'final straw' was the one that broke the proverbial 'camel's back' – so that we moved out and away to Ipswich in mid-July 2005. More than five years on, in early August 2010, the issue of the utilisation of our London flat remains an unresolved problem. Although it is nominally our PPR (principal private residence), we have, more recently, used it only from time to time – for our visits to London and/or as a stop-over base for us on our trips to foreign parts by the Channel Tunnel from Waterloo or, more recently, St Pancras, or from Heathrow and the other London airports for more distant locations.

CHAPTER 10

Five Twilight Years from 2005

SHORTLY AFTER RESETTLING in Ipswich in July 2005 I found there was little changed here from our pre-2000 sojourn – except for my decision to resign from the membership of the Ipswich and Suffolk Club for reasons of costs and of concern for the dictatorial way in which it seemed to be run by a clique of Johnny-make-good directors! I also decided not to seek re-election to the Chair of the Ipswich Society given what seemed to be its much closer relationship with the Borough Council and especially with the then Chief Executive Officer, whose policies were not in my view highly favourable for the further development of Ipswich.

I was still involved in visits to Geneva where early in February I had been commissioned by a firm of internationally orientated lawyers to provide information and analyses on a dispute between Iran and Israel over a period of more than twenty years, when an earlier agreement for Iran to ship oil to Israel had been eliminated by the radical change of Iran's government. The two parties both claimed huge recompense so that by 2005 no agreements had been reached. My commission from the Iranian Oil Company (INOC), through the Swiss lawyers, was to demonstrate the validity of the Iranian claims. Thus in the first half of 2005 I had already made several suggestions as to the validity of the Iranian Oil Company's claims and had made numerous journeys to and from Geneva for discussions on and evaluations by the lawyers.

Further progress was now made from my analyses undertaken in the UK with my conclusions on the issues necessitating two further visits to finalise the lawyers' presentations to the Zurich Arbitration Tribunal. Meanwhile, however, I had also been asked to attend meetings in Hamburg and Köln in Germany over a period of nine days (so allowing time for looking around the two cities as well as making a visit to Bremen over the week-end between the meetings). Even more impressive was an invitation from a study-centre in Abu Dhabi to attend a conference on the global prospects for oil – and to present my own paper on 'Gulf Oil in a Global Context; Strategies for Supply and Demand Security'. This first visit to Abu Dhabi was climatically oppressive, through the heat at up to 40°C, and

64. *My presentation from the rostrum at a large conference in Abu Dhabi in September 2005*

impressive, given the modernity of the developments under way based on high revenues from oil exports.

Meanwhile, Jean and I, following discussions with our son, Nigel, who had recently moved home in Melbourne with his family, decided to take a lengthy trip to Australia, with intermediate stop-overs in Dubai and Brunei.

This foreign travel extended from late November 2005 to late February 2006 and so gave time enough for a long stay with our elder son and family in their very pleasantly located home in the suburb of Alphington, about 8 km from the centre of Melbourne. This, by and large, ran very smoothly – except for the consequential failure of a retailing venture which Nigel's wife, backed by funds from Nigel and through him, from us, had undertaken, as a purveyor of ladies' lingerie.

Unhappily, the poor sales in the last months of 2005, plus a couple of burglaries of the premises, put paid to any chance of success. Naturally, creditors had to be paid, so that once more, we had to help with financial difficulties. Meanwhile, our two grandchildren, Thomas and Kasia, kept us on our toes in the context of both sporting games and of sights to see in downtown Melbourne.

Outside these family components of our visit, we managed stop-overs in Brisbane and Sydney en route by rail to Melbourne. These created opportunities for meeting old colleagues and friends, most notably Donald and Margaret Stephenson whom we had known through many years in Rotterdam. Unhappily, this call in Brisbane proved to be our final meeting with Donald, whose death occurred less than a year ahead. At the time we were there, Brisbane was growing apace as the capital city of Queensland with its rapidly expanding port based on the export of coal and minerals located in inland locations. It was, indeed, rapidly becoming a metropolis of large dimensions and with a multi-racial population from other parts of eastern Asia as well as from Europe. On our subsequent short visit to Sydney we noticed attempts to up-date the city within which easy movements no longer existed, given transport facilities which demanded improvement. An attempt there, at the largest university, to secure greater knowledge of Australia's energy resources proved to be impossible – Christmas' vacation was, it seems, already wielding its power!

On our arrival in Melbourne in early December we prepared for the first occasion for us of an Australian Christmas. This provided enjoyable traditional food and events outdoors in Nigel's garden, followed on Boxing Day with a visit to the massive Melbourne Cricket Ground to see an Australia v South Africa test match: for a somewhat disappointing display! On the following day we all set off in two loaded cars to the holiday resort of Bright, located in the Barry mountain range in north-eastern Victoria. Unexpectedly the town's weather turned out to be much warmer than normal for late-December. Indeed, the day temperature rose to upwards of 40° Celsius! The air conditioning in the lodge was much appreciated.

Thereafter, in January we made subsequent visits to Ballarat, some 100 km or so from Melbourne, the home of the parents of Nigel's wife. Of Irish/English descent, they pulled together all of the family's children, spouses and grandchildren. A few days later we were driven further west to the Grampian Mountains from the top of which the plains of South Australia stretched to the distant horizon. Needless to say, as grandparents of the respective families, we spent some of the time in their home sharing doubts over Nigel's continuing interests as an Australian film-producer and his wife as a lingerie shopkeeper and over future successes in those careers!

Later in the month we flew over from Melbourne to Tasmania to visit long-since lost Australian members of the Liverpudlian McKintosh family.

Gossip over the past was accompanied by pleasant and extensive visits along the northern coast and the inland mountains (of volcanic origin) of this smallest state of the Commonwealth of Australia. Similarities over many physical aspects of the countryside, together with people's attitudes to the British way of life, were very apparent.

On returning to Melbourne we were attracted by, and tempted to purchase, an apartment in a magnificent new building located on the city's inner harbour – transformed to an even greater extent than the downstream developments on the north and south sides of London's former port facilities along the river Thames. Prices for Melbourne's high-rise apartments were then modest compared with London, so that we were sorely tempted to buy possible future facilities for ourselves and for the visits of our UK-based family members. We were, however, unable to take the plunge! In retrospect – on a 2009 renewed visit to Melbourne – we much regretted our earlier negative decision and shall continue to do so!

Finally, after our more than two month's sojourn in the south-east areas of the Australian continent, we started on our return journey home, first, by plane from Melbourne to the Australian Northern Territories' capital, the small city of Darwin. In the mid-1940s the town had suffered extensively from air attacks by the Japanese air force during that country's occupation of the Dutch East Indies directly to the north. By the time of our visit, of course, Darwin had recovered completely from the destruction incurred by the wartime attacks. Over the same period, moreover, the city had become rail-linked to the centre of Australia (at Alice Springs) and thence further on to the south of the country as far as Adelaide (and thence to Sydney and Melbourne). Darwin has thus become attractive for both international trade and for tourists. The latter were, and remain, able to visit its surroundings of magnificent countryside and of many relics of long-since Aboriginal occupation. We were impressed – and even overwhelmed – by what was to be seen.

Thence, we were able to take a direct flight by Brunei Airlines from Darwin to the small state of Brunei on the island of Borneo (mainly part of Indonesia and also of Eastern Malaysia). After spending a night in Brunei we then commenced our journey towards home.

First we had a ten-hour flight to Dubai in the Middle East on the western side of the Gulf. We stayed there for three days to witness the frenetic expansion of this hitherto modest waterside state – in the manner of Hong Kong, but on an even greater spacious scale. Even in mid-

February, however, the city's daytime temperature reached the high-30s so that expeditions such as the day-trip to Buraimi at the frontier with Oman and thus an important Arab trading centre for many centuries, were necessarily in an air-conditioned car.

In Dubai itself we were able to take a tour of the city in the late afternoon on the open top-deck of the tourist buses going to various sectors of the rapidly expanding suburbs, involving vast hectares of up-market homes along the country's Gulf coast, together with hotels of formidable size and height. Elsewhere, outside the old city, there were skyscrapers galore, some already occupied, but with many more in the process of construction with the work undertaken almost entirely by immigrants from the Indian sub-continent – working mainly for a pittance and with most of that transmitted home to enhance their families' well-being. Two developments stood out: first, the 'Snoasis' – for European style indoor winter sports; and second, the ongoing work for what was to become the world's highest building, so overtaking Melbourne's claim to this phenomenon! The former was eventually achieved late in 2009.

Meanwhile, the 'old city' of Dubai along the river waterfront was one we had visited and enjoyed on our visit in 2005. By then previously rundown buildings had been restored and the level of activities along the river and coastal waterfront had also been much expanded. Only the city's extensive areas of bazaars, with their multitude of stalls and sellers, remained as always: as still a place of 'sojourn and price negotiations' with buyers from many other Middle Eastern countries galore – as well as from European and Russian lands.

On our return to the UK, in the approaching spring of 2006, there was a great deal of necessary catching up on house, home and external contacts – mainly of a financial nature within the 2005/6 tax year! There were helpful hands required by our four children: first in helping out Nigel over the failure of his wife's lingerie shop; second, to Mark for his responsibilities in looking after his two children, Robin and Lucy, following the break-up of his marriage; thirdly, for Susie with her two sons, George and Lucas, each attending his local village school/pre-school respectively as she tried to maintain her outside catering business in the Ipswich area and planned for the family to migrate to Melbourne; and, fourthly, to Deborah's only child, Kirsten, who had been admitted to the University of Aberdeen, the most distant university of some 800 km from Ipswich, involving not insignificant costs in terms of fees, accommodation and travel. Fortunately, by the transfer of savings from the so-called Discretionary Settlement for the family, finances were available and thus helped to cover the costs incurred by Kirsten over the next four years.

Through the spring, summer and autumn of 2006, I was also kept busy on matters relating to oil and gas subjects. In early May, for example, I was invited to the University in Aberdeen to contribute my views – along with those of a dozen other people – on the forty years to 2006 during which much of the exploitation of Britain's oil and gas resources under the UK's territorial waters took place. I shall return to this issue and the implications thereof towards the end of this Chapter.

Relatively few days later, I flew to Rotterdam from City airport to celebrate the final presentation of my hitherto regular three-monthly contribution to the Dutch publication *PetroVision*. This required my giving an overview on the prospects for the short to medium development of carbon fuels, in the context of the Dutch enthusiasm for large-scale alternative renewable energy resources. There followed a terminal reception for my many years of contributions to the journal.

I then had my travels to Geneva for discussion with the international lawyers prior to the forthcoming hearings on the dispute between Iranian and Israeli oil companies. This was by no means a walk-over, given that it was related directly to an agreement made between the two countries in the 1970s. The hearings were then confirmed for two weeks later in Zurich, at which I was to be heard by the city's International Arbitration Tribunal on the huge volumes of monetary claims being made by the two parties over the issues involved. These hearings lasted for a whole week, from 9 a.m. to 6 p.m. each day, plus evening sessions as required for the following day's issues. Given the millions of US dollars at stake, I am now, in November 2010, amazed that I have still not been advised of the Tribunal's decisions – let alone of the attentions which were given to my submissions. Maybe I shall be called again to defend my arguments!

Going back to 2006, however, I find that following the demands on my knowledge and time by the Tribunal, I was almost immediately requested to contribute to a 'keynote session' of the Annual Meeting of the International Association for Energy Economists in the city of Potsdam, very close to Berlin, where the Conference dinner was set in the summer retreat for prior German Royalty and at the location for the 1945 agreements to end Europe's World War Two! The five-day meeting, with some 250 attendees, proved to be a 'humdinger', as a result of conflicting views on carbon fuels versus alternative energies (in parenthesis I should report that, on taking a long walk for fresh air in the extensive forest adjacent to the conference centre, I became lost – but was rescued by a passing motorist!).

Back in Ipswich, I was almost immediately requested to go to London's Savoy Hotel, where LSE had organised a breakfast presentation and my delivery of expectations on the future of oil and gas in the global energy system. Moreover, in early July, I was again requested to attend and speak at a Royal Dutch/Shell seminar in Den Haag on international oil and gas prospects for the long-term.

Thereafter, however, through the rest of the summer life was more relaxed with family visits and a five-day trip to Hereford and mid-Wales. September, however, proved to be a formidably complicated period; first, in the early days of the month to the wedding of a second son of my only Odell-named cousin, Timothy, who had been a resident and schoolmaster for many years in Cheltenham. Our participation in this event was, however, constrained by a last-minute, unexpected and more distant development: a notification by the Secretary General of OPEC that 'the Board of Governors had selected me to be the recipient of the 2006 Biennial OPEC Award'. The honour to be awarded to me was based on the OPEC member countries' conclusions as set out below:

> That I had '*made outstanding contributions to the petroleum industry and its oil-related issues, so enhancing internationally orientated cooperation*', especially as my work had '*contributed to enhanced cooperation between oil producers and consumers*'.
>
> In particular, the Award made to me was stated as '*meeting the following attributes*:
>
> <u>first</u>, *for dedication to research and analysis of oil-related issues.*
>
> <u>second</u>, *by making a contribution to an enhanced dialogue between producers and consumers of oil.*
>
> <u>third</u>, *by demonstrating the independence and integrity of the work involved.*
>
> <u>fourth</u>, *in presenting critical, yet impartial, views on oil-related issues in public debate.*
>
> <u>fifth</u>, *in having a substantial record of publications at the international level and*

sixth, by enhancing further knowledge of the oil industry in encouraging and promoting young researchers, particularly within OPEC member countries and the developing world.'

Needless to say, I was more or less instantly flabbergasted by the receipt of this formidable range of attributes which the OPEC's Governors had linked to my work for a period covering more than four decades. Indeed, later, in the aftermath of the ceremony that followed, my wife, who had been invited to the Award meeting, spoke of my shock on receiving the letter from OPEC's Secretary General and told the audience of my collapse into the nearest easy-chair at home! This was as late as the last day of August, with only twelve days to go prior to the opening of the OPEC International Seminar in the Hofburg Palace in Vienna, at which the award was to be made.

Family issues, however, posed problems, pertaining first to the Odells' wedding event in Cheltenham and second to the arrival from Australia of

65. A photo of me receiving the 2006 OPEC International Award

our son Nigel and his two children just a few days later. Jean and I were already committed to look after the latter, so that Nigel could proceed to Halifax in Nova Scotia to attend a meeting on film affairs! Fortunately, other family members, Deborah and Susannah, sorted out these problems.

Jean and I thus succeeded in accepting OPEC's invitation to the two-day conference incorporating the Award presentation and ceremony. The Hofburg Palace, dating back to the days of the Hapsburg Empire, with its mighty red-carpeted stairway from the entrance doors to the still-magnificent ballroom of the Palace, was to be the location for the Award ceremony at which some 300 + delegates would be assembled. The presentation was not only forthcoming from OPEC's officers and representatives of its member countries but it was also filmed – and, in the following month, duly recorded at length in OPEC's *October Bulletin*. Some parts of the text of the latter are featured below:

> 'Economist Professor Peter Odell was the recipient of the 2006 OPEC Award, which he was handed by Nigerian OPEC Governor, Ammuna Lawan Ali, during a special presentation at the Third OPEC International Seminar. The award, made every two years, was in recognition of his lifetime achievement as an energy analyst.
>
> Ms Lawan Ali referred to Odell as a "gift to academia" and a legend of the global energy sector. She paid tribute to his "unparalleled commitment and contribution" to the energy industry with over five decades of academic and research excellence in energy economics. "This is a man who has devoted his whole life to research in petroleum economics," she said. Ms Lawan Ali pointed out that Odell was a prolific writer. "He believes in sharing his thoughts and research findings with the larger academic and research community so that knowledge of the industry can be enhanced globally."
>
> In accepting the award, Odell said he wanted to express his appreciation of the honour which OPEC had bestowed upon him in the context of the criteria employed by the Organisation's Board of Governors in reaching their collective decision. "This award to me is totally unexpected and I will endeavour to ensure that my efforts to understand the international oil and gas industry continue to meet the criteria on which the award has been made."

Following three years with Shell International's Economic division from 1958, Odell returned to academia via the London School of Economics and subsequently in 1968 to a Chair in the Netherlands School of Economics, now part of the Erasmus University in Rotterdam. He retired from his directorship of the University's Centre for International Energy Studies in the 1990s and now has the status of Professor Emeritus.

In 1991, he was honoured by the International Association for Energy Economics for his "outstanding contributions to the subject and its literature" and in 1994 by the award of the Royal Scottish Geographical Society's Centennial Medal for his studies on North Sea Oil and Gas.

Over the years, he has advised many public and private bodies on energy related issues and has lectured on his research interests at well over one hundred academic and professional institutions around the world.

Of his books, *Oil and World Power* ran to seven UK editions and 13 translated editions between 1970 and 1986. More recently, he has published a two-volume selected collection of 70 of his studies and commentaries, entitled *Oil and Gas: Crises and Controversies, 1961–2000*; and, in 2004, the book, *Why Carbon Fuels Will Dominate the 21st Century's Global Energy Economy.*'

In my immediate response to the receipt of the Award, I presented the following comments of relevance from my thoughts over the relatively short period between receiving the notification of OPEC's decision and my acceptance of it:

> 'First and foremost may I express my appreciation of the honour which OPEC has bestowed upon me in the context of the criteria employed by its Governors in reaching their collective decision. This Award to me was totally unexpected, and I will endeavour to ensure that my efforts to understand the international oil and gas industry continue to meet the criteria on which the award has been made. On this occasion I thus take the opportunity briefly to set out what I perceive to be the most significant elements in the long-term evolution of the international energy developments:
>
> First, that the current 60 per cent contribution of oil and gas to world energy supplies will be only modestly reduced by mid-

century; thereafter, hydrocarbons' contribution to energy demand will slowly decline, but will still account for over 40 per cent in 2100. By then, however, natural gas will be two-and-a-half times more important than oil; though the latter will still be an industry larger than that of 2000, albeit one which will become up to 90 per cent dependent on non-conventional oil. Natural gas will undoubtedly become the prime energy source by the second quarter of the twenty-first century (streets ahead of renewables) – initially through a near three-fold increase in conventional gas production by 2050 and, thereafter, through the continuing rapid exploitation of prolific non-conventional gas supplies.

Second, that the ultimate physical sufficiency of global oil and gas resources is not in doubt so that one can ignore the present-day Jeremiahs. Their predecessors in the 1960s, the 70s and the 80s were all quickly proven wrong and a like fate will overcome the so-called "peak oilers" by the end of the present decade. Any underachievement in future oil and gas production will be the result of a combination of organisational, economic, political and environmental factors, all of which can be overcome, as they always have been in the past – except for very short-term lapses.

Third, that the current generally accepted wisdom favouring globalisation, liberalisation, market competition and dependence on speculative trading exchanges (such as NYMEX and the IPE) for price determination will soon fall from favour, as a consequence of the turmoil which they have created over the past three years. This has been to the detriment of consumers the world over and is having adverse impacts on economic and social development in many countries, especially in the developing world. The continuing – albeit modest – expansion of the world's demand for oil now necessitates the establishment of an international oil organisation whereby order can be brought to the markets. The current unacceptability of this by policy makers in the OECD countries will hardly be relevant beyond the middle of the next decade, in the context of the rapidly declining importance of these countries in the global oil system.

Fourth, that oil from non-OECD countries already accounts for almost 80 per cent of world reserves and production, with most of this from state-owned or state-controlled exploration and production facilities. Even the remaining four largest multi-national oil corporations already appear unable to secure significant new production rights, except as minority partners in state-run systems. This process is unlikely to be reversed, as all the large oil consuming nations of the developing world view self-sufficiency as a prime objective, and will feel assured of this only in the context of nationally owned and operated companies.

Fifth, that in such potentially adverse circumstances for the oil majors, the fact that they have in recent years been pursuing policies which hardly endear them to countries in which expanding demands for energy are of the essence, is not helpful for their survival. The companies are seen as responsible for high prices, leading to high profits, from which extortionate remuneration is paid to their executives and shares are "bought-back" to enhance their stock-markets' status; whilst they make too little investment in new upstream operations, as they cannot count on a rate of return in excess of 16 per cent.

Sixth, that as with those "majors" that have already failed to survive, so those remaining may well be playing out their last few years. A Chinese bid for Exxon and/or Chevron and/or a Russian bid for Shell and/or BP, backed by funds provided by the wealthy member countries of OPEC, seem likely to be only a matter of time. With the "majors" gone, there will be concern in the main OECD countries for the future security of supplies. In this context, one can reasonably forecast a revival and/or the resuscitation of their own state-owned oil and gas industries. The two currently booming and expanding state oil companies in OECD countries (Statoil of Norway and ÖMV of Austria), could thus soon have new bedfellows: for example, a new British National Oil Corporation, a revived Petro-Canada and a de-privatised Total in France-Belgium.

Seventh, that above and beyond all these developments, we may anticipate the creation of a formal UN International Energy Organisation designed to deal with the world's twenty-first century energy matters. Such an organisation will, of course, include a major input from a now more powerful than ever Organisation of Petroleum Exporting Countries, given its members' interests in tomorrow's much expanded and ordered global oil markets.

Eighth, that the world's continuing regionalised gas markets will massively expand. In Europe the current obsession for liberalisation will be inevitably abandoned, as producers wisely insist on long-term contracts to ensure security of demand in the context of importing nations' search for security of supply. The EU's current commitments to fully liberalised gas market, in general and, in particular, the UK's hopelessly failed experiment with "perfect competition" for securing infrastructural developments and low pricing, will not survive the present decade.

Post-2020, an ordered gas market will emerge, with continuing long-term benefits based on the near-limitless supplies available from a range of gas-rich countries from Russia, the Caspian region, the Middle East, North Africa and Norway, and on the consuming countries' overwhelming preferences for natural gas over the high-cost alternatives of renewables and/or nuclear power and the high CO_2 emission levels from the use of oil and coal. The establishment of a Greater European Strategic Gas Authority will be the precursor to similar developments in Latin America, sub-Saharan Africa, south-east Asia and the western Pacific Rim over the first quarter of the twenty-first century.'

Now, in late-2010, four years on, global events on energy issues are proceeding in ways which are very close to the octet of suggestions I presented in Vienna. During the relatively short period between now (November 2010) and then (November 2006), there has been a notable resurgence in demands on my time for both written and verbal presentations. Thus, meetings and publications in a number of countries have been requested: usually leading to a positive reply from me with a title setting out my intended presentation: for example, on 'Our Long-term Energy Future: a Reality Check', incorporating several major issues, such as carbon fuels' supply potentials in the context of renewable energy development, given the possibility of global warming, particularly within the world's developing countries' requirements for the continuing growth of energy resources. The second half of this first decade of the twenty-first century has for sure been of this ilk.

In the context of these developments, I have thus continued along the entitled axis of the title of this book: *An Energetic Life*. I have now decided that my eight decades of long and generally positive life and livelihood have reached its embodied peak. Thus, by late-2010 my final contribution to global energy issues has arrived. The largely inept procedures taken by the UK in the context of the global energy system is challenged in a short paper which I wrote early in 2010 for publication later this year on the failure of successive UK governments to optimise the exploitation of hydrocarbons located in the extensive geological formations lying under the seas around most parts of the country, so creating the relatively modest status which now undermines Britain's position in the totality of European, Commonwealth and even global terms. In 2010, just less than a hundred years from Britain's top-dog international role on the exploitation, use and export of coal, we now stand twentieth in the rank order of the world's nations energy supply systems.

It is thus with some degree of sadness that I reach the near end of my energetic life, downhearted by my failure to contribute enough knowledge and understanding of the global energy system's importance in the twentieth century. I am even more dejected by the potential imposition of prospective carbon energy limitations during the twenty-first century. These will arise from the scientists' and politicians' claims and fears for global warming, as a result of which limitations on the production and use of carbon fuels will be at prices beyond those which can be met by many of the world's consumers and thus serve to constrain the otherwise possible growing population of the world from achieving higher standards of living and of longer life-spans.

My hopes and expectations for the achievement of an energised total world population cannot now be foreseen before the prospective end of my life. The world's governments are now frittering away the potential universality of global energy supplies for the 9 + billion population which will be 'sharing' the world before the end of the mid-21st century.

My contribution to developments and policies whereby this universality could have been achievable is now virtually at an end. Quite the contrary, over the modest lifetime yet to come I shall inevitably be no more than an observer of 'energy' developments. For my present view, I visualise more for 'worse than for better', given the continuity of ongoing fears for global warming and its attributes. Unhappily, those who recently secured the Nobel Peace Prize for the demise of the use of carbon fuels have committed a negative rather than a positive achievement. The award winners – notably a former US Vice President (Al Gore) and an Indian energy technocrat (Dr R.K. Pachauri) are now insisting on actions which are more likely to enhance than to diminish global economic and social difficulties.

Meanwhile, as an 'also-ran' from my conclusions concerning global energy futures, I must turn instead to parochial and family issues: the former through my location in the almost 800 year-old Borough of Ipswich in a 108-year-old Edwardian house with its beautiful and productive garden; and the latter embracing the communities of the Odells (few in number) and of my wife's clan, the McKintosh's (large in number) across various parts of the UK and of the Commonwealth.

This year's fifty-third anniversary of Jean's and my wedding, together with our eightieth birthdays, generated a family party from across the country, but it was also a celebration for our younger daughter Susannah and her partner and two boys, as they have fulfilled their plans for emigration to the other side of the world, to the Tasmanian State of Australia (where they will be in much greater proximity to Nigel, our elder son and his family, in the State of Victoria). Our other two children, Deborah and Mark, plus their spouses and children, seem likely to remain with us in the UK.

Collectively, our intra-families will, through the use of modern technology, enable us to maintain instant – as well as lengthy – contacts. Little of this will take me any further into 'An Energetic Life' of almost eight decades – but still dependent perhaps on potential developments as shown in the Epilogue which follows this final chapter!

An Epilogue

IN LATE JUNE 2010, after one of the longest and coldest winters since 1947, my previous last successful publication – on a matter of the UK's diminishing offshore exploitation of its oil and natural gas hydrocarbons – was accepted by the editors (Professor Philip Wright and Dr Ian Rutledge) for a book entitled *UK Energy Policy and the End of Market Fundamentalism*.

It is, in part, a sad story that I have related: that is, the inability of succeeding British governments over the past forty years to generate favourable conditions for the continuing exploitation and production of significant volumes of the UK's offshore resources. The cause of this phenomenon, I consider I may claim, has been derived from the government's failure to accept the conclusions of my advisory work for Tony Benn, the Secretary of State for Energy in the late-1970s.

Unhappily, the fall of the then Labour government and its replacement by the Thatcher regime eliminated the possibility of radical changes that had become necessary for securing the longevity of Britain's hydrocarbons production. Now, however, in the early part of the twenty-first century, national and international conditions and new technologies have created a potential outlook for an additional thirty years of substantial British oil and gas production.

But this potential is, it now seems, unlikely to be exploited over the rest of my remaining lifespan, as a consequence not only of the widespread disbelief in my claims, but also because a number of parliamentary decisions which have already been made require up to 80 per cent of energy use in the country to be 'green' and 'renewable' by mid-century. This is a prospect which I believe to be absurd – on the basis of the data and arguments which I set out in my 2004 published book, *Why Carbon Fuels will dominate the Global Energy Prospects for the 21st Century*. In this book I have shown how renewable energies will, over the century, account for no more than about 25 per cent of total energy use around the world – a widely unbelieved and an unacceptable proposition!

Meanwhile, I already have more mundane requirements set out for my prospective future. First, the protection of our four children and seven grandchildren in the context of European and US financial systems which are falling apart. The transfer of assets to other parts of the world would appear to be logical, and so involve investments in China, India, Brazil, Indonesia and even Russia. Other countries of the non-Western world and in hitherto 'Western orientated' countries – such as Australia and New Zealand – are now disengaging their current economic and societal links and engaging instead to the emerging countries named above. Likewise, with the oil and natural gas rich countries of Latin America, the Middle East and North Africa and other present member countries of OPEC such as Venezuela, Angola and Nigeria. The potential oil and gas energy riches of other countries of west and east Africa and of east and south-east Asia will also become relatively more important.

In the context of these future radical changes, there should still be modest family wealth from the continuity of our fifty-plus years of careful housekeeping and associated savings. The Australian states of Victoria and Tasmania, in which half of our offspring and their families are already residents, now seem more likely to offer brighter prospects of successful lifespans and of more secure financial situations than the other half of our family which have so far chosen to remain in the UK. For this latter group, however, our accumulations of global energy interests, ideas and information from 1958 to today, may engender something of a solace; or even of elements that could help to minimise the problems and issues of the first quarter of the twenty-first century: possibly with profitable gains from the returns of my *Energetic Life*. Only time will tell!

APPENDIX 1

Books, Papers and Articles Written between 1961 and 2010

A. Books and encyclopaedia entries written by Professor Peter R Odell

An Economic Geography of Oil, Bell, London, 1963.

Oil: the New Commanding Height, The Fabian Society, London, 1965.

Geografia Econômica do Petroleo, Zahar Editôres, Rio de Janeiro, 1966.

Natural Gas in Western Europe, De Erven F. Bohn, Haarlem, Netherland, 1969.

Oil and World Power, Penguin Books, London, 1st Edition 1970 and subsequently in seven updated editions in English, 1972–1986 and also published in 13 other languages from 1970, viz. Italian, Spanish, Dutch, Norwegian, Japanese, Finnish, French, Greek, Brazilian, Arabic, Farsi, American and Canadian.

'Oil and Western European Security', in *Brassey's Annual*, London, 1972.

Energy; Needs and Resources, MacMillan Education, Basingstoke, 1974 (2nd Edition, 1977).

'Oliepolitiek: de Ontwikkelingen sedert 1968', *Winkler Prins Encyclopaedie Supplement*, Den Haag, 1976.

'The international companies in the new world oil market', *The Yearbook of World Affairs*, Stevens, London, 1978.

British Oil Policy: a Radical Alternative, Kogan Page, London, 1980.

Energiecrisis of crisis van het energiebeleid?, *Jaarboek 1979, Heideland-Orbis/Oosthoek*, Hasselt/Utrecht, pp. 161–165, 1980.

The Oil and Gas Resources of the Third World Importing Countries and their Exploration Potential, The United Nations Development Research and Policy Analysis Division, New York, 66 pp., 1984.

'Energy', in A. Kuper en J. Kuper (Eds.) *The Social Science Encyclopaedia*, London, pp. 250–255, 1985.

'Changes in Western Europe gas markets', Memorandum 31, in Seventh Report of the *United Kingdom House of Commons Energy Committee*, 2, pp. 324–338, 1985.

'North Sea oil and gas and the Western European energy economy', 1985–2000, *Jaarboek van de Mijnbouwkundige Vereniging*, Delft, 54, pp. 145–156, 1986.

'After the Oil Price Collapse', *The Encyclopaedia Britannica Book of the Year*, London, pp. 211–212, 1987.

'Prospects for West European Energy Markets', Presented at the *School of Advanced International Studies*, John Hopkins University, Washington, pp. 12–28, 1987.

'A Carbon Energy Tax', Report of the *House of Lords European Communities Committee*, February 1992.

'Energy', in A. Kuper and J. Kuper (Eds.), *The Social Science Encyclopaedia*, 2nd Edition, Routledge, London, pp. 243–8, 1995.

Fossil Fuel Resources in the 21st Century, *Financial Times Energy*, London, 97 pp., 1999.

Oil and Gas: Crises and Controversies, Vol. 1; Global Issues, Multi-Science Publishing Company Ltd, Brentwood, England, 2001.

Oil and Gas: Crises and Controversies, Vol. 2; Europe's Entanglement, Multi-Science Publishing Company Ltd, Brentwood, England, 2002.

'Energy', in *The Social Science Encyclopaedia*, 3rd Edition, Routledge, London, 2003.

Why Carbon Fuels will Dominate the 21st Century's Global Energy Economy, Multi-Science Publishing Company Ltd., Bentwood, England, 2004.

'Reserves and Resources', *The Encyclopaedia of Hydrocarbons*, Vol. IV–2, Economics, 40 pages, 2008.
'Future Outlook: the Qualitative Aspects', *The Encyclopaedia of Hydrocarbons*, Vol. XIV, 2008.

B. Books and articles written jointly by Professor Peter R Odell and colleagues (as indicated)

Estimating World Oil Discoveries up to 1999 – the Questions of Method, *Petroleum Times*, 79, no. 2001 (with K.E. Rosing), 1975.
A Predictive Simulation Model of Oil Province Development: the North Sea Example, *Proceedings of the A.A.G.* (with K.E. Rosing), 1975.
The North Sea Oil Province: an Attempt to Simulate its Exploration and Development, Kogan Page, London (with K.E. Rosing), 1975.

An optimization of the U.K. sector's North Sea oil pipelines, *Energy Policy*, 4, no. 2 (with K.E. Rosing and H. Beke-Vogelaar), 1976.

Optimal Development of the North Sea's Oil Fields: A Study of Divergent Government and Company Interests and their Reconciliation, Kogan Page, London (with K.E. Rosing), 1977.
Optimal Development, The Reply, *Energy Policy*, 5, no. 4, pp. 295–306 (with K.E. Rosing), 1977.
Optimal Development of the North Sea's Oil fields, *The Chemical Engineer*, No. 321, pp. 393–396 (with K.E. Rosing), 1977.

The political economics of offshore oil, *Natural Resources Forum*, No. 2, pp. 229–239 (with K.E. Rosing), 1978.
The pressures of oil: a strategy for economic revival, Harper and Row, London, 215 pp. (with L. Vallenilla), 1978.
Political Economics of Offshore Oil, *Natural Resources Forum*, 2, no. 3 (with K.E. Rosing), 1978.

The Future of Oil: a Simulation Study of the Interrelationships of Resources, Reserves and Use, 1980–2080, Kogan Page, London (with K.E. Rosing), 1980.

Energie: Geen Probleem?, Uitgeverij Bert Bakker, Amsterdam, 189 pp. (with J.A. van Reijn), 1981.
The Future of Oil: Hypothesis and Conclusions, *GeoJournal*, Supplementary Issue 3, pp. 93–107 (with K.E. Rosing), 1981.

The Future of Oil, 2nd Edition, Kogan Page, London/John Nichols, New York (with K.E. Rosing), 1983.

The Future of Oil: a re-evaluation, *OPEC Review*, 3, pp. 203–228 (with K.E. Rosing), 1984.
Estimating the ultimate economically recoverable hydrocarbon reserves of the North Sea Province: Phase 1, The Theory, *The Statistician*, 33, pp. 75–89 (with K.E. Rosing), 1984.

East-west differ on estimates, *Petroleum Economist*, 52, pp. 329–331 (with K.E. Rosing), 1985.

The Politics of European Gas: Dutch Play for a Return to Centre Stage. *Geopolitics of Energy*, Vol. 18, No. 9, pp. 7–10 (with A.F. Correljé), 1996.

Groningen: Catalyst for European Gas, *FT Energy Economist Briefing*, No. 213, July, pp. 7 (with A. F. Correljé), 1999.

Four Decades of Groningen Production and Pricing Policies and a View to the Future (with A.F. Correljé), *Energy Policy*, Vol. 28, No. 1, January, pp. 19–28, 2000.

C. Professor Odell's contributions to edited books

'The Oil Industry in Latin America', in *The Large International Firm in Developing Countries*, E. Penrose, Allen and Unwin, London, 1968.

'Relationships Between the International Oil Industry and National Interests in Latin American Countries' in *International Oil and the Energy Policies of Producing and Consuming Countries*, OPEC, Vienna, 1969.

'The Location Component in Oil and Gas Reserves' Evaluation with Special Reference to Western Europe's Oil Supply, 1970–1980', in the *Economic Intelligence Unit International Oil Symposium Book*, London, 1972.

'North Sea Basin Oil and Gas and Western Europe's Energy Problems', in *The Jaarboek van de Mijnbouwkundige Vereniging*, T.H. Delft, no. 45, 1975.

'The Oil Dimension', in J. McGill (Ed.), Investing in Scotland, Collins, Glasgow, 1975.

'Oil', in C. Payer (Ed.), *Commodity Trade of the Third World*, MacMillan, London, 1975.

The Western European Energy Economy: Challenges and Opportunities, The Athlone Press, London, 1975.

'The Economic Background to North Sea Oil and Gas Development', in M. Saeter and I. Smart (Eds.), *The Political Implications of North Sea Oil and Gas*, Universitätsforlaget, Oslo and I.P.C. Science and Technology Press, London, 1975.

'European alternatives to oil imports from OPEC countries: towards self-sufficiency based on indigenous oil and gas', in F.A.M. Alting von Geusau (Ed.), *Energy in the European Communities*, Sijthoff, Leiden, 1975.

'OPEC und die Multi's: Amerikanische Politik und Europäische Optionen', in W. Hager (Ed.), *Erdöl und die Internationale Politik*, Piper, München, 1975.

'The E.E.C. Energy Model: Structure and Integration', in R. Lee and P. Ogden (Eds.) *Economy and Society in the E.E.C. Spatial Perspectives*, Saxon House, London, 1976.

Energy Policies in Western Europe and the Geography of Oil and Natural Gas, in J.T. Coppock and D. Sewell (Eds.), *Spatial Dimensions of Public Policy*, Pergamon Press, Oxford, 1976.

'Constrained Random Simulation: The North Sea Oil Province', in I. Masser (Ed.), *Theory and Practice in Regional Science*, Pion Press, London, pp. 105–123 (with K.E. Rosing), 1976.

'Predicting the Future Development of the North Sea Basin', in V.M. Gokham, G. A. Prevalovckaye, Yu. G. Saushkin (Eds.), *International Geography 1976*, Moscow, pp. 247–250 (with K.E. Rosing), 1976.

'Optimizing an Energy Transport System: Oil and Gas Pipelines' in the North Sea, in F.E.I. Hamilton (Ed.) *Proceedings of the Symposium on the Organization of Spatial Systems*, London (with K.E. Rosing), 1976.

'Oil and gas exploration and exploitation in the North Sea', in E.M. Borgese and N. Ginsburg (Eds.), *Ocean Yearbook I*, University of Chicago Press, pp. 139-159, 1979.

'Soviet energy policy, some resource base and geo-political considerations', in R.G. Jensen (Ed.), *Soviet Energy Policy*, Association of American Geographers, Washington, 1979.

'Towards a more rational view of the energy policy options open to the Western oil-consuming countries', in K.E. Davis and P. De Wit (Eds.), *Energy – what now?* Elsevier bv, Bonaventura, Amsterdam, pp. 31-47, 1979.

'The Maritime Dimension: Oil and Gas Resources', in R.P. Barston and P. Birnie (Eds.), G. Allen and Unwin, London (with K.E. Rosing), 1980.

'Energy Policies in the E.E.C. and their Impact on the Third World', in C. Stevens (Ed.), *Survey of E.E.C. and the Third World*, Hodder and Stoughton, London, 1980.

'International Energy Issues: the next 10 Years', in P. Tempest (Ed.), *International Energy Options: an Agenda for the 1980s*, Graham and Trotman, London, pp. 187-202, 1981.

'Energy Policies in the EEC and their Impact on the Third World', in C. Stevens (Ed.), *EEC and the Third World*, Hodder and Stoughton, London, pp. 84-91, 1981.

'The Electricity Sector and Energy Policy', in C. Sweet (Ed.), *Energy Requirements and the Fast Breeder Programme*, MacMillan, London, pp. 18-29, 1981.

'Oil and Gas potential in developing countries: prospects for and problems of its development', in United Nations (Ed.), *Petroleum Exploration Strategies in Developing Countries*, Graham and Trotman, London, pp. 17-26, 1982.

'Simulating the future of oil 1980-2080', in W.B. Fisher and P.W. Kent (Eds.) Resources, Environment and the future, *Deutsche Akademische Austauschdienst*, Bonn, pp. 263-342, 1982.

'World oil energy potential', in Y. Elizur and E. Salpeter (Eds.), *Energy: the Oil Glut and Beyond*, Naaviv Books, Tel Aviv, pp. 15-22, 1982.

'Institutional and Economic Constraints on the Utilization of Natural Gas Resources, with Particular Reference to Western Europe and North America', in C. Delahaye and M. Grenon (Eds.), *Conventional and Unconventional World Natural Gas Resources*, International Institute for Applied Systems Analysis, Laxenburg, pp. 313–338, 1983.
'The International Oil Industry: A Case Study', in H.P.S. Althuis and A.L. Vervuurt (Eds.), *Technological Movements on a World Scale*, Delft University Press, Delft, pp. 37–49, 1983.
'The Significance of Oil', in J.E. Peterson (Ed.) *The Politics of Middle Eastern Oil*, The Middle East Institute, Washington, pp. 5–14, 1983.
'Towards a System of World Oil Regions', in P. Tempest (Ed.) *International Energy Markets*, Graham and Trotman, London/Oelgeschlager, Gunn and Hain, New York, pp. 27–34, 1983.

'Energy issues', in J.R. Short and A. Kirby (Eds.) *The Human Geography of Contemporary Britain*, Basingstoke, pp. 97–114, 1984.
'Dimensions of Resource Dependence in Exporting Countries', in H.Siebert and I. Walter (Eds.) *Risk and the political economy of resource development*, Basingstoke, pp. 134–136, 1984.
'Constraints on the development and use of natural gas resources with special reference to Western Europe', in C.C. Watkins and L. Waverman (Eds.), *Adapting to changing energy prices*, Toronto, pp. 57–70, 1984.

'Natural gas in Western Europe: major expansion in prospect', in W.F. Thompson (Ed.), *World Energy Markets: Stability or Continued Cycle?*, Boulder, pp. 286–329, 1985.
Discussion of 'H. Franssen's; The Development of energy demand', *Energy – Economics and Politics*, Statens Energiverk, Stockholm, pp. 140–142, 1985.
Discussion of 'F. Fesharaki's, Energy supply: the power of the producers', *Energy – Economics and politics*, Statens Energiverk, Stockholm, pp. 158–165, 1985.

The International Oil Industry: an Inter-Disciplinary Perspective, London, 181 pp. (with J.A. Rees), 1986.
Gas and Electricity Markets in Europe: Prospects and Policies, Brussels, 553 pp. (with J. Daneels), 1986.

'The Prospects for the Oil Sector by 1995', in V. Marcha (Ed.) *Nos future; Wegen naar een toekomst voor de Nederlandse Antillen*, Zutphen, pp. 337–344, 1986.

'Institutional constraints on the development of the Western European gas market', in P. Stevens (Ed.) *International Gas: Prospects and Trends*, London, pp. 89–106, 1986.

'The changing structure of the oil industry in the Caribbean', in H.E. Chin (Ed.) *The Caribbean Basin and the Changing World Economic Structure*, Groningen, pp. 17–49, 1986.

'Draining the world of energy', in R.J. Johnston and P.J. Taylor (Eds.) *A World in Crisis? Geographical Perspectives*, Oxford, pp. 68–88, 1986.

'The economic and political geography of a century of maritime oil transport', *Met Olie op de Golven*, Rotterdam, pp. 41–54, 1986.

'Gas Demand Prospects', in P. Stevens (Ed.) *Energy Demand: Prospects and Trends*, Basingstoke, pp. 71–81, 1987.

'The World Petroleum Market: the Current Situation and Prospects', K. Khan (Ed.), *Petroleum Resources and Development*, Bellhaven, London/New York, pp. 3–17, 1988.

'The Improving Economics of North Sea Oil and Gas', in M. Goldring (Ed.) *The World in 1989*, Economist Publications, London, 1988.

'Draining the World of Energy', in R.J. Johnson and P.J. Taylor (Eds.) *The World in Crisis*, 2nd edition, Blackwell, Oxford, 1989.

'Energy: Resources and Choices', in D. Pinder (Ed.), *Challenge and Change in Western Europe*, Belhaven Press, London, 1990, 2nd Edition, 1998.

'Continuing Long-Term Hydrocarbons' Dominance of World Energy Markets: an Economic and Societal Necessity', in *Proceedings of the World Renewable Energy Congress, Reading*, Pergamon Press, Oxford, September 1990.

'World Oil Resources, Reserves and Production', *The Energy Journal*, Special Issue on the Changing World Petroleum Market, pp. 89–114, 1994.

'Towards the Regionalization of Oil Markets', in K. Gillespie and C.M. Henry (Eds.) *Oil in the New World Order*, University Press of Florida, Gainesville, pp. 74–86, 1995.

'The Exploitation of the Oil and Gas Resources of the North Sea: Retrospect and Prospect' in G. MacKerron and P. Pearson (Eds.), *The UK Energy Experience: a Model or a Warning*, Imperial College Press, London, pp. 123–133, 1996.

'Hydrocarbons: the Pace Quickens', in G.H. Blake et al (Eds.), *Boundaries and Energy: Problems and Prospects*, Kluwer, Law International, London, pp. 28–42, 1998.

'Gulf Oil in a Global Context: Strategies for and Challenges to Demand Security', *Gulf Oil and Gas: Ensuring Economic Security*, The Emirates Center for Strategic Studies and Research, Abu Dhabi, pp. 282–310, 2007.

'Managing the UK's Remaining Oil and Gas Resources: A Future Role for the State?' Chapter 2 in the book of Prof. P. Wright and Dr. I. Rutledge (Eds.), *UK Energy Policy and the End of Market Fundamentalism*, O.I.E.S., 2010.

D. Professor Peter R. Odell's published articles

'Impact on the West of Growing Russian Oil Exports', *The Times*, 19th–21st December, 1961.

'Russia in the Oil World', *New Statesman*, 16th February, 1962.
'Argentina's Natural Resources', *Manchester Guardian*, 28 March, 1962.

'Labour's Policy for Oil', *New Statesman*, 14th June, 1963.
The Development of the Caribbean and Middle Eastern Refining Industries, *Tijdschrift voor Economisch en Sociale Geographii*, September, 1963.

'What will Gas Do to the East Coast?' *New Society*, May 1966.
'Three point Approach Necessary to Exploit Sea Gas', *The Times*, 7th July, 1966.

The Right Price for Sea Gas, *The Times*, 8th December, 1966

'The North Sea Gas Boob', *New Statesman*, 7th February, 1967.
'Energy Resources: a Basis for Regional Growth in the 1970s', *Regional Studies*, April, 1967.
'Energy and Economic Development', *Power and the 1970s*, London, April, 1967.
'North Sea Gas: a Report on the Advisability of Public Ownership', *Labour Party Publication*, July, 1967.
'The North Sea Gas Price War', *New Statesman*, London, August, 1967.
'Cheap Energy: the Costs of Killing off Coal', *New Society*, London, September, 1967.
'Britain's Fuels Problems: wanted a Socialist Energy Policy', *New Statesman*, December, 1967.
'The North Sea Gas Price War', *New Statesman*, 18th August, 1967.
'The Empire of British Petroleum', *Socialist Commentary*, November, 1967.

'Oil and Politics in Latin America', *Latin America and the Caribbean*, A. Blond, January, 1968.
'The Significance of Oil', *Journal of Contemporary History*, Vol. 3, No. 3, 1968.
'The Oil Industry's Perpetual Promise', *The Financial Times*, 9th April, 1968.
'The British Gas Industry', *The Geographical Journal*, March, 1968.
'The Cost of Richard Marsh', *Tribune*, 12th July, 1968.

'North West Europe's Energy Revolution', *The Geographical Magazine*, London, June 1969.
'Competition for Groningen Gas', *The Petroleum Times*, Vol. 73, no. 1878, London, June 1969.

From Monopoly to Competition in the Marketing of Natural Gas in Western Europe, UN Commission for Europe, Geneva, Switzerland, 1970.
Energy and Regional Economic Development in Western Europe, International Geographical Union, Budapest, 1970.

'North Sea Oil and Gas: Perspectives, Problems and Policies', *Bergen Private Bank Review*, No. 2, 1971.

'Europe and the International Oil and Gas Industry in the 1970s: challenges and Opportunities', *Petroleum Times*, February, 1972.

'Natural Gas in the European Energy Economy: Emerging Prospects for 1975', *Petroleum Times*, October 1972.

'Europe's Oil', *NatWest Bank Review*, pp. , 6–21, August, 1972.

'Natural Gas as a European Energy Source', *Petroleum Times*, Vol. 70, November, 1972.

'Can the Oil Producing Countries hold Europe to Ransom', *New Europe*, 1972.

'Europe and the International Oil and Gas Industries in the 1970s', *Petroleum Times*, Vol. 76, no. 1929 and no. 30, 1972.

'On from 1975: Towards another New Geography of Europe's Energy Supply', *Institute of Fuel*, London, 1973.

'Norway, Europe and the International Oil System: Standing Options for a New High Cost Oil Producer', *Bedrifts økonomenon*, Bergen, 1973.

'Indigenous Oil and Gas Developments and Western Europe's Energy Policy Options', *Energy Policy*, Vol. 1, No. 1, June, 1973.

'Het Nederlandse Aardgastekort: Onbeantwoorde Vragen en een Alternatieve Hypothese', *Economisch Statistische Berichten*, Rotterdam, 1973.

'Oil: Strategic Importance on Future Supplies', *Royal United Services Institute*, March, 1973.

'The Future of Oil: a Rejoinder', *The Geographical Journal*, Vol. 139, 1973.

'The Exploitation of Siberia's Energy Resource Potential: in Competition with Other Frontier Resource Regions', *NATO Economic Committee Round Table*, Brussels, 1974.

'Energy Alternatives; Planning Implications', *Town and Country Planning Journal*, 43, no. 1, 1975.

'Settlements and Energy', *Planning and Administration*, No. 1, 1975.

'E.P.O.C. and the Powerhouse of Europe', *Profile*, 3, 1975.

'The Friendly Neighbourhood Generator', *The Architect's Journal*, 161, no. 14, 1975.

'The Energy Outlook for the Western World: International and National Responsibilities', *Foreign Affairs*, no. 5, Tokyo, 1975.

'Small Power Stations or the National Grid', *Geographical Magazine*, 42, no. 9, 1975.

'The World of Oil Power in 1975', *The World Today*, 31, no. 7, Chatham House, London, 1975.
New Economic Map of Europe, *Geographical Magazine*, 47, no. 12, 1975.
The West European Energy Economy: Challenges and Opportunities, Athlone Press, London, 1975.
'North Sea Oil Production by 1990', Proceedings of the Second Scandinavian and the North Sea Conference, Oslo, *Financial Times*, 1975.
'The Oil Crisis', *New Society*, October, 1975.
'De Toekomstige Energievoorziening van de Westerse Landen', *Economie in Limburg*, 1975.
'Britain's Oil and the North's Future; a European View', Proceedings of the Energy North Conference, Newcastle upon Tyne, *Financial Times*, 1975.
'A Fundamentally Changed Outlook for Oil in Western Europe: the Implications for Associated Industrial and Associated Facilities', *Fairplay International Shipping Weekly*, 257, no. 4819, 1975.

'Western Europe's energy economy: the case for self-sufficiency, 1980–2000', *Bedrijfskundige Signalementen*, H.E. Stenfert, Leiden, 1976.
'Toekomstige Energievoorziening van de Westerse Landen', *Noodzaak*, 25, no. 5, 1976.
Europe and the Cost of Energy: Nuclear Power or Oil and Gas, *Energy Policy*, 4, no. 2, 1976.
'North Sea Activity and Industrial Energy Demand', *Proceedings of the Financial Times Conference, The North Sea in 1976*, Oslo, 1976.
'Oil and Gas from the North Sea: The Key Elements in Western Europe's Energy Supplies 1980–2000', *Proceedings of the International Natural Gas Congress*, Copenhagen, 1976.

'The Potential for Natural Gas from the North Sea in Relation to Western Europe's Market for Gas by Mid-1980s', *Geoforum*, 8, 1977.
'Energy and planning', *Town and Country Planning*, 45, 1977.

'Energy Policy: there's more Oil than People Think', *Euromoney* (April), pp. 147–150, 1978.
'Fuel for 50 years', *The Consulting Engineer*, 42, pp. 19–22, 1978.
'An Energy Supply Crisis – how soon?' *The Journal of Canadian Petroleum Technology*, 17, pp. 10–14, 1978.

'Olieproduktie kan nog halve Eeuw met Drie pct. Groeien', *Bouw*, 12, pp. 40–42, 1978.
'An Application of Integer Programming to Economic Studies of Offshore Oil Development', *Recherches Economiques de Louvain* (with K.E. Rosing) 44, pp. 53–69, 1978.

'World Energy in the 1980s: the Significance of non-OPEC Oil Supplies', *Scottish Journal of Political Economy*, 26, no. 3, pp. 215–231, 1979.
'Western Europe's Natural Gas Resource System', *Zeszytv Naukowe Uniwersytetie Jagiellonskiego* (Kraków), 48, no. 2, pp. 133–143, 1979.
'The Energy Economy of Western Europe: A Return to the Use of Indigenous Resources', *Geografisch Tijdschrift*, 13, no. 5, pp. 361–372, 1979.
'The future Supply of Indigenous Oil and Gas in Western Europe: with Special Reference to the North Sea', *Workshops on energy supply and demand*, International Energy Agency (O.E.C.D.), Paris) pp. 130–172, 1979.
'The World's Energy Needs and Resources', *Built Environment*, 5, no. 4, pp. 254–264, 1979.
'Energy: an alternative perspective', *Economenblad*, 1, no. 26, p. 3, 1979.
'Constraints on the Development of Western Europe Natural Gas Production Potential in the 1980s', *Oil-Gas international*, 5, no. 3, pp. 21–30, 1979.
'Exploration and Development of the United Kingdom Continental Shelf', *Institute of Energy Review*, 1979.

'Oil: an Overpriced Abundance', *Energy Policy*, 8, no. 2, 1980.
'Energie in de Jaren Tachtig. De Betekenis van het Olie aanbod uit niet-OPEC Landen', *Economisch Statistische Berichten*, 65, no. 3252, 1980.
'Energy Prospects in Latin America', *Bank of London and South America Review*, 14, no. 2, 1980.
'Missing Oil', *the Petroleum Economist*, 47, no. 1, 1980.
'The Great Oil Shortage Mystery', *Chelwood Review*, 7, pp. 18–23, 1980.

'The Energy Economy of Western Europe: a Return to the Use of Indigenous Resources', *Geography*, 61, part 1, January, pp. 1–14, 1981.
'Third World Oil and Gas; Underexplored and Underdeveloped', *Long Range Planning*, 14, February, pp. 10–14, 1981.

'Where there's Energy, there's Industry', *Geographical Magazine*, 53, no. 9, pp. 593–597, 1981.

'Energiecrisis, Ja of Nee?', *Tijdschrift van de Koninklijke Vereniging van Transport Ondernemingen*, 33, no. 14, pp. 446–447, 1981.

'Prospects for and Problems of the Development of Oil and Gas in Developing Countries', *Natural Resources Forum*, 5, no. 4, pp. 317–326, 1981.

'Lower Oil Prices: Dangers to the North Sea', *Lloyds Bank Review*, 142, October, pp. 26–38, 1981.

'Towards a Geographically Reshaped World Oil Industry', *The World Today*, 37, no. 12, pp. 447–453, 1981.

'Too exposed to Political Pressure: Oil and Gas in Western Europe', in *Times Higher Educational Supplement*, 517, pp. 13–14, 1982.

'An Alternative View of the Outlook for the International Oil Market', *Petroleum Economist*, 50, pp. 392–394, 1983.

'Beware of the Oil Shock in Reverse', *Euromoney*, pp. 261–262, 1983.

'Energy Policy 1973–83: Retrospect and Prospect', *Energy Policy* 8, pp. 99–100, 1983.

'The Future Supply and Price of Oil: Proof of Evidence presented to the Sizewell B power station public inquiry', *Town and Country Planning Association*, London, 1983.

'De Ontwikkeling van de Wereldenergieprijzen', *Economisch Statistische Berichten*, 64, pp. 384–385, 1983.

'The Future of Oil: A Response to the Review Article by H.V. Dunnington', *Energy Exploration and Exploitation*, 1, pp. 109–315, 1983.

'Hydrocarbons in Northern Europe: an Evaluation of the Situation and Outlook', *Oil and Enterprise*, 13, pp. 19–24, 1984.

'Outlook for the International Oil Market and Options for OPEC', *Energy Policy*, 12, pp. 5–12, 1984.

'The Changing Role of OPEC', *The Annual Review of the Commercial Bank of Kuwait*, pp. 24–29, 1984.

'The Oil Crisis: its Nature and its Implications for the Developing Countries', *Manuscript Reports of the International Development Research Center*, Ottawa, 2, pp. 23–46, 1984.

'The UK Oil Refining Industry: a Case of Neglect', *Oil and Gas Law and Taxation Review*, 2, pp. 185–188, 1984.

'The Western European Energy Market under Conditions of Constrained Demand and Increasing Competition', *Oil and Gas Law and Taxation Review*, 3, pp. 59–64, 1984.
'Intervention, Regulation and the Western European Natural Gas Industry', *House of Commons (UK) Energy Committee*, Session 1983–1984, pp. 40–44, 1984.

'Back to cheap oil', *Lloyds Bank Review*, 156, pp. 1–15, 1985.
'Energy Resources: the Next Fifty Years', *Geographical Magazine*, 57, pp. 231–235, 1985.
'OPEC, Oil Prices and the West', *The World Today*, 41, pp. 82–84, 1985.
'Energy and Regional Development: a European Perspective', *Built Environment*, 11, pp. 9–22, 1985.
'De OPEC, de Olieprijzen en de Westerse Economieën op Lange Termijn', *Economisch Statistische Berichten*, 3495, p. 198, 1985.
'The Western European Energy Market under Conditions of Constrained Demand and Tripartite Competition', *International Energy Policy, 1985*, BIEE, Bedford, pp. 155–160, 1985.

'De OPEC en de Industrielanden: Confrontatie of Coöperatie?', *Economisch Statistische Berichten*, 3568, pp. 799–801, 1986.
'Falling Oil Prices: a Commentary', *Zeitschrift für Energiewirtschaft*, 10, pp. 68–70, 1986.
'Nordsø Olie og Naturgas of den Vesteuropaeiske Energiøkonomi', *Økonomisk Perspectiv*, 8, pp. 3–7, 1986.
'OPEC and the West, Longer-Term Needs and Perspectives', *Geopolitics of Energy*, 8, pp. 7–10, 1986.
'The Political Costs of The Long-Run Supply Price of Oil', *Financial Times Energy Economist*, 58, pp. 2–4, 1986.

'Aardgas en de Nederlandse Sameleving', *De Gids*, 150 pp. 121–128, 1987.
'The Prospects of Oil Prices and the Energy Market', *Lloyds Bank Review*, 165, pp. 1–14, 1987.
'Gorbachev's New Economic Strategy: The Role of Gas Exports to Western Europe', *The World Today*, 43, pp. 123–125, 1987.
'Gas Market Developments in Western Europe', *MIES Energy Newsletter*, 8, pp. 10–23, 1987.

'Pakistan: Needs Conservation, Iranian Gas and ... Nuclear?', *Energy Economist*, no. 77, pp. 10–13, 1988.

'Der Europüsche Gasmarkt: Gegenwärtige Situation und Alternative Zukunftsaussichten', *Zeitschrift fur Energiewirtschaft*, 12, no. 2, pp. 110–118, 1988.

'Dutch Gas Policy Changes Essential and Inevitable', *Norsk Olje Revy*, 14, no. 7/8, pp. 4–5, 1988.

'De Westeuropese Gasmarkt', *Economisch Statistische Berichten*, 73, no. 3672, pp. 822–828, 1988.

'Gas Markets in Western Europe', *Energy Exploration and Exploitation*, Vol. 6, Nos 4/5, 1988.

'The West European Gas Market: the Current Position and Alternative Prospects', *Energy Policy*, 16, no. 5, 1988.

'European Gas 'Club' lacks Entrepreneurial Approach', *Gas World International*, October, 1989.

'Restructuring the Dutch Electricity Sector', *Energy Economist*, February, 1989.

'Energy and the Environment', *Ditchley Foundation Report*, Oxford, 1991.

'Spotlight on Middle East Dims', *Oxford Economic Forum*, No. 7, November, 1991.

'Oferta di Energia: Favole e False Teorie', *Energia*, Vol. 12, No. 4, pp. 4–17, 1991.

'Global and Regional Energy Supplies: Recent Fictions and Fallacies Revisited', *Energy Policy*, Vol. 20, No. 4, pp. 284–296, 1992.

'Prospects for Non-OPEC Oil Supply', *Energy Policy*, Vol. 20, pp. 931–411, 1992

'Prospects for Natural Gas In Western Europe', *The Energy Journal*, Vol. 13, No. 3, pp. 41–59, 1992.

'World Energy Resources and Global Sustainable Development', *OPEC Review*, Winter, pp. 369–381, 1992.

'Indigenous Hydrocarbons and the Western European Energy Economy', *The Mining Engineer*, Vol. 152, No. 374, pp. 143–150, 1992.

'Do Countries need an Energy Policy?' *Oxford Economic Forum*, January, 1993.

'Energy Markets: Future Supply Potentials', *International Energy Agency*, Paris, June 1993.

'International Developments in the Energy Sector', *Benelux Dossier-Energie*, pp. 12–19, 1994/1.
'Global Energy Markets: Future Supply Potentials', *Energy Exploration and Exploitation*, Vol. 2, No. 1, pp. 59–72, 1994.
'International Oil: a Return to American Hegemony', *The World Today*, Vol. 50, No. 11, pp. 208–210, 1994.
'U.S Companies to take the High Ground', *Petroleum Economist 60th Anniversary Special Issue*, July, pp. 40–41, 1994.
'The Prospects for North Sea Oil and Gas: an Overview', *Energy Week*, London, 1994.
'United States-Saudi Arabia Compact: a European Perspective', *The Geopolitics of Energy*, Vol. 16, No. 12, pp. 5–7, 1994.

'Netwerken voor Energy', *Europa Periodiek*, Vol. 12, No. 2, pp. 32–34, 1995.
'West Europe's Indigenous Gas Prospects, UK', *C.E.E.D. Bulletin*, No. 47, pp. 8–11, 1995.
'Europe's Energy; Panic Over; Opportunity Knocks', *The World Today*, Vol. 51, No. 10, pp. 191–3, 1995.
'Petrolio: Inevitabile il Dominio del Medio Oriente', *Energia*, Vol. xvi, No. 4, pp. 38–45, 1995.

'Britain's North Sea Oil and Gas Production; a Critical Review'; *Energy Exploration and Exploitation*, Vol. 14, No. 1, pp. 3–11, 1996.
'The Geopolitics of Western Europe's Energy: from Problems to Opportunity', *Geopolitics of Energy*, Vol. 17, No. 10, pp. 1–5, 1996.
'The Cost of Longer Run Gas Supply to Europe', *Energy Studies Review*, Vol. 7, No. 2, pp. 94–108, 1996.
'International Oil Market Prospects for the longer Term – Middle East Domination or Regionalisation', *Erdöl Erdgas Kohle*, Vol. 112, No. 4, pp. 138–149, 1996.
'Europe's Energy Prospects: Supplies, not Structure, the Key'. *PetroChem*, Vol. 8, Issue 8/9, pp. 28–9, 1996.

'The Exploitation of Off-shore Mineral Resources', *GeoJournal*, Vol. 42, No. 1, pp. 17–26, 1997.

'Europe's Gas Consumption and Imports to Increase with Adequate Low-cost Supplies', *Energy Exploration and Exploitation*, Vol. 15, No. 1, pp. 35–54, 1997.

'Oil Shock – a Rejoinder', *Energy World*, No. 247, March, pp. 11–14, 1997.

'Higher Oil Prices: the Result of a Political Agenda', *PetroChem*, Vol. 10, No. 1, pp. 22–3, 1997.

'The Global Oil Industry: Middle East Domination or Regionalisation', *Arab Oil and Gas*, Vol. xxvi, No. 607, January, pp. 42–8: and in *Revue de l'Energie*, No. 484, January, pp. 37–43, 1997.

'The Location of Oil Production – Middle East Domination or Regionalization', *Regional Studies*, Vol. 31, pp. 309–320, 1997.

'Oil Reserves: much more than meets the eye', *Petroleum Economist*, Vol. 64, No. 11, November, pp. 29–31, 1997.

'Restructuring the World's Oil Markets: the Options', *Pipeline*, No. 16, September, pp. 21–22, 1997.

'Mehr Öl als Nötig', *Erdöl Informationsdienst*, 50 Jahre, pp. 20–28, 1997.

'*Fossil Fuel Resources in the 21st Century*', a Report for the Planning and Economic Studies Section of the International Atomic Energy Agency, Vienna, June 1998.

'Energy, Resources and Choices: Retrospect and Prospect', *Energy Exploration and Exploitation*, Vol. 16, No. 2/3, pp. 117–124, 1998.

'Changing the Face of the International Oil Market', *Petroleum Review*, Vol. 52, No. 2, pp. 2–4, 1998.

'The Geopolitics of European Gas', *Geopolitics of Energy*, Vol. 20, No. 1, pp. 2–5, 1998.

'The New Great Game in International Oil Markets', *Geopolitics of Energy*, Vol. 20, No. 10, October, pp. 2–5, 1998.

'Oil and Gas Reserves: Retrospect and Prospect', *Geopolitics of Energy*, Vol. 20, No. 12, December, pp. 13–20, 1998.

'Natural Gas and Renewable Oil: the Likely Recipe for 21st Century Energy Growth', *FT Energy Economist*, No. 209, March, pp. 16–22, 1999

'Plentiful Energy Supplies for the 21st Century', *Petroleum Review*, Vol. 53, No. 625, pp. 35–37, 1999.

'Le Fonti non-rinnovabile all'alba del terzo Millenio', *Energia*, Vol. 20, No. 2, June, pp. 20–25, 1999.

'Dynamics of Energy Technologies and Global Change' (a rejoinder to Grübler et al, 1999)', *Energy Policy*, Vol. 27, No. 12, October, pp. 737–742, 1999.

'A Response to Müller, B. and Barsch, U., The Kyoto Protocol and Its Impact on Global Oil Markets', *Oxford Energy Forum*, No. 41, May, p. 18, 2000.

'The Global Energy Market in the Long-term: the Continuing Dominance of Affordable Non-renewable Resources', *Energy Exploration and Exploitation*, Vol. 18, No. 5, pp. 599–613, 2000.

'Long-term future oil supplies from non-conventional sources', *Pipeline*, No. 29, February, pp. 12–13, 2001.

'Prospects for Energy in the 21st Century', *Energy Policy*, Vol. 29, pp. 12–13, 2001.

'L'offerta potentiale di energia nel Lungo periode', *Energia*, Vol. 22, No. 3, pp. 2–9, 2001.

'The UK Gas Industry in the Long Term: and the Liberalisation of European Markets', *The House of Commons Trade and Industry Committee*, 2nd Report, Vol. 1, January 2002.

'Commentary on the PIU Energy Report', *Oxford Economic Forum*, Issue 58, pp. 18–19, 2004.

'International Oil's Dysfunctional System', *Geopolitics of Energy*, Vol. 26, No. 10, pp. 2–4, 2004.

'Das Märchen van der Knappheit', *Schweiger Monatslufte*, Vol. 84, No. 7/8, pp. 13–15, 2004.

'Re-vitalising the UK's Offshore Oil and Gas Industry', *Geopolitics of Energy*, Vol. 26, No. 9, pp. 2–4, 2004.

'Odell takes his leave', *Geopolitics of Energy*, Vol. 27, No. 12, pp. 11–12, 2005.

'High oil prices: a Self-inflicted Wound on the Global Economy', *Geopolitics of Energy*, Vol. 27, No. 11, pp. 6–7, 2005.

'Carbon Fuels to Dominate World Energy Demands', *Geopolitics of Energy*, Vol. 26, Nos. 3/4, pp. 2–8, 2006.

'The Long-term Evolution of the Global Oil Industry', *Geopolitics of Energy*, Vol. 26, No. 9, pp. 2–3, 2006.
'Public/Private Partnerships on the UKCS', *Oxford Economic Forum*, Issue 67, November, pp. 8–10, 2006.
'Why Carbon Fuels will Dominate the 21st Century's Global Energy Economy', *Energy Focus*, Vol. 23, No. 3 pp. 1–9, 2006.
'Porque los Combustibles de Carbon Doninairáu la Economia Energetica en al Sigle xxi', *La Vanguardia*, No. 18, Enero/Marzo, pp. 104–9, 2006.
'Gulf Oil in a Global Context: Strategies For and Challenges to Demand Security', in *Gulf Oil and Gas: Ensuring Economic Security*, E.C.S.S.R., Abu Dhabi, pp. 287–310, 2006.
'An Insight into the Future Direction of the Global Energy Industry', *OPEC Bulletin*, Issues 9/10, pp. 70–76, 2006.

'Conventional Wisdom Challenged', *Energy and Environment*, Vol. 18, No. 2, pp. 289–291, 2007.
'A New World Energy Order is Coming', *European Energy Review*, Vol. 1, No. 1, p. 28/9, 2007.

'A Self-Interested Forecast of Oil's Decline', *Energy and Environment*, Vol. 19, No. 5, pp. 777–778, 2008.

'The Long-term Future for Energy Resources Exploitation', *Energy Politics*, No. 18, pp. 78–105, 2009.
'A Long-term Production Scenario; Supply Price Issues; Abiogenic Oil and Gas; and the Peak Oil Debate', *Global Energy Assessment Report, KM7*, 2009.

'Our Long-term Energy Future: a Reality Check', *European Energy Review*, January, 2010.
'Why we do not have to worry about "peak-oil"', *European Energy Review*, February, 2010.
'The British Government must take Control of Oil and Gas', *European Energy Review*, April, 2010.
'Uno Scenario Realistico sul Futuro Energetico', *Revista Trimestrale Sui Problemi Dell'Energia*, Giugno 2010, Anno xxxi/N.2, pp. 2–13.

APPENDIX 2

Professor Odell's Appointments, Affiliations and Awards from 1954 to date

A. Appointments

1954–1957	Education officer in the Royal Air Force
1958–1961	Economist with Shell International Petroleum Co. Ltd., London
1961–1965	Lecturer in Economic Geography, London School of Economics, London
1965–1968	Senior Lecturer in Economic Geography, London School of Economics, London
1968–1981	Professor of Economic Geography and Director of the Economic Geography Institute, Netherland School of Economics, Rotterdam (from 1973 renamed Erasmus University)
1977–1979	Special adviser to the Secretary of State for Energy, UK
1982–1991	Professor of International Energy Studies and Director of the Centre for International Energy Studies, Erasmus University, Rotterdam
1983–1990	Visiting Professor, College of Europe, Brugge
1983–2000	Visiting Professor, London School of Economics, London
1992 to date	Professor Emeritus, Erasmus University, Rotterdam
1996–2000	Visiting Scholar, Department of Geography, University of Cambridge
1997–2004	Visiting Professor, Department of Geography, University of Plymouth

B. Other significant academic/professional affiliations

Member, Royal Institute for International Affairs (London) since 1963
Fellow, Institute of Petroleum (London) since 1973 (re-named Energy Institute from 2003.
Lord Stamp Annual Memorial Lecture in Economics, University of London, 1976

Canadian Council Fellow, University of Toronto, 1978
Annual Lecture, Scottish Economic Society, 1979
Visiting Scholar, Faculty of Science, University of Southampton, 1980/81
Wilkinson Lecture, University of Reading, 1982
Scholar-in-Residence, Rockefeller Study Centre, Bellagio, October/November 1984
Academic Visitor, Fridtjof Nansen Institute, Oslo, September 1987
Member, Editorial Board, *Journal of Energy Policy*, 1976 to 1991
Member, Editorial Board, *International Journal of Energy Research*, 1979 to 1991
European Editor and Member of the Editorial Board, *The Energy Journal*, 1986 to 1990
Member, Scientific Committee, *Energia* (Italy), 1991 to date
Chairman, Benelux Association of Energy Economists, 1983 to 1988
Director, London School of Economics/Erasmus University Joint Summer School on the International Oil and Gas Industries, May/June 1987
Killam Visiting Fellow, Dept of Economics, University of Calgary, Canada, Fall Semester 1989
Member, Council of the International Association for Energy Economics, 1990/1
Member of the Editorial Board, European Energy Review, 2009 to date

C. Invitations to lectures/seminars at universities and other academic institutions around the world (generally in each section by date order of visits)

i. The Netherlands

University of Amsterdam
University of Utrecht
Europa Institute, Amsterdam
Vrije University, Amsterdam
Technological University, Delft
Bouwcentrum, Rotterdam
ISS Den Haag
University of Groningen
University of Leiden
Technological University, Eindhoven
University of Nijmegen

Economisch Hogeschol, Limburg
Institute of Chemical Engineers, Den Haag
Clingendael Institute, Den Haag
Society of Petroleum Engineers, Den Haag
Den Helder Petro-Institute
University of Limburg
Shell Training Centre, Den Haag
University of Leiden
University of Tilburg

ii. The Rest of Europe

London School of Economics, England
University of Leuven, Belgium
Vrije Universiteit, Brussels, Belgium
NATO Round Table, Belgium
EEC Energy Directorate, Brussels, Belgium
International Energy Agency, Paris, France
Atlantic Institute, Paris, France
UN Economic Commission for Europe, Barcelona, Spain and Evian, France
University of Grenoble, France
University of Durham, England
Leeds Polytechnic, England
University College, London, England
Birkbeck College, London, England
Trinity College, Dublin, Ireland
University of Aberdeen, Scotland
University of Edinburgh, Scotland
Heriot-Watt University, Edinburgh, Scotland
University of Glasgow, Scotland
University of Newcastle, England
University of Plymouth, England
University of Liverpool, England
University of Hull, England
Energy Research Centre, University of Cambridge, England
University of Warwick, Coventry, England
University of Leicester, England

University of Oxford, England
Chatham House, London, England
Imperial College of Science and Technology, London, England
Royal Military Staff College, Camberley, England
N.C.B. Staff College, Chalfont St. Giles, England
Royal United Services Institute, London, England
University of Copenhagen, Denmark
Danish Technological University, København, Denmark
Royal Institute of Technology, Stockholm, Sweden
Lund University, Sweden
University of Oslo, Norway
University of Trondhjem, Norway
Norwegian School of Economics, Bergen, Norway
Norwegian School of Management, Sandvik
University of Budapest, Hungary
University of Bucharest, Romania
University of Krakow, Poland
International Institute for Management Education, Milan, Italy
Petroleum Exploration Society, London, England
International Institute for Applied Systems Analysis, Laxenburg, Austria
Royal Scottish Geographical Society, Glasgow, England
Bristol Polytechnic, England
Institute of Petroleum, London, England (subsequently the Energy Institute)
Centre for European Policy Studies, Brussels, Belgium
University of Antwerp, Belgium
University of Sheffield, England
Frederick Alexander University, Nürnburg, West Germany
University College, Cork, Ireland
University Association for Contemporary European Studies, London, England
University of Nottingham, England
Institut Européen d'Administration des Affaires, Fontainebleau, France
South Bank Polytechnic, London, England
University of Reading, England
University of Essex, England
British Institute of Energy Economists, London
University of Göteborg, Sweden
University College Dublin, Ireland

Gesellschaft für Energiewissenschaft und Energiepolitik, Bonn, West Germany
UN International Atomic Energy Agency, Vienna, Austria
University of Vienna, Austria
Institut Universitaire des Hautes Etudes Internationales, Geneve, Switzerland
National Energy Administration, Stockholm, Sweden
University of Surrey Energy Economics Centre, England
Swedish Society for Energy Economics, Stockholm, Sweden
Stockholm School of Business, Sweden
SNS Stockholm, Sweden
University of Helsinki, Finland
The Ditchley Foundation, Oxford, England
Norsk Forening for Energiøkonomer, Stavanger, Norway
Chr. Michielsen Institutt, Bergen, Norway
UK Society of Business Economists, London
Fridtjof Nansen Institutt, Oslo, Norway
University of Durham Centre for Middle East Studies, England
School of Oriental and African Studies, University of London, England
European Association of European Geologists, København, Denmark
Academy of Sciences, Energy Institute, Kaunus, Lithuania
University of Tallinn, Estonia
Rockefeller Study Centre, Bellagio, Italy

iii. North America

University of Toronto, Toronto, Canada
Institute for Environmental Studies, Toronto, Canada
Scarborough College, Toronto, Canada
Erindale College, Toronto, Canada
University of Waterloo, Ontario, Canada
University of Calgary, Alberta, Canada
University of Alberta, Edmonton, Canada
Alberta Society of Economists, Calgary, Canada
Simon Fraser University, Vancouver, Canada
United Nations Energy and Natural Resources Centre, New York, USA
Resources of the Future, Washington, USA
Ministry of Mines, Ottawa, Canada

Calgary Society of Petroleum Geologists, Canada
International Development Research Centre, Ottawa, Canada
Stanford University, California, USA
Fletcher School of Law and Diplomacy, Medford, Mass., USA
Harvard University Energy and Environmental Centre, Cambridge, Mass., USA
City University, New York, USA
Centre of Advanced International Studies, Johns Hopkins University, Washington
University of Halifax, Canada
University of San Juan, Puerto Rico, USA

iv. Latin America

University of the West Indies, Trinidad and Jamaica
University of Caracas, Venezuela
University of Colombia, Bogota
University of Lima, Peru
University of Santiago, Chile
Da Fundaçao Getulio Vargas, Rio de Janeiro, Brazil
University of Vitoria, Brazil
University of Panama, Panama
University of San Jośe, Costa Rica
Colegio de Mexico, Mexico City
University of Mexico
University of the Nederland Antilles, Curaçao
Centro de Estudios do la OPEP, Caracas, Venezuela
Federal University of Rio de Janeiro, Brazil

v. Australasia

University of New South Wales, Sydney
University of Melbourne, Melbourne, Australia
Australian National University, Canberra, Australia
University of Wellington, New Zealand
University of Auckland, New Zealand
University of Palmerston, New Zealand
Australian Petroleum Institute, Melbourne, Australia
New Zealand Institute of Petroleum

vi. Asia

Indian Technological Institute, Kharagpur, India
University of Patna, India
University of New Delhi, India
Tata Energy Research Institute, New Delhi, India
Indian Association of Energy Economists, New Delhi, India
Pakistan Institute of Hydrocarbons, Islamabad, Pakistan
Centre for South East Asian Studies, Singapore
Xiamen University, China
Iranian Petroleum Institute, Teheran

D. Awards

i. The W.A. Cadbury Prize for 1st Class BA honours degree in the 1951 University of Birmingham examinations and a University postgraduate scholarship for 3 years' study for a Doctorate.
ii. An International Rotary Foundation Fellowship at the Fletcher School of Law and Diplomacy. Tufte University, Boston, 1957/8.
iii. The International Association for Energy Economics 1991 Award for Outstanding Contributions to the Profession of Energy Economics and to its Literature, May 1992.
iv. The 1994 award of the Royal Scottish Geographical Society's Centennial Medal for Studies on North Sea Oil and Gas.
v. The 2006 OPEC Biennial Award in recognition of 'five decades of academic and research excellence in petroleum economics: so making an outstanding contribution to the petroleum industry and oil related issues.'

Index

11+ Scholarship Examination 17, 18
1944 Education Act 18

Aberdeen, University of 168
Adelman, Professor M.A. 135
AGI Petroli 117
Air Products Inc. 118, 135
Aldeburgh, Suffolk Coast 115
American University 47
American War of Independence 67
An Economic Geography of Oil 77
Andorran Pyrenees 106
Anglesey 115
Anglo/Dutch Society 107
Appalachian Mountains 67
Arab/Israeli conflict 134
Argentina 72
Aruba 99
Ashford, Middlesex 134
Assistant District Commissioner (ADC) 46
Atlee, Clement 35
Australia 111, 125, 132, 147, 163, 165–178
  Ballarat 166
  Brisbane 166
  Darwin 167
  Melbourne 165–168
  Sydney 166–167
  Tasmania 166, 178, 180
Austria 90, 175
Aylesbury 54

Bahrain 41–42
Balogh, Lord Tommy 101
Bardon Hill railway station 5–6, 11
Battle of Hastings 1

Baxendale, Peter (of Shell) 94
BBC (see British Broadcasting Corporation)
BBC World Service 75
Belgium 88–90, 111, 118, 157, 175
Benn, Rt. Hon. Tony 50, 98–104, 179
Bexxon, Mr (of BP) 94
Bharat Airways 41, 47
Birmingham 2, 19, 25–41
Birmingham, University of xiii, 22–59
Bishopsgate Institute, London 162
Black Country 30, 39
Blackpool 12
Borneo, Sultanate of 167
Bosworth Constituency 20, 35
Bournemouth 12
Brazil 72
  Rio de Janeiro 111
Bridge Road Primary School 7–16
British Association of Energy Economics 128
British Broadcasting Corporation (BBC) 94, 149
British Empire 75
British Library 34
British National Oil Corporation (BNOC) 100–104
British Oil Policy: a Radical Alternative 102, 109
British Petroleum (BP) 80, 94, 104, 128, 175
Broomhall, Mr (head of physics at Grammar School) 20
Browne, Lord John (former head of BP) 128
Burke, Terry 36
Butcher's boy in Coalville 22

INDEX

Burton-on-Trent 5, 12, 25
Buxton, Derbyshire 12

Calgary, University of 110
Callaghan, James 100
Cambridge 2, 130
Cambridge, University of 71, 125
Canada 45, 70, 98, 112, 132
   Lake Huron 66
   Lake Superior 66
   Montreal 66
   Niagara Falls 66
   Ottawa 66
   Quebec 66
   Sault Ste Marie 66
   Sudbury 66
Caracas, University of 111
Carbon dioxide emissions 149–158
Central Electricity Generating Board 115
Centre for Energy Research 104
Centre for International Energy Studies 120, 134, 173
Chandler, Sir Geoffrey 71, 133
Chiang Kai-shek 73
Charles River 64
Chatham House (see Royal Institute for International Affairs)
Chevron Oil Corporation 175
Children's Medical Centre, Boston 62–66
Chile 72, 157
Chiltern Hills 54
China 73, 111, 132, 180
Christian Science Monitor (newspaper) 65
City of London Galleries 160
Climate change (see global warming)
Coalville, Leicestershire 1–70, 80, 83
   Bridge Road School 7, 11, 16
   Christ Church Primary School 11
   Co-operative Society 16
   Grammar School 18–36, 68
   Rotary Club 62
   Technical College 16
   Town F.C. 21
   Urban District Council 1, 13
College of Europe, Brugge 110
Collyns, Napier 133
Colston's School, Bristol 96
Columbia, University of (USA) 99
Commonwealth Club, Rotterdam 107, 128
Conservative Party, UK 81, 100, 103, 133
Constitution Hill, Ipswich 100, 148–149
Continuing Long-Term Hydrocarbons' Dominance of World Energy Markets: an Economic and Societal Necessity 109
Controller of Her Majesty's Stationery Office 102
County Durham 30
Cromer 12
Controversy 89, 105, 117, 119, 127, 151
Cub scouts (see Scouting)
Cunard Shipping Company 62–67
Curaçao, University College of 111
Cyprus 41, 49, 54
Czechoslovakia (now Czech Republic) 38
   Prague 38

Daily Herald (newspaper) 35
Danube River 38
De Telegraaf (Dutch newspaper) 81
Den Haag, Netherlands 70, 96, 110–119, 170
   British School 96
   Clingendael 110
Derby 2, 12
Derbyshire 2, 7, 12, 30
Dijon, University of 55
Ditchley Park Centre, Foreign Office 111
Doris, Aunty 10, 19
Draining the World of Energy 109
Dresdner 131

Dubai 165–168
Dulwich Gallery 160
Dutch Ministry of Economic Affairs 120
Royal Dutch Geographical Society (KNGS) 88

East London Gallery 160
Economic Geography Institute (EGI), Rotterdam 92, 106, 108
Economist, The (journal)
Egham 70–71
Elizabeth II's coronation 41
Energie: Geen Probleem? 109
'*Energy*' (*chapter from The Social Science Encyclopedia*) 109
Energy Advice Ltd 117, 131
Energy Policies in the E.E.C. and their Impact on the Third World 109
Energy Policy (journal) 119
English Heritage 160
Erasmus University Centre for International Energy Studies (EURICES) 108–118, 134
Erasmus University, Rotterdam (see also Nederlandse Economisch Hogeschool) xiii, 91–119
Esso/Exxon 80–114, 175
Estonia 111
  Tallinn 111
Ethel, Aunty 96
European Atomic Energy Community 141
European Coal and Steel Community 141
European Commission 118, 128, 155
European Institute 90
European Parliament 130
EURICES (see Erasmus University Centre for International Energy Studies)

Fabian Society 78
Faulkner, Kenneth 64

Festival Hall 159
First World War 3
Fletcher School of International Law and Diplomacy, Boston 62–73
Foreign Office 68, 111
Forest Road Allotments Society 3
France 30, 90, 127
  Chamonix, French Alps 48
  Normandy 1–2
  Paris 41–48, 99, 118
Friends of Kew Gardens 162

Garston Labour Exchange 67
Gas Council 80–82
General Motors, Detroit 67
Geographical Studies (journal) 35
Geography of world oil and gas supplies 137
Germany 54, 90–91, 111
  Berlin 37–40
  Köln/Cologne 111, 164
  München/Munich 111
  Nuremberg 111
  Potsdam 169
Gibraltar 18
Glenny, Stan 33
Global and Regional Energy Supplies: Recent Fictions and Fallacies (lecture) 119
Global warming 30, 66, 136–159, 176–177
Gore, Al 177
Grant, General 67
Greece 47
  Athens 47
  Corinth Canal 47
  Piraeus 47
Groningen gasfield 90, 120, 133, 143
  Price 134
  Production 134
Guatemala 76
Guild of Undergraduates' Union, Birmingham University 28–29, 37
Gulf Oil 104

Gulf Oil in a Global Context: Strategies for and Challenges to Demand Security 164

Hamilton, Dr (family doctor) 7, 17, 59
Hapsburg Empire 172
Harley Foundation 24
Harley Trust Fund 18
Harvard University 62, 111
Harwich, East Anglia 83, 107, 183
Hathern, Leicestershire 4
HAVO Dutch School 96
Hayward Gallery 161
Higher School Certificate 20–29
Hong Kong 132, 167
House of Commons 102, 149
House of Lords 98, 101
Houston, University of 111
Huishoudelijke School, Rotterdam 84
Hull, University of 94, 106
Humboldt University 39
Hungary 36–39
    Budapest 37–39
    Lake Balaton 39
    Miskolc 39
Hydrocarbons 77–78, 103, 137–144, 174–179

IATA, Geneva 92
India 41–47, 84, 88, 111–112, 161, 168, 177, 180
    Bombay 41–47
    Deccan 45
    Hyderabad 46
    Madras 46
    Mysore 41, 46
    New Delhi 88
    Poona 45
    Western Ghats 45
Indian Railways 45
Inland Revenue 107, 121
Institute of Petroleum/Energy Institute 72, 128, 149
International Association of Energy Economists (IAEE) 126–127

International Court of Justice 113
International Energy Agency, Paris 118, 155
International Energy Issues: the Next 10 Years 109
International Geographical Union 88, 98
International Institute for Applied Systems Analysis (IIASA), Vienna 112
International Union of Students (IUS) 25, 38–40
Institutional Constraints on the Development of the Western European Gas Market 109
IPCC 158
IPE 174
Ipswich 2, 64, 97–107, 121–130, 146–178
Ipswich and Suffolk Club 164
Ipswich School 97, 106
Ipswich Society 130, 146, 164
Iran 98, 164
Iranian Oil Company (NIOC) 113, 169
Iranian Revolution 95, 100, 107–108
Ireland 63, 111
    Cork 63
    Dublin 111
Irish Peat Board 131
Isle of Man 51–53, 83
    Jurby RAF Base 51–53
    Ramsey 52
    Sulby Glen 52
    Villa Marina, Douglas 52
Islington Business Centre 161
Israel 164, 169
Italy 47, 90, 111
    Bellagio 111
    Brindisi 47
    Corinth Canal 47
    Florence 48
    Naples 47
    Pompei 48

Rome 47
Turin 48
Vesuvius 49
Ivory and Sime, Edinburgh 93, 118, 211

Jamaica 76
John Bull (magazine) 76
Journal of Common Market Studies 89
Journal of Contemporary History 89

Kearton, Lord 104
Kempston, Bedfordshire 2
Kinvig, Professor 33–34, 50
KLM 92–94, 114
Kuwaiti National Oil Company 104
Kyoto Treaty 153–156

Labour Party, UK 78, 82, 90, 98, 100–104, 129–130, 159, 179
Lager, Miss (primary school headmistress) 17
Lansdowne Club, London 125
Latin America 72, 82, 87–92, 111, 137, 176, 180
Left Book Club 35
Leicester 2–13, 27, 34–35
Leicestershire Education Authority 30
Lensbury Club, Teddington 74
Liberal Party, UK 129–130
Liberal Democratic Party, UK 130, 159
Lithuania 111
   Kaunas 111
Liverpool 51–71, 86, 115
London Institute 72, 77
London Midland and Scottish Railway 5
London School of Economics (LSE) 87, 110, 125–135, 173
London, City of 71, 105, 148, 160
London, University of 35, 55, 62, 74–82, 95
Long Eaton, Derbyshire 2
Loss, Joe 52

Luxembourg 90

Mabon, Dr 101
Manx Railway 51
Maritime Museum, Rotterdam 138
Marlborough School, Wiltshire 96
Marnix Gymnasium, Rotterdam 96
Marsh, Richard 81
Massachusetts Institute of Technology (MIT) 111
Mayor of London 148
McKintosh, Mr (father-in-law) 59, 62
Mexico 72, 76, 111–112
Midland Electricity Board 131
Midland Railway (see London Midland and Scottish Railway)
Middle East 41, 47, 89, 112, 115, 133–145
Milkman in Coalville 25, 33
Ministry of Fuel and Power 81–82, 133
Ministry of Power 78, 80
Mississippi River 67
Morecambe, Lancashire 12
Ms. Ammuna Lawan Ali
Mysore
   Maharajah of 42
   University of 41

NAAFI, Jurby 52
National Art Fund 160
National Coal Board 112
National Deposit Friendly Society 7
National Gallery 160
National Newspaper Library 34
National Oil Agency 78
National Service 24, 51–55
National Trust 160
National Union of Mineworkers 36
National Union of Railwaymen 11
National Union of Students 34–39
Natural gas
   Discoveries 72, 90
   Production 92, 100–102, 134, 145, 152, 159, 174, 179

INDEX

Pipelines 82, 90, 100, 145
Prices 78, 90, 134, 137, 143
Nederlandse Antillen Government 94, 99
Nederlandse Economisch Hogeschool/Netherland School of Economics (NEH) (see also Erasmus University) xiii, 81–173
Netherlands 70–120
  Amsterdam 90–92, 113–114
  Hoek van Holland 83, 97, 107, 121
  Rijswijk 70
  Rotterdam xiii, 70–173
  Vught 90
New Society (journal) 78, 81, 92
New York Times (newspaper) 65
New York, University of 111
New Zealand 92, 111
  Auckland 92
Newcastle-upon-Tyne 33
Nieuwe Rotterdamse Courant (NRC) (newspaper) 94
North Sea Oil and Gas 44, 73, 78–144
North Sea Oil and Gas Committee 90
Northampton 2
Northern Universities School Matriculation Certificate Board 20
Norway 32–33, 92, 94, 103, 111–113, 175–176
  Bergen 33, 111
  Bodô 111
  Oslo 33, 111, 118
  Skien 32–33
  Stavanger 111
  Telemark 33
  Trondheim 111
Norwich 2
Nottingham 2, 4
Nottinghamshire 2–7, 132
Nuclear power 81, 98, 115, 116, 129, 135, 141–143, 154, 176
NYMEX 174

Odell, Bedfordshire (village) 1–2
Odell (family) 1–12
  Deborah Grace (daughter) 79–83, 97, 121–122, 168, 172, 178
  Frank James (father) 3–22, 30–34, 48
  Frederick Charles (paternal grandfather) 2
  George (grandson) 168
  George (great-grandfather) 2
  Kasia (granddaughter) 165
  Kirsten (granddaughter) 168–169
  Lucas (grandson) 168
  Lucy (granddaughter) 163, 168
  Mark John (son) 79–84, 94–100, 121–124, 147, 163, 168
  Lucy, nee Clark (grandmother) 2
  Jean Mary, nee McKintosh (wife) xiv, 57–178
  Nigel Peter (son) 79–84, 96–97, 106–125, 147, 165–172, 178
  Patricia Mary (sister) 7–19, 33–34, 48, 55, 83
  Robin (granddaughter) 163, 168
  Susannah Mary (daughter) 79–84, 96–100, 121–124, 172–178
  Thomas (grandson) 165
  Timothy (cousin) 170
OECD 137, 155–158, 174–175
Oil
  Discoveries of 33, 72, 136, 143
  Prices 90–177
  Production 70–95, 112, 137, 157
  Refineries 70, 94–99, 115–117
  Transportation 70, 120, 152
Oil: the New Commanding Height 78
Oil and Gas Potential in Developing Countries: prospects for and problems of its development 109
Oil and Gas: Crises and Controversies 95, 132, 149, 173
Oil and Politics in Latin America 89
Oil and World Power 92, 95, 109, 111
ÖMV 175

Optimal Development of the North Sea's Oil Fields: A Study of Divergent Government and Company Interests and their Reconciliation 101
Organisation of Petroleum Exporting Countries (OPEC) xiv, 92, 117, 137, 145, 170, 180
Osnabruck, University of 97, 106
Our Long-term Energy Future: a Reality Check 176
'Oxbridge' University 21, 28, 73
Oxford 2, 80

Pachauri, Dr R.K. 177
Pakistan 111–112
Park Road, Coalville 1–13, 23, 49
Peak District, Derbyshire 30
Penrose, Professor Edith 89, 133
Peterborough 2
Petrobras 72
Petro-Canada 175
Petroleum 70, 170–172
PetroVision (journal) 169
Philips 113
Plymouth, University of 125
Poland 111
   Kraków 98, 111
   Warsaw 98, 111
Posner, Michael 80–81, 113
Post Office Worker's Union 104
Preston, Dr David 77
Princess Mary's Royal Air Force Nursing Service 58
Prospects for the West European Energy Markets 109
Public Record Office 34, 148
Puerto Rico 76

Queen Beatrix of the Netherlands 108
Queen Charlotte's Maternity Hospital, London 70
Queen Juliana of the Netherlands 81

RAF Ely Hospital, Cambridgeshire 58–59
RAF Grantham, Lincolnshire 52
RAF Halton, Buckinghamshire 54, 63
Randon (family)
   Albert (uncle) 4
   Bill (uncle) 4
   Elizabeth (great-grandmother) 4
   George (grandfather) 4
   George (great-grandfather) 4
   Grace Edna (mother) 1–21, 33–34, 48–50
   Margaret (cousin) 10
   Grandmother, nee Miss Fisher 4
   Reg (uncle) 4
Regent's Park 162
Renewable Energy 152–178
Reynolds's News (newspaper) 35
Rhine delta 89
River Soar 4
River Trent 4
Rockefeller Study Centre 111
Rosing, Dr Kenneth E. 94–95, 109
Rotary International Foundation Fellowship 62
Rothschild Family 54
Royal Academy Summer Exhibition 161
Royal Air Force (see also RAF) 18–19, 51–63
Royal Albert Hall 159
Royal Dutch/Shell Company (see Shell)
Royal Geographical Society/Institute of British Geographers 128
Royal Institute for International Affairs/Chatham House 75–77, 149
Royal Scottish Geographical Society 127
Royal Scottish Geographical Society Centennial Medal 173
Royal Society of Arts 128, 160
Runton Hill School, Norfolk 97

Rutledge, Dr Ian 179

School Certificate 20–29
Scotland 12, 100, 104, 111 165
   Edinburgh 93, 99, 104–105, 116, 127–128
   Glasgow 127–128
Scots Church, Rotterdam 91, 107
Scouting 17, 21, 39
Second World War 7, 12–22, 51, 59, 66 141–143, 170
Selly Oak, Birmingham 27
Senate House 74, 95
Shell
   Economic Division 73–74
   International 68–175
   International Junior Management Course 68–69
Silk, Miss (head of geography at Grammar School) 20
Singapore 54, 111
Sizewell nuclear power plant 116, 129
Smailes, Professor 35
Smith, Sir Paul of Beeston (second cousin) 7
Snibston Colliery 49
Soames House 160
Social Democratic Party, UK 129–130
Society for Latin American Studies 77, 82
South Africa 120, 166
Southend 12
Southern Rhodesia (now Zimbabwe) 120
Soviet bloc 37, 158
Soviet Union 47, 72, 111, 140–154
Spain 76
   Fuengirola 76
St Matthew's Church of England School, Ipswich 97
St Paul's Cathedral 159, 162
Stalin, Joseph 40
Stamp Memorial Lecture 95
Stanford, University of 111

Statoil of Norway 103, 175
Stephenson, Donald 166
Stephenson, Margaret 166
Stratford-upon-Avon 2, 21
Student's Union Labour Society 36
Switzerland 90, 118, 125
   Geneva 90, 164, 169

Talenpracticum (Language School), Rotterdam 86, 90
Tate Britain/Tate Modern 160
Thatcher, Margaret 103, 179
The British Gas Industry 89
The Changing Structure of the Oil Industry in the Caribbean 109
The Electricity Sector and Energy Policy 109
The Future of Oil: a Simulation Study of the Interrelationships of Resources, Reserves and Use, 1980–2080 95, 109
The Hinterlands of Melton Mowbray and Coalville 35
The Maritime Dimension: Oil and Gas Resources 109
The North Sea Oil Province: an Attempt to Simulate its Exploration and Development 101
The Oil and Gas Resources of the Third World Importing Countries and their Exploration Potential 109
The Oil Industry in Latin America 89
The Pressures of Oil: A Strategy for Economic Revival 95–100
The Significance of Oil 89
Times, The (newspaper) 78, 94
Toronto, University of 110
Total of France 175
Total Energy Leasing Systems (TELS Ltd) 99, 117
Total Energy systems 93
Town and Country Planning Association (TCPA) 115, 129
Trade Unions 36

Transactions of British Geographers (journal) 35
Travels
  Intercontinental 120
  In the UK 26
Treaty of Rome 141
Trinidad 76
Tufts University, Boston 65
Turkey 140, 157
  Istanbul 41, 47
Turner (family)
  Ernest (uncle) 12
  Kenneth (cousin) 3, 12
  May (aunty) 12, 14
Tyrrhenian Sea 48

UK Institute of Petroleum 72, 128, 149
United States of America 62–66, 92, 111, 113, 132
  Amherst, Massachusetts 65
  Bergenfield, New Jersey 63, 67
  Boston, Massachusetts xiii, 62–71, 111
  California 67
  Chicago, Illinois 67
  Delaware 67
  Detroit, Michigan 67
  Galena, Illinois 67
  London, Connecticut 65
  Manhattan Island, New York 63, 67
  Michigan 66, 118
  Minnesota 66
  Montana 66
  New England 63–66
  New Jersey 63, 67
  New York 59–67, 76, 95, 99, 111, 118
  North Dakota 66
  Ohio 67
  Oregon 67
  Pennsylvania 67, 118
  Rocky Mountains 66–67
  Vermont 64

Washington D.C. 113
Wisconsin 66
Yellowstone National Park 66
Urban Spheres of Influence in Leicestershire in the Mid-Nineteenth Century 35
US Air Products 131
US Internal Revenue Service 113–114

Valenilla, Dr Luis 95, 99
van Put, Elly 84
Venezuela 95–99, 112, 117, 180

W.A. Cadbury Prize 30
Wales 12, 30, 59, 86, 170
  Bala 59, 86
  Llandudno 15
  Prestatyn 14
Wallace Collection 160
Washington, University of 111
Wellingborough 2
Wendover 55
West European Energy Markets in the 1990s 109
What will Gas do to the East Coast? 78
Whitehaven, Cumbria 98
Whitwick Colliery 16, 49
Why Carbon Fuels will Dominate the 21st Century's Global Energy Economy 149, 173, 179
Will, Uncle (Jean's Uncle) 63
William the Conqueror 1
Wilson, Harold 100
Windscale Nuclear Plant 98, 115
Wise, Professor Michael 73
World Oil Energy Potential 109
Wolverhampton 39
World University Service 34–46
Wright, Professor Philip 179

Yarmouth 12

Zurich Arbitration Tribunal 164